THE BAD CADET

GROWING UP IN THE CHURCH OF
SCIENTOLOGY'S SEA ORGANIZATION

KATHERINE SPALLINO

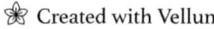

Dedicated to the Ranchers

PREFACE

"We're not playing some minor game in Scientology. It isn't cute or something to do for lack of something better. The whole agonized future of this planet, every Man, Woman and Child on it, and on your own destiny for the next endless trillions of years depend on what you do here and now with and in Scientology." ~ L. Ron Hubbard

FOREWORD

A midwife delivered me in a small room in an eight-story apartment building on Hollywood Boulevard. The luminescent, bright green Scientology sign outside my window reflected off the Hollywood stars that lined the sidewalk below. I was a Sea Org baby. My parents had dedicated their lives to the Church of Scientology and its Sea Org, and in doing so, dedicated my life as well. Instead of being raised by my parents, my brothers and sister and I were trained among a couple hundred other Sea Org children to be the future leaders of Scientology. I was a cadet. And I was going to help save the planet.

If only I could follow the rules.

PART I

THE CADET ORG

1

THE ATA

"Wake up!" The door to my dorm flew open. Eleanor strode in, panting from the short flight of stairs leading from the lobby to the first floor. "Muster, in the lobby in fifteen minutes ladies!"

I opened my eyes and stretched my arms out, yawning. Eleanor was dorm mom to me and my dormmates, all of us six or seven years old. She was a hefty woman with a perpetually frazzled expression, as if things weren't quite under control. Eleanor had been with us for as long as I could remember. We were the children of Sea Org parents. Sea Organization members worked for the Church of Scientology, using L. Ron Hubbard's technology to clear the planet. I didn't know what it meant to clear the planet, but I loved this idea of my parents rescuing it from danger. Because our parents worked long hours from morning to late in the evening, they didn't have time to take care of us, so instead, we had Eleanor.

At six years old, I knew the drill. I crawled out of bed and drew my white sheet taut against the mattress to tuck in the corners and pulled the blanket across and smoothed it flat. I ducked to avoid my friend Mandy's legs dangling from her middle bunk as she sat there in a groggy daze. My bed was the bottom one of our three-tier bunk bed, with gray metal poles that reached up to the ceiling. I finished the last two corners of my blanket and crawled out from beneath Mandy, whose legs still hung over my bed like ornaments. I laughed as I looked up at her, then walked barefoot across the thin carpet toward the bathroom, leaned against the wall and waited for my turn. With sixteen of us in this dorm, there was always a line in the morning.

Almost everyone was out of bed now and the room was a flurry of motion as girls made their beds. Several others dressed by the brown battered dressers all lined up in a row near where I stood. It was getting cramped with girls in line to pee and others pulling on their clothes with arms flying up in the air as bright colored shirts were pulled over heads, pants or leggings pulled on and hair brushed haphazardly.

"Katherine, it's your turn," the girl in the bathroom said as she slid past me.

"Thanks," I replied as I stepped inside. I sat on the toilet and tried not to look at the two cockroaches in the corner as I peed. Cockroaches were everywhere, and while I should be used to it, they still grossed me out. I finished peeing, then stepped up on the stool to reach my toothbrush, which was sticking out of one of the cups, bristles pushed flat from overuse. Turning on the dripping faucet, I held the brush underneath it. I stared in the mirror and looked at my coarse brown hair, poofed out as usual. With my brown hair, muddy brown eyes, and light brown skin, I knew I was ugly. I was all one color. I yearned for blue or hazel eyes, like most of my fellow dorm mates, and hair that was long, smooth, and perfectly straight. I got one hand wet and tried to smooth my hair, but it fluffed back up.

Ugh, stupid hair.

I sighed and began to brush my teeth.

Mandy came in and sat down, chatting happily about her dream as I scrubbed away.

Eleanor poked her head in. "Your minute's up, Katherine," she ordered.

I nodded my head at her and leaned over to spit. After I rinsed my toothbrush, I jumped off the stool, squeezed through the girls waiting by the door, and headed to my dresser.

My clothes occupied the top two drawers of the dresser I shared with Mandy, who joined me a minute later. As I pulled my clothes out, she grabbed hers from the bottom drawer. We joked around as we dressed until Eleanor silenced the room with another shout.

"Everyone chicken pick!" she demanded. We crouched down on the floor and picked up any tiny pieces of garbage we could see. I gathered as much as I could, and then raced Mandy to the small trash can near the hallway, pushing and shoving as we ran. Eleanor scolded us to stop goofing off and get out the door for muster.

Mandy and I dropped our bits of trash into the garbage and skipped to the lobby, which was just down a few steps away from our dorm. We gathered here every morning before heading off to our school, the Apollo Training Academy.

The Apollo Training Academy, or the ATA for short, was named after one of L. Ron Hubbard's original Sea Org ships, called the Apollo. L. Ron Hubbard was the founder and leader of the Sea Org. He had dropped his body in 1986 but that didn't matter. His presence was everywhere. Framed photographs and portraits lined the walls of our dorms, our school, and every Sea Org building. In every photo, he

seemed to stare right at me, as if he knew what I was thinking. With his pockmarked skin, bad teeth, and bushy
reddish-blond hair, LRH was kind of ugly. But he seemed to
possess some sort of magic. Whenever I passed by a photo, I
felt his eyes follow me. It wasn't spooky or anything; I felt
like he was watching over me, making sure I was doing a
good job.

Mandy and I lined up with the girls from our dorm as
more children spilled into the lobby from other dorms. We
were in a four-story apartment building called the Anthony
Building. The AB for short. The top three floors were occupied by Sea Org members, many of whom were our parents.
They were gone for the day, working hard at their posts in
organizations in the Sea Org.

The lobby was a cavernous room. The hardwood floor
was warped and wavy and creaked with every step. Posters
of L. Ron Hubbard hung on every wall. A bust of his head
sat on a pedestal near the entryway, as if greeting anyone
who walked in.

The noise in the lobby rose as our high voices competed
against each other's and echoed off the high plaster ceiling.
The dorm moms shouted over us to be heard. The room was
crammed now, a whirling mash of children with adults
sprinkled in like chickens trying to coral their chicks. I
glimpsed my mom off in the distance with her group of children, aged four to five, but she was too busy for me to wave
at. My mom was a dorm mom, so I was lucky to be able to
catch glimpses of her throughout the day, unlike the other
kids who only saw their moms on Saturday evening and
Sunday morning.

An adult roared for silence and a hush descended as she
began roll call. After attendance had been taken, the whispers and giggles returned with a slow rumble and rose to a

deafening roar as each dorm mom ushered her charges out the front door, grabbing arms and yanking kids away from whomever they were talking to. Soon it was my dorm's turn. Eleanor led us out the double glass doors, down the cracked cement stairs to the sidewalk outside.

It was eight blocks to our school. As we walked, I stared at the gray LA sidewalk, with dried bubblegum gone black from age, empty Coke bottles littering the gutter, and dog poop ignored by the pet's owner. I distracted myself and played silly games with my friends. We skipped over cracks and sang, "Step on a crack, you'll break your back, step on a line, you'll break your spine." Then we segued into another favorite, chanting this Scientology mantra at the top of our lungs:

WE ARE THE UPSTATS, the mighty, mighty upstats.
    Wherever we go, people want to know,
    Who we are, so we tell them, we are the upstats,
    The mighty, mighty upstats.

AFTER SEVEN BLOCKS, I saw the bright silver Scientology cross on top of a tall, sky-blue building that towered over the brown houses and one-story businesses that lined Fountain Avenue. We were almost to PAC Base. With manicured lawns, bushes flowering along the sidewalk, and freshly painted buildings, the Church of Scientology's block stood in stark contrast to the dirty streets around us. It was utopia. And across the street from this paradise, in its shadow, was the Sea Org school—the ATA.

. . .

THE ATA WAS a one-story building painted in the same blue hue as the Scientology buildings. It looked like a mini Sea Org base, but without the pretty flowers surrounding it. Instead, there was a chain-link fence covered in blue tarp. With the holes in the tarp and the chipped paint on the walls, the school had begun to show its age. But this wasn't something I paid attention to. Today as I walked with the other kids into our school, all I noticed was my stomach growling. I couldn't wait to get breakfast. I followed the other girls and boys in line as we walked through the chain-link gate into the front yard. Once inside, we scattered like wild animals and ran toward the front door, eager for our first meal of the day.

"Slow down!" the adults shouted as we dispersed. We ignored them and barreled our way through the tiny hall-way, our bodies bouncing off the walls and each other. As I passed the classroom where my mom taught, I glanced in and saw her with her charges. I gave her a quick wave and just caught her smile, her eyes crinkling, before I passed in a blur. My stomach warmed with happiness. I loved when I managed to catch a bit of her attention.

I refocused and joined the others running to the buffet but got caught in the crowd in the doorway. I pushed through and joined the line as more and more kids rushed in behind us. I craned my neck to see what was on the table. Cornflakes and milk—yum! Finally, I reached the front and grabbed a bowl of cereal and a carton of milk. I went to sit down in my usual seat. Mandy and a few of our friends joined me. When we were done, we cleaned our table and got a pass from Eleanor to go outside.

My friends and I headed to the front yard and squeezed ourselves into a corner of the fence where the two tarps didn't quite meet, so we could peer out onto the sidewalk.

We could see everyone passing by from there. Most importantly, we could see the Sea Org base. We always tried to time our trips with the Sea Org's break time in hopes of spotting one of our parents. If we did, we would shout their name, trying to get them to wave. It was rare to see your parents across the street because they were always inside their work building, so when one of my friends did, it felt like a huge accomplishment. I never saw my dad, though, because his org was farther up the street, but I liked to help my friends whose parents' org was in sight. Eventually, one of the teachers caught us and told us to stop yelling out onto the street, saying it was bad PR. We ran off to do something else, since this wasn't worth getting spanked for, which could happen if you riled up an adult too much.

It was time for morning roll call, so we headed back inside to our classroom. After that came Chinese School. I didn't know why it was called Chinese School. Maybe this was how they taught Chinese kids? All I knew was it was something we did every day. Today's word was "backflash." The definition of backflash was read out to us, and then we had to recite it back, loud and Tone 40. Tone 40 meant enthusiasm, which was the highest level on the tone scale that L. Ron Hubbard had created to measure a person's energy level. I stood straight and tall, shouting with enthusiasm, "Backflash: An unnecessary response to an order!" The room reverberated with the noise as every one of us screamed in unison.

"Good job!" Eleanor commended.

I sat down, exhilarated from my screaming. It was kind of fun getting to shout, since that was normally something we got in trouble for.

After Chinese School, Eleanor had an announcement to make. We were going to the L. Ron Hubbard Life Exhibition!

Cheers erupted around me, and I joined in. I loved the L. Ron Hubbard Life Exhibition. We went on this field trip almost every week, but I never tired of learning about the man who was the founder of the Sea Org.

L. RON HUBBARD

The L. Ron Hubbard Life Exhibition was located on Hollywood Boulevard, in the heart of Hollywood. The building was so tall you had to crane your neck to see the top. With its high columns and fancy walls, you could tell that it was an important place. The exhibition occupied the first floor and was open to any members of the public who passed by and were curious about Scientology.

We parked in front of the building and scrambled out of the bus. The adults directed us into the building and led us to the far end of the lobby. As we waited for our tour guide, my friends and I rushed over to the fountain, where water streamed over bronzed metal. I loved watching the water trickle across the inscribed words, *L. Ron Hubbard Life Exhibition*.

Soon Eleanor called us back, as the Sea Org member who was to give us the tour had arrived. She led the way through the door with our ragtag group in tow. Her frame was slim, and with her red hair, sharp clothes, and silky voice, she was the perfect guide for L. Ron Hubbard's life.

She stopped at the first photo gallery and began listing

all of L. Ron Hubbard's achievements. There was L. Ron Hubbard at age three and a half, riding a wild mustang on a ranch in Montana. At age six, L. Ron Hubbard became a blood brother to the local Blackfoot Native American tribe, and then became the youngest-ever Eagle Scout. He had traveled all over the globe before he was twenty, studying with the world's most famous scientists and Buddhists. During all this, he was writing often and became a best-selling science fiction author. When we arrived at the science fiction section, there was an *entire* wall of books that he had published. And right next to it were huge, life-size characters from his book *Battlefield Earth* that moved. There was even a lifelike human in a cage, captured by a horrible monster called a Psyclo. The creatures used to scare me but now I was used to them. Just next to the cage was another exhibit, where two men were flying to outer space to represent L. Ron Hubbard's book *Mission Earth*.

Now came my favorite part of the tour. I followed the tour guide into a theater. Sinking into the velvet red chairs, I wiggled with excitement. The lights dimmed as a rumble came through the speakers. Mist appeared from the front of the room, enveloping us so we couldn't even see our feet. A lifelike volcano was on the stage! I watched enthralled as the lava frothed over and ran in rivulets down the volcano. A voice came over the speaker announcing the birth of Dianetics, discovered by L. Ron Hubbard. The volcano looked just like the one on the cover of the book *Dianetics*. As the lava flowed, the room darkened. A large, thin screen lowered and began playing a movie.

I learned about how L. Ron Hubbard created Dianetics and disseminated it all over the world. How L. Ron Hubbard had healed so many people and helped them find a path to a better life. How his book was the best-selling book of the year! How he was revered! How he was praised! Oh, how I loved L. Ron Hubbard! When the movie ended, I jumped up, clapping and cheering along with all the other children.

I chatted excitedly as we moved through the final exhibits, then down a narrow hallway that fed into a large room with a ceiling almost two stories high. There were bright lights everywhere. We were at the finale. The awards L. Ron Hubbard had received over the last few decades were on display. There must have been *thousands*, on wall upon wall, each wall sliding open to reveal another. Meanwhile triumphant music played and a voice on a loudspeaker exclaimed how wonderful L. Ron Hubbard was. There were awards from government officials thanking him for his humanitarian work, others for his fiction, for the Way to Happiness Campaign, Narconon, and on and on. As I stood there, looking at these twenty-foot walls with certificates and medals from top to bottom, I knew I was part of something special. We, in Scientology, were lucky to have L. Ron Hubbard as our leader and founder. Yeah, he wasn't present with us now, but you could almost feel like he was here, watching over us. When I cheered for him at the end, I shouted "Hurray" with gusto, bursting with pride.

DITCHING SCHOOL

I was eight years old when I ditched school for the first time. I was leaving my dorm to join the line of kids in the lobby for our morning walk to the ATA when I saw my brother, Judson, peeking around the corner of the hallway. I didn't get the chance to hang out with him often, since he was two years older than me and lived in a dorm with older boys. I hurried over to say hi. As I neared him, Judson reached out, grabbed my hand, and pulled me around the corner.

"Guess what?" he said with a mischievous look on his face.

"What?" I asked, squeezing Judson's hand. Everyone in the school loved Judson, and they always wanted to hang out with him. But in this one way, I was the lucky one, because he was *my* brother, and now he wanted to hang out with *me*.

"Me and Patrick are going to stay here and hang out in Patrick's mom's room instead of going to school!" Judson gestured back to his dorm room, where I could see Patrick's head peeking around the door. Patrick was a year older than me, one of the boys my friends and I would chase around the ATA, trying to capture him for a kiss. He would scream "Cooties, cooties!" until an adult shouted at us to cut it out.

"I wanna stay too! Can I?"

Judson smiled. "Are you sure? You might get in trouble."

"I don't care. Let's do it!" I had never skipped school before, never even thought of it really, but hanging out with my brother and Patrick all day sounded too good to pass up.

My dorm mates assembled in front of the lobby with the normal chaos and confusion as the dorm moms tried to get everyone lined up. Judson put his finger to his lips and turned, gesturing at Patrick to start walking. I walked quietly behind them, feeling at any moment Eleanor would be shouting my name. My heart pounded. But nothing happened. The sound of the lobby receded behind me.

Wow. It had never occurred to me before how easy it would be to sneak off after attendance had been taken. Judson, Patrick, and I stopped around the corner of the long hallway and listened as the last high-pitched voices faded away, the front doors banging shut with a metallic clang.

"They're gone," my brother said with an impish grin on his face.

"Hey, Monkey, let's go to the store on the corner and buy candy and stuff," Patrick said. Judson's nickname was Monkey because his friends said he looked like one. With his buzzed head, brown skin, brown eyes, and slightly bucked teeth from sucking his thumb, I guess he sort of did. I never called him Monkey though. To me he was always Judson.

"Yeah! Let's go to our parents' rooms and get change from their drawers. Then we can get all the candy we want. We'll meet you in the lobby. C'mon Katherine!" Judson said. He grabbed my hand and jogged up the stairs leading to the third floor as Patrick continued down the hallway toward his mom's room.

Our parents had recently been moved into another apartment. It was much smaller than their old one, with hardly enough space for their bed and a beat-up dresser. The first apartment had at least had a second room with a bunk bed for me, my brothers, and sister to sleep in, two per bed. But now that we were older, we didn't get to spend Saturday nights with our parents like we had when I was six. These days we just met up with them on Sunday mornings for CSP time. I didn't know what CSP meant, other than we got to hang out with our parents and maybe walk to the 7-Eleven down the street to do their laundry at the laundromat because the AB's laundry room was always full and in use. On those days, they would let us get an ice cream from Thrifties, which was special. The few times we did get to sleep in their room, I slept with my parents in their queen-size bed while my brothers slept on the floor. Our sister Darcy was always gone at the older kid's school, which was far away, so it wasn't too squished at least.

Judson jingled the key to our parents' room in the lock and pushed the door open.

"Yes!" He walked over to the dingy dresser and rifled through our mom's jewelry box, then began pulling out change. "You look in this drawer," he said. I pulled the drawer open and heard change clinking. I couldn't believe how many coins there were. We could buy so much candy with this. I picked out the coins and piled them on the top of the dresser.

"No pennies," Judson said glancing over at my pile. I weeded them out, cutting my stash to half its original size. I slid the coins over to Judson, who added them to his own and stuffed them all in his pockets. We headed out the door, me giggling as my brother jingled next to me.

"We sound like a piggy bank," he said as he slung his arm around me. We met up with Patrick in the lobby and headed out the glass doors to the convenience store at the end of our block. I swung my arms and skipped to keep up with Patrick and Judson's longer strides, smiling from ear to ear. When we got to the store, we ran through the cramped aisles shouting what we wanted until the lady behind the counter yelled at us to stop running and buy what we wanted or get out. We scrambled to pick out candy and chocolate and then dumped it on the counter.

"$8.99," the lady said, glaring at us over the glasses perched on her nose. Judson poured coins out of his hands, and Patrick did the same. The lady stood there, arms crossed, as we slowly counted out the money. I was worried she would say it was too many coins, but she was quiet as Judson slid them across to her. She flicked her hand toward the door, and we grabbed the plastic bag, pushed the door open, and stepped out into the humid air of Los Angeles.

"Yes!" Patrick pumped his arm in the air.

"We have so much candy," I said in wonder as I stared at the white plastic bag dangling from Judson's hand. We didn't get candy often, other than Sorbees, sugarless "treats" that Eleanor gave out if my dorm mates and I were being extra good.

"Let's go eat it!" Judson exclaimed. We raced each other to the AB and up the stairs to my parents' room. We moved fast, not wanting any Sea Org members to catch us. Most of them were on post for the day, but we had to be careful just in case.

We plopped down on the bed and divided up the candy.

We ate Now-and-Laters, Skittles, Hershey's chocolate, red and black licorice, and each of us got our own gigantic lollipop. We stuffed ourselves with as much as our stomachs could hold and stashed the rest away for later. For the rest of the day, we played hide-and-seek and tag in the hallways and watched TV in Patrick's parents' room. My parents hadn't had a TV in a year since the Sea Org Security came and confiscated them all. Patrick told us his mom had hidden theirs that day. I don't know why they were taken. Maybe they had too much entheta and other bad news. Patrick's mom's TV was small with bad reception, but if you gave it a good smack, it worked okay.

Just before the kids returned from school, we headed to the lobby and hid in the far corner where we couldn't be seen. Soon the patio doors banged open, and the sound of noisy kids filled the room. Judson, Patrick, and I glanced at each other and nodded. We silently joined the mass of kids casually, acting like we had been with everyone the whole day. No one seemed to notice. As I made my way back to my dorm, I saw Eleanor glance my way. I swallowed.

"Get ready for showers," she ordered.

"Okay," I said with a wide grin. Eleanor looked at me as if she wanted to say something, then turned away.

Phew.

I gathered my hygiene supplies and towel and headed toward the communal showers down the hall.

4

1-2-3-4 I DECLARE WAR

Wars were common among the girls at the ATA. We scratched, punched, kicked, and even bit. As soon as a scuffle broke out, an adult would race over to break it up, but the ones involved would already be tangled up in each other, hair wrapped around each other's hands, faces screwed up in anger and swear words flying. After the adult managed to separate them, they were sent on a time out. If they had been swearing, they might even get their mouths washed out with soap or, if the fight was extremely bad, they got a spanking.

Whenever a conflict happened, I'd have to choose a side. I'd sit at that table at mealtime, snubbing the other girl and her friends. At recess, we would get into cussing matches in the backyard until an adult screamed at us to stop, and more mouths were washed with soap. Knowledge Report wars usually came next. By the time I was able to read and write, I remember writing Knowledge Reports on other girls at the ATA, even my friends, and they would write them on me. Knowledge Reports were statements that described an incident where you observed someone doing something wrong.

They were submitted to your teacher and saved in the report subject's permanent ethics file. During our wars, we submitted ten or more reports on a single girl in one day. I never was the ringleader in these fights, and that suited me just fine. But one day I found myself in an argument in my dorm, and the attention was on me.

"You're so stupid!" I shouted at Emma.

"Whatever. Your hair is so ugly," she sneered.

"Shut up!" I screamed as the girls around us shrieked with laughter. They had no idea how lucky they were that their hair just stayed flat on their head while mine acted all crazy like it had been electrocuted.

"Is that your only comeback?" She laughed. "Shuuut uuup," she said in a squeaky imitation of my voice.

Martha, one of the dorm moms from down the hall, strode into the room. "What's going on here?"

I ignored her, instead screaming at Emma that she was a loser.

"Just get a brush," Emma said. The laughter from the other girls rose all around me.

I lunged at Emma. Martha's arms snagged me as my hand swung toward Emma's face.

Emma pretended to duck.

"You missed," she said.

"Fuck you!" I shouted, saliva dripping from my mouth.

Everybody laughed.

I shrieked, my arms swinging, trying to get out of Martha's hold, to punch that smirk off Emma's face. The faces around me blurred, mouths open in a swirl of laughter.

"Knock off the HE&R, Katherine," Martha said sharply, her arms gripping me like a tourniquet. "I don't want to give you a spanking!"

"I hate you all!" I screamed as Martha picked me up and staggered out with my legs flailing in the air. She carried me through the hallway until we were a few doors down and the sound of the girls had faded. I gave up my struggle and became dead weight in her arms. She grunted and set me down. I slid to the floor and put my arms around my knees, sobs racking my body.

Martha put her arm around me as I shook.

"Katherine, you need to calm down," she said. "We are going to do a locational, okay?"

I looked up at her through my tears, snot running down my nose. I wiped it with my sleeve and shrugged. Another sob ripped through me. I didn't want a stupid locational. I just wanted to curl up in a corner and go to sleep. I closed my eyes as more tears dripped out. I knew she would do it anyway, because it was meant to help me. A locational was technology developed by L. Ron Hubbard to calm you down. I opened my eyes as Martha pushed herself up and put her hand down for me. I put my hand out and she pulled me to my feet.

"Katherine, look at that picture," she said as she pointed to a framed image on the wall. I looked, taking in the man climbing up the mountain, his fist raised up in the air. "Thank you," she said. "Look at the ceiling." I craned my head up and looked at the white plaster, cracks lining it like decoration. "Thank you," she said.

"Look at the stairs."

After a few minutes of the locational, I felt better. My sobs had disappeared. There was only a slow thudding in my head and exhaustion.

"I feel better now," I said to Martha.

"Good," she said. "End of assist. Why don't you go splash

your face with some water, then head to bed." She glanced at her watch. "It's already lights out now."

I nodded and trudged off to my dorm. I was glad everyone was in bed. I didn't want to see their faces sneering at me. Or worse, their pity. Then I might start crying again. After rinsing my face and brushing my teeth, I slipped into my bunk and covered my face with my blanket. Within minutes I was asleep.

THE NEXT DAY Emma came up to me as I was making my bed and asked if I wanted a piece of gum. I looked at her, surprised. She gave me a small smile, and I could tell she felt bad.

"Yeah," I said. "Thanks."

I accepted the gum and returned to smoothing my sheets. Had I overreacted yesterday? Why had I acted so crazy? Remembering how my mouth had filled with salvia that burst out as I screamed made me cringe. I thought about Martha telling me to "Knock off the HE&R." Maybe I was just too emotional. I hoped that when I did the Scientology Communication Course, I would be able to control my emotions better.

SISTER TIME

As soon as the lights went out in our dorm, I pulled out the *Boxcar Children* book and began reading using the light that streamed in from the hallway.

Wood creaked under footsteps. I shoved my book under the blanket. Someone was coming. I saw their dark shadow as they approached, with long hair that wasn't Eleanor's.

Who was it? I peered out over the metal pole of my bed as they entered the room.

My eyes widened in surprise. It was my sister! Darcy was thirteen and didn't live at the AB like the rest of us, so she rarely got to have family time on Sunday mornings.

"Hi Katherine," she whispered as she crouched next to me.

"Hi Darcy!" I reached to pull my covers back so I could get out of bed, but she gestured at me to stay.

"I brought you some licorice," she said handing me two Red Vines.

"I *love* licorice! They're my favorite. How'd you know?" I took a big bite and let the red, gummy chewiness flood my mouth.

"I didn't. I just love them too." She smiled. "Well, that and chocolate." Darcy nodded to the book I had tried to hide. "What's that?"

"Oh, it's my book," I said. I grabbed it and held it up for her to see. "Have you read it?"

"Oh, yeah, I read all of the Boxcar Children when I was your age," Darcy said as she glanced around. "But you probably shouldn't read in the dark. It's not good for your eyes."

"It isn't?"

"Yeah, you could get bad eyesight." Darcy glanced at her watch. "Okay, I better run. It was good to see you!"

With a swirl of her long hair, she was gone. I flopped down on my bed and stared at the metal spirals above me that held up the bunk above. Where was she off to in such a hurry, and why was she here at all? Was she sleeping in my parents' room? Maybe she would stick around for CSP on Sunday morning. For a while I'd been hearing about a place where a lot of the older kids stayed called The Ranch. I figured that's where she probably lived now. If you were thirteen like my sister, you were no longer a kid. You were a cadet.

One day I would join her there. It sounded important and exciting. I was only eight, so had a few years to go, but I loved knowing I would follow Darcy's footsteps eventually.

THE RANCH

M andy and I sat in the van and watched trees rush past as the car drove up the windy road into the mountains somewhere far from Los Angeles. We had been chosen to attend the Canyon Oaks Ranch, a Sea Org-run boarding school where my sister was. At eight years old, we would be two of the youngest cadets at the Ranch. I hadn't expected to go to the Ranch so soon, but I was proud that we had been chosen before all our friends —even before my two older brothers.

The snaking two-lane road hugged the side of the mountain. I held my breath each time the van was at the edge, the guardrail the only protection from us plunging down into the valley below. It didn't scare me though. It exhilarated me. This place was so high up. It felt like we were above the world, looking down on it. We rounded another curve, and I fell silent as I looked down at a brilliant blue lake far below.

"That's the reservoir," the staff member driving said as she slowed a little so we could take in the view.

"What's a reservoir?" I asked.

"It's where water is held and purified for people to drink," she answered.

I nodded and continued to gaze at the bright blue water, contrasting with the light blue sky with the fluffy white clouds above. Mandy leaned over me, hanging onto my arm. We stared, mesmerized by the startling hue. As we passed the reservoir, the road slowly gave way to an open valley with mountains rising high on both sides. The van slowed.

"Here we are," the Sea Org member said. She turned left onto a dusty asphalt road with a latched wooden gate blocking it.

A majestic wood sign hung high above, with the words carved into it declaring, "Canyon Oaks Ranch." The driver got out of the car and opened the gate, then got back in and drove through. I looked around, as the car bounced down the long road that led to a tan building at the far end. The green lawn in front was the only grass in sight. Everything else was dirt and brush. I craned my head to look out Mandy's window and caught sight of a row of tan one-story buildings and a large log cabin in the distance. The cabin seemed familiar.

"Have we been here before?" I asked Mandy.

"Yeah," she said. "Remember the riots?"

"Oh yeah! When people were lighting the buildings on fire!"

"Yep!" Mandy laughed. "That was so crazy. They sent us to the Ranch, and we camped here so none of us got shot!"

"This is the main office," the Sea Org member said, interrupting our giggles as she pulled into a marked parking spot next to one of the buildings set apart from the others at the end of the long drive. "You two can go on inside and meet the Cadet Coordinator. Although Mandy, you might already know her. You are her daughter after all." She chuckled.

We grinned and scrambled out of the van. Mandy dropped her bag on the asphalt and ran into the building ahead of me. I followed suit but stopped inside the doorway and watched as Mandy and her mom hugged. Near Mandy's mom's desk I noticed a small side table with a telephone. I wondered if I would be able to call my mom sometime soon and let her know how I was doing. It would be a long time until I saw my parents again, but maybe one of them would be able to catch the bus from the Sea Org base at PAC and visit during their time off on a Sunday morning.

"Katherine," Mandy's mom gestured me over. "Welcome to the Ranch. You and Mandy will be buddies and do an orientation checklist together. One thing that is new here at the Cadet Org is that you will call every adult *Mister*, whether they are male or female. I am called Mr. Miller."

I nodded my head.

"You will always answer "Yes sir" or "No sir" when spoken to." Mr. Miller paused.

"Yes sir," I said. I glanced at Mandy and tried not to laugh. This seemed so serious.

Mandy muffled a giggle.

"You too," Mr. Miller said to Mandy.

"Yes sir," Mandy replied with a grin.

"At least try to say that when we're with the cadets." Mr. Miller chuckled. "Oh, here is the cadet that will be showing you two to your new dorm." An older cadet stood at the door waiting. "Make sure to set an example and show what upstat cadets you can be."

Mandy nodded. She straightened her shoulders and saluted. "Yes sir."

"Yes sir," I responded dutifully. I puffed out my chest with pride.

At eight years old, we were now part of the Cadet Org.

THE NEXT MORNING, I woke with a start to a cadet hollering into our dorm, "Time to get up, fifteen minutes to muster!" For a moment I had déjà vu. This was just like Eleanor, my old dorm mom, except now it was an older cadet ordering us around.

I jumped out of bed and pulled on my new cadet uniform, a red polo shirt with a Sea Org symbol on the left breast pocket and khaki pants with a belt that had a shiny buckle I had never seen before. The silver buckle was shaped like a rectangle and snapped onto the canvas belt. It looked sleek. I felt so professional. I made my bed like I had been shown yesterday, pulling the thin blue blanket so it was taut. Our dorm had bunk beds, but instead of the ugly metal ones in Los Angeles, these were made from thick, gleaming wood. Seven other cadets, including Mandy, moved around me, making their beds with their identical blue blankets.

Our dorm was one of three squat buildings evenly spaced from each other a hundred yards or so behind the main office. We were Dorm 9, and from our west windows you could see Dorm 8, where the boys lived, and in the east was Dorm 10, which housed the older cadets, including my sister. I'd seen Darcy for a second yesterday during my orientation. That had been cool. I couldn't wait to see her again.

· · ·

THE BELL RANG, signaling muster. Mandy and I trotted out, down the cement path toward the schoolhouse. Once there, we entered a door a cadet held open to find a long, narrow room filled with cadets crammed in like sardines. Mandy and I edged our way inside.

Where were we supposed to go? I looked at my friend, and she seemed just as confused as I was. A cadet noticed us standing there and told us to go join Division I, pointing at the line at the far end of the room.

Mandy and I got there just as one of the older cadets shouted, "A ten-hut!" Everyone present immediately stopped talking. We stood at attention, our arms at our sides, facing the cadet who had given the command. She looked like an adult, although she was probably my sister's age, fourteen or so. She stood ramrod straight, her uniform ironed crisp, her hair in a high ponytail. This must be the Commanding Officer, which meant she ran the Cadet Org. She called another cadet up to the front of the room and ordered them to take attendance.

"Div I?"

The cadet at the front of our line snapped out, "Present and accounted for!"

"Div 2?"

"Present and accounted for!" the cadet at the head of the next line reported.

Roll call continued. I looked around, hoping to spot my sister. I finally saw her far across the room, but she was standing at attention, staring straight ahead. I didn't think I should wave during attendance, but maybe I would get to talk to her after muster.

After attendance, the CO made a few announcements, cleared her throat, and then shouted, "Start!" Everyone moved and hurried about. I turned to where I had seen

Darcy, but before I could make my way over to say hello, she was striding out the door with her unit.

That's okay, I thought to myself, *I'll catch her another time.*

As the crowd dispersed, a cadet in her mid-teens called to Mandy and me. She walked us over to a desk, announcing that she held the Hubbard's Association Secretary post, HAS for short.

"Okay," she said as she shuffled through some papers. "Your post is expeditor. An expeditor is someone who does work wherever it's needed until they get a specific post title assigned to them. Today they need more deckies deweeding on the hillside this morning, so that's where you will work this morning. Got it?"

"Yes sir," Mandy and I said in unison.

"Okay, good. But before we do anything, you two need to go get your lice check. Go report to the Medical Liaison Officer in the Qualifications office. We call her the MLO."

We looked at her, confused.

"Didn't you get a tour?" she asked.

"Uh, yeah, but we don't remember where that room is," I said apologetically. Mandy nodded in agreement.

The cadet rolled her eyes. "Follow me," she said. She strode out of the room, us eight-year-olds chasing her heels. Down the hall, she took a quick left and opened a door into a little room.

"Hey," she stuck her head inside. "Two new cadets need a lice check," she informed the MLO.

A girl of about thirteen years old stood up and sighed. "You first," she indicated to me.

She sat me on a folding chair and stood behind me. Parting my hair, she was stopped by a tangle. As she pulled it apart, I tried not to wince. She stopped suddenly, grabbing a piece of my hair between two fingernails. I winced as she yanked hard.

Her hand appeared in front of my face, inches from my nose. "Lice," she announced to me. On her fingernail was a little round opaque thing with a small tail, almost like a comma.

Shoot. My cheeks burned. This wasn't my first time getting lice. The dorms at the AB constantly had breakouts. But I never imagined I'd have to deal with this during my first couple of days at the Ranch.

The MLO told me to wait nearby, then indicated for Mandy to sit. I looked toward the mountain towering above the dorms and tried not to cry as the MLO methodically went through Mandy's hair.

"You're a pass," she told her. "Go tell the HAS you need a new buddy. Katherine can't be on post till her lice is gone."

Mandy looked over at me. "I guess I'll see you later?"

"Yeah," I shrugged, unable to meet her eye. This was not how I expected my first day as a cadet to go. Mandy left, and I watched as the door swung shut behind her. The MLO sighed.

"We better get you some lice shampoo," she said with a grimace, like she would rather do anything but touch my hair. I couldn't blame her. I was disgusting.

WE SPENT the first hour washing my hair with lice shampoo that made my eyes and ears sting. Next, I stripped my bed of its sheets to be washed. My hair wet and dripping, I walked down the long asphalt path behind the dorms, carrying my bedding like a weight on my shoulders. When I arrived, I gave it to the cadet inside and headed back to MLO office at the schoolhouse. I sat in front of the MLO's office while she picked my head free of lice. Cadets gave me a wide berth as they passed.

Midway through the lice-picking, a group of older cadets walked by, my sister Darcy among them. I cringed, worried she would judge me or ignore me like everyone else. But she stopped and said hi, not even acknowledging my predicament. She headed off after a minute, saying she had to go to work on her post.

THE NEXT DAY, I passed my lice check and was back to being Mandy's buddy. Mandy and I were assigned to go work with the deckies on the hill above the woodshop and laundry room. We were given tools they called weed whackers, that had sharp, curved ends and instructed on how to wave them back and forth like pendulums against the weeds to cut them from the dirt ground.

The sun beat down on me as I swung the weed wacker back and forth. Soon I had a rhythm going and was making fast work. After an hour, my skinny arms ached. When I saw the cadet in charge walk to another area of the hillside, I slowed and chatted to Mandy. Anytime the cadet walked back our way, we would stop chatting and focus on our work. Despite our talking, we managed to clear out all the weeds in a ten-foot radius. I was impressed with the two of us. I had done hard work before, like times when I had stayed late at night at the ATA to help wax all the floors with one of the teachers, or when we would paint walls in Los Angeles for the Way to Happiness, but this was a new kind of work. I loved being on the hill and the sense of accomplishment I felt watching the weeds get cut down.

The bell rang for lunch. We brought our tools to the woodshop and walked up the path to the dining room.

Mandy and I ate quickly and headed out to the patio to hang out until PE muster. It was large enough to fit all hundred or so of us for muster. It was so spacious that there was plenty of room for the older boys to set up their ramps to skateboard on. Mandy and I sat on the short brick wall that surrounded the patio and watched the boys do tricks and ollies.

The CO walked over to the long rope dangling from the arched overhanging roof and yanked hard. The bell clanged. The ramps were quickly shoved to the side as we all lined up.

PE was free exercise time, so after muster Mandy and I went to see if we could go horseback riding. There were five mustangs kept in the corral on the far end of the Ranch, past the dorms. I'd wanted to go riding since seeing them on my first day. We walked into the shed to ask the cadet who looked after the horses, but she informed us that there was a list. My heart sank.

"Maybe in a couple days we can go," I said. I added my name, along with Mandy's.

"Let's go ride my new bike instead," Mandy suggested.

"Okay. But remember, you need to show me how," I said.

"Yep, don't worry. It's easy!" Mandy grabbed my hand, and we skipped down to Dorm 9, where her bike was locked on the bike rack. Mandy's mom had given it to her when she arrived at the Ranch. It was a girly bike, with a bright pink frame and pink-and-white tassels flowing from the handles. I loved it. I wished I could have a bike like that, but I knew there was no point in even asking my parents. They wouldn't have the money for it. I don't know why, but they never seemed to have money. At least I was lucky that I had a best friend with a bike.

"Here," Mandy said. "Let's walk it up to Dorm 10, and then you sit on the handles and we'll ride down together."

We walked her bike to the top of the hill, and I climbed on the handles.

"Hold on!" Mandy cried out. She pushed off with one leg, and we were off, picking up speed as we flew down the small stone path past each dorm, then the schoolhouse.

I screamed the whole way down as the wind rushed past me. We reached the patio and Mandy slowed to a stop.

I laughed as I hopped off the handles. "Let's do it again!"

We walked the bike up and went a few more times, laughing and shrieking the whole way down.

"Okay, time for you to learn how to ride it," Mandy said after we had brought it back up to the top of the hill for the fifth time.

"I'm nervous."

"Don't worry! You can do it," Mandy said. She had me straddle the bike and told me how to push off with the pedal that rose up from the ground.

"Okay, here I go," I said. I pushed my remaining foot off the ground and onto the pedal. The bike wobbled for a few seconds, but I figured out how to balance and I soared down the hill, smiling as the wind pushed my hair back from my face. I was biking! I made it down to the patio, biked in a circle, and then pedaled back up to Mandy, who was now a tiny figure at the top of the hill. She jumped up and down as I pedaled hard up the last bit.

"You did it!" Mandy cried.

"I can't believe how easy it was!"

"Now you bike with me on the handles," Mandy said.

She hopped up and soon we were off again, flying down the hill, our hair streaming behind us.

7

GETTING PAID THE BIG BUCKS

Three weeks after getting to the Ranch, I sat perched on the patio wall outside the dining room on a cool Saturday afternoon.

"Katherine Spallino!" a voice called out. I looked up and saw our fifteen-year-old Treasury Secretary across the large patio, surrounded by a crowd of cadets. She called my name again and waved an envelope in the air. I squeezed through the crowd, wondering why she was asking for me.

"Here you go," she said, passing me the envelope. I took it as she called another name, and another kid jostled through the crowd toward her.

I pushed my way back out of the crowd and peeked inside the envelope as I went.

Money! Yes!

I knew what this was. My first weekly cadet paycheck! I hurried over to the patio wall and sat down to examine the envelope's contents. I pulled out a ten, then a few dollar bills and some change. The final item was a thin yellow slip of paper. I looked at it and saw my name, my post title, and the amount of money issued. Fifteen dollars before FICA was taken out.

"What's FICA?" I asked an older cadet standing near to me.

"It's what the government takes out for taxes," she replied.

"Oh." I pushed the paystub and cash back into the envelope. "Awesome," I whispered to myself. I had never held that much money in my life, and it was all mine!

I hugged the envelope to my chest, then started off across the patio to the canteen window near the galley. The canteen was only open during lunch and break times. When it was, the wooden shutters were unbolted, and you could order through the window, which looked into a small room filled with shelves crammed with everything you could ever want. There were chocolate and blueberry muffins, red licorice, Hansen sodas, frozen Capri Suns that were perfect for a hot summer day, ramen noodle soup, cheese and peanut crackers, Pringles, and more. I had never bought anything from the canteen because I didn't have any money. But now I could. I stood on my toes and looked over the counter at the goodies lining the shelf. After a few minutes of mulling it over, I decided on a large chocolate chip muffin and a Hansen's soda.

I paid and walked away with my bounty. I still had $11.00 left. I munched on my muffin and pondered what to buy next.

I decided to hold on to my money for now. Every other Sunday, the bus took cadets down to Walmart to buy any essentials. I couldn't wait for my chance to go shopping for treats and hygiene supplies.

. . .

EVERY SATURDAY I got my envelope with $15 inside, until one morning late in the spring, when the Treasury Secretary began to read the names, one by one, but skipped mine. I looked up in surprise.

Was it just a mistake? I listened to the rest of the list, but still my name wasn't called. When she was finished, I walked over as she gathered up the silver-colored metal safe box that stored the pay envelopes.

"Um, you didn't say my name," I said as I scuffed my sneaker against the cement patio.

"Oh." She looked up. "That's weird. Have you been paid before?"

"Yeah."

"Well,"—she shrugged—"I'll ask an adult when I return the safe."

"Okay, thanks." I stepped aside so she could pass me to head down to the main office. I watched her go, hoping that maybe later today she would come find me and tell me that my pay had just dropped out of the box or something. But I didn't hear anything. The next day I asked again, and still got no answer.

Finally, a few days later, the Treasury Secretary tracked me down and told me that I didn't have a Social Security number, so they couldn't pay me anymore.

"What's a Social Security number?" I asked.

"It's a number you get from the government when you are born, and you have to have it to get paid. Apparently, you don't have one," she said.

"How do I get one?" I asked.

"I guess you have to call your parents and they need to get it." She shrugged.

"Okay," I mumbled. Getting ahold of my parents was kind of hard. But I would try during my next lunch break.

My mom was still a teacher at the ATA, so she was always busy.

At lunch, I called, but just as I expected, my mom was unavailable to talk. I tried again when I had my next break, but still no luck. I left another message and hoped eventually she would call. There wasn't anything else I could do.

THE NEXT DAY, I was playing jump rope with two friends on the patio during lunchtime. A cadet came over and told me to go to the office because my mom was on the phone. I sprinted down the asphalt road, blazing by the log cabin, laundry building, and woodshop before arriving at the main office. I hoped that when I spoke with my mom, this thing with my Social Security number would be resolved. I opened the door to the main office and walked quickly to the phone.

"Mom?" I panted.

"Hi honey!" she said.

I launched right into what I needed, telling her what had happened with my pay, and asked her if she knew what a Social Security card was. My mom explained that when you are born in the hospital you are assigned a Social Security number. I asked if she knew why I didn't have one and she said that because I was born in the Scientology apartment building and not in a hospital, I was not given one.

"So, what am I supposed to do?"

"Let me talk to Mr. Williams," she requested. I turned to Mr. Williams, one of the adult Sea Org members staffed at the Ranch, who sat at the desk next to me.

"My mom wants to talk to you," I told her. I handed her the phone and slumped into a nearby chair. I still didn't understand why my mom couldn't have just gotten me a Social Security number when I was a baby.

Mr. Williams handed the phone back to me. My mom talked for a few minutes, but I barely listened to what she said. She was going on about a need to request a birth certificate for me and then send in an application for me to get my Social Security card. Blah blah blah blah. All it meant was that she didn't have a solution.

"How long will it take?" I demanded.

"Oh, it may be a few months, but I don't think that long," she said.

"A few months! Shit, Mom! But I won't have any money to buy hygiene supplies or even go to the canteen. This sucks." I blinked hard, trying to keep my tears in.

"It's okay, honey," my mom's voice crackled over the line. "I'll try to send you money each week. And I'll work on getting your Social Security card as soon as possible."

"Okay, fine. But don't take forever." I turned toward the wall to avoid looking at the adults coming in for their muster.

"I won't," she promised.

We said our goodbyes and I trudged back to the patio for cadet muster.

LATER, I told Mandy and some other girls in my dorm what had happened.

"Wait, so you don't exist?" a girl teased.

"What do you mean?"

"If you don't have a Social Security number, then that means the government doesn't even know you're alive." She smirked. "I guess you're nonexistent."

"Well, then at least I won't get drafted into the army," I said as I gave her my best smile.

"Girls don't even get drafted," she replied with a laugh.

"Never say never," I retorted. I turned and marched out of the room and crossed the hallway to my own dorm. I flopped on my bed and closed my eyes. I wanted to crawl under my covers and just ignore everyone for the rest of the day but I knew that wasn't possible unless I faked being sick. But even then, it was hard to get an adult to believe you were sick, and if they did, I would just be sent off to isolation, a tiny two-room space that smelled like disinfectant, vitamins, and old puke. I reached over and pulled out my book from underneath the pillow. I opened it and read. I focused on the words, the pages in my hands, and soon my troubles seemed to float away as I got lost in *The Babysitters Club* that I was reading.

8

GALLEY DUTY

After a few months as an expeditor, I was assigned to a new post. From now on, I'd be working in the galley. I was excited to hear the news. I had never cooked before.

After muster, I hurried across the patio, through the dining room and into the galley. Industrial-sized stainless steel counters stretched across the room. There were pots larger than my body and ovens and stove burners so high I would need a stool to reach them. I spotted the cook's office off to the side and walked over to find out where I should work.

The cook was Eleanor. She had been transferred to the Ranch and placed in charge of the galley. Now that she was at the Ranch, we weren't allowed to call her Eleanor anymore. She was now Mr. Ellis. Having her at the Ranch didn't really change anything for me since I had never been one of her favorites. We got along fine, but I didn't expect special treatment.

I poked my head into the small office where she sat reviewing paperwork.

"Hi, Mr. Ellis," I said as I gave a small wave.

"Hi, Katherine," she said. She gestured to a girl standing next to her. "Bella is going to give you an orientation and get you started on your post."

Bella was my sister's best friend and was also fourteen years old, like Darcy. She always seemed so put together, just like my sister.

"K, follow me," Bella said with a smile. She strode around the galley, her long, tan legs moving so fast that I had to jog after her. After giving me a quick tour, she stopped by the pots and pans.

"This is what you will be doing." Bella pointed to the dirty pots stacked next to the large sink.

"But I was . . . " I trailed off.

Bella smiled. "Don't worry, you will get to cook. Everyone does pots first, and then they rotate to another position in the galley. After a couple weeks you should be able to man the grill."

"Okay," I said. I stepped up to the large sink, dipped a baking pan in the water, and began to scrub.

After two weeks of grunt work, I was finally allowed to cook. I was assigned to make scrambled eggs for the entire Ranch along with another cadet. His name was Derek. He was two years older than me, with hazel eyes and straight blond hair that fell just over his eyebrows. Even though we were both in the galley, we hadn't really spent much time together. Derek always hung out with the older kids and was considered one of the "cool" boys. I couldn't believe how lucky I was to be paired with him.

He gestured me over and showed me how to crack two eggs at the same time. I grabbed one in each hand and cracked them against the side of the large pot. Three chunks of shell dropped in.

"Whoops!" I glanced at Derek to see if he was mad.

"Don't worry." He smiled. "It took me a little bit to get a hang of it. That's why we have this." He held up a slotted silver spoon with a long handle and leaned over the pot to fish out my shells. "All better. Now try again."

I gave it another go, and this time the eggs cracked perfectly. No shells in the pot. "Yes!" I declared.

"See?" Derek smiled.

"Yep." I grinned and got to work. Quickly I worked my way through over twenty of them. Soon I was scrambling my own eggs alongside Derek, although I needed to stand on a stool to reach the back of the stovetop. We laughed and talked the whole time. I loved this post. Maybe I could request to stay in the galley permanently.

A WEEK LATER, I was on lunch shift making hot dogs. I stood on a stool so I could reach the back of the griddle and used a spatula to roll them so they wouldn't burn on one side. I chatted with another girl my age who was manning the griddle next to mine. I was leaning over to get the hot dogs in the back when the stool slipped out from under me. I fell, my arm landing on the scalding hot griddle. I cried out in shock as a searing pain shot through me. I couldn't move. It felt as if I was pinned.

Two hands gripped my shoulders, lifting me off the grill and setting me on the tile floor. I curled over, tears streaming down my face. The pain was like red hot lava eating my arm to the bone.

"What happened?" I heard dimly.

I looked up and saw Bella, the head galley cadet, leaning over me. Other cadets appeared and looked on. I had no idea where Eleanor was. She was probably supervising the dining room set up for lunch.

"I . . . fell . . . on . . . the grill," I gasped.

"We need to get your arm under water right now." Bella's face was white. She leaned over and pulled me up, supporting my weight and guiding me over to the sink on the far wall.

"Keep your arm under the water," she instructed. I leaned against the sink while it rushed over my arm. I gasped shallow breaths and tried to listen to what Bella was saying, but her words faded in and out.

". . . main office . . . need to take you . . . keep water . . ."

I squeezed my eyes shut as tears slid down my cheeks. Would the pain ever stop? The water continued to wash over me as I held onto the sink for dear life. It felt like if I let go, I would collapse. After what felt like hours, I heard Bella again.

"Katherine? Is it any better?"

I took a deep breath. The pain had receded from its initial burn, but my arm throbbed sharply.

"A little," I whispered.

"Okay." Bella rubbed my back. "Let's pat your arm dry and walk to the main office. I think we've let the water run long enough."

I lifted my head and looked at my arm. It was bright pink, and large blisters had popped up like balloons. Bella turned off the water and then took a towel and lightly patted the burned area. I jerked involuntarily with each pat.

"Okay, done. Let's go," Bella said softly. I followed her out through the back of the galley, my throbbing arm cradled against my body.

Bella gave me a locational as we walked toward the main office.

"Look at that tree," she said, pointing to the large oak by the art room. I looked over.

"Good. Look at the clouds in the sky," she said. I looked.

"Thank you. Look at the propane tank." She pointed at the large cylinder by the laundry room. She continued pointing to different things as I hobbled down the road next to her. By the time we had reached the main office, my tears had stopped, and I felt calm.

BELLA LED me to the door and pushed it open. Mr. Williams heaved herself up from her desk chair when she saw me.

"What's going on?"

Bella explained what had happened as I stared at the carpet, my arm extended out for show.

Mr. Williams shook her head as she examined my arm. "Okay, this may be a second or third degree burn, so we are going to head to Urgent Care and have it looked at."

I nodded. I hadn't been to a doctor in a while, and the prospect gave me a shot of excitement. Trips off the Ranch were always fun. Yeah, my arm hurt like hell, but at least I could skip Scientology studies and go on an adventure. Kind of.

"Here, we'll just wrap it up like this." Mr. Williams wound a cloth loosely around my arm. She guided me to the staff car and helped me in. As we drove through the gate, Mr. Williams told me I could pick what to play on the radio. I leaned over and tuned the radio to Star 98.7. An Ace of Base song came through the speakers. I leaned my head against the door and watched the trees rush by. My arm was now just a dull throb as the music floated over me.

By the time we made it to the doctor's office, I was more interested in my surroundings and observing the world outside the Ranch than my arm. As we sat in the waiting room, I looked out the window, and watched a woman walk by holding the hand of a little girl who was licking a lollipop. The moment made me smile.

"Katherine, it's time," Mr. Williams said.

I looked away from the window and followed her and a nurse to a small room down a hall.

The doctor said I had a second-degree burn, but I was lucky. If it had been a third-degree I could have had nerve damage. I had to keep my arm loosely wrapped in a bandage and apply a thick, white, creamy ointment every morning and evening to help it heal.

I followed these instructions for the next few weeks and watched as my arm turned from bright red to dark brown and slowly scabbed all over. Eventually, it was like one large scab from wrist to elbow. After another week, my scab flaked off, with bright-pink, shiny skin underneath.

I was almost as good as new.

———

9

GOODBYES

I t was a warm spring afternoon, and I was skipping along the narrow stone path to my dorm when I heard my name called. I looked over and saw Charlotte, a friend of my sister's walking toward me from Dorm 10.

"Oh, hey Charlotte!" I stopped and gave her a hug.

"Did you hear the news?" She tucked her hair behind her ears.

"What news?"

"Your sister got recruited for the Sea Org! Isn't that great?" Charlotte grinned.

My sister was joining the Sea Org already? We hadn't even had a chance to hang out since I'd come to the Ranch. I knew I should be happy for her. This was a huge accomplishment. But my insides were telling me something else. *Shut up, Katherine*, I told myself. We had been told our purpose was to join the Sea Org. Darcy was helping save the world!

"Cool!" I squeaked out. I swallowed and tried again. "Is Darcy in her dorm packing? I'd like to say goodbye."

"She already left," Charlotte said. "They wanted her on the EPF before Thursday at 2 p.m. so that the stats would be up."

"Oh. Good for her, helping the stats get up!" I forced a smile.

"Yeah, it's great! She is going to be in CMO. That's an executive org."

My mind raced. Darcy, at age fourteen, was going to have a higher post than our parents! Did that mean Mom and Dad would have to call her "Sir?" That was impressive.

I thanked Charlotte for telling me and wandered up to my dorm to think. One minute Darcy was at the Ranch with me, and the next she was gone. I came here hoping we would get to see each other more, but we rarely did. It was like I never had a sister here at all.

Well. She *was* fourteen. At the Ranch, that was practically an adult. She was ready for the Sea Org. I had known this would happen. The Cadet Org's whole purpose was to create Sea Org members. The L. Ron Hubbard quote "Many are called, few are chosen" had come to fruition. My sister had been chosen. I had to admit, that was pretty awesome.

A FEW WEEKS LATER, Mandy found me after lunch muster was dismissed. "I have to tell you something," she whispered. She grabbed my arm and tugged me toward the stone path leading to the dorm.

"What is it? Did you get libs?" I asked. Libs was short for liberty, the word the Sea Org and cadets used for taking a day off. As a cadet, you issued a request for libs in writing when your production was high enough. It had to be approved by your seniors, including the CO cadets.

Mandy glanced at me as we walked along the path. We

were passing the pool, so I stopped to look for ripe grapes on the vines that grew on the fence surrounding it. Mandy crouched next to me and started searching too. We hadn't yet swum in the pool because it was still spring, but I couldn't wait until the day it opened.

"So, what is it?" I asked again.

Mandy stood up and shoved her hands in her uniform pants. "I'm going to Flag."

I froze and stared up at her. "What do you mean?"

"My mom is being transferred to Flag, so I am going with her. I'm going to be posted in the Flag Cadet Org." Flag was the Mecca of Scientology, all the way across the country in Clearwater, Florida.

"So . . . you're leaving?"

"Yeah." Mandy continued to dig through the grapevines.

"Ripe grapes!" She crouched down and reached underneath a branch, snapping off a dark purple bunch.

"Nice," I said in a daze.

We walked over to the oaks that lined the creek. Mandy stopped underneath our favorite tree and hitched herself up onto the rickety wooden fence that ran alongside the creek, her feet propped on the rail below.

"Here," she said, handing me grapes. I threw them in my mouth and felt the warm, sour juices explode against my tongue. I was used to the sour taste. The grapes that grew around the pool were meant for making wine, not for regular snacking. Someone had planted them here long before it became a Scientology Cadet Org. We liked to eat them despite how sour they were. The adults reprimanded us for it, but they were never around, so we ate them anyway.

"So, you're going to a whole different Cadet Org? That's crazy."

"I know. I'm kind of nervous. I don't know why my mom has to go. Her senior told her she was being transferred. My mom says I'll really like it." Mandy shrugged. "I mean, it can't be harder work than here, right?"

"Well, it's not on a Ranch, so no deweeding," I joked.

"Yeah, that's true. Just sucks that none of my friends will be there," she said.

I nodded. Ever since Darcy's departure a few weeks ago, a steady stream of cadets had been leaving the Ranch for the Sea Org. Bella and Charlotte were already gone, and it seemed like soon there would be no older cadets left. But with so many joining the Sea Org, more kids had been arriving from the ATA. Just last week, my brothers Judson and Lucas had arrived, along with many of my friends from the ATA. It got to the point where any time I saw the Ranch car pulling up the long driveway, I'd run to the main office to see who might be among the new arrivals. Mandy and I now had so many friends here that we hadn't had before.

"But it seems so exciting," I mused. "Like a whole new adventure. New place, new friends . . ."

"Yeah, I know, that part is kind of cool. Oh! Annnnd . . ." Her eyes widened.

"What? Tell me!"

"I am giving my bike to you!"

My mouth dropped open as I stared at her in shock. Mandy grinned at me, her eyes shining. I hopped off the fence and pulled her into my arms, hugging her fiercely. "Are you serious?" I shrieked into her ear.

"Ow." She laughed, rubbing her ear. "Yes. For reals. My mom said that we couldn't take it on the plane."

"Wow. Thanks so much!" I couldn't stop grinning. Only the rich kids at the Ranch had bikes. I never thought I would get to own one myself.

The next day, Mandy left. We promised to write each other often, and that night I wrote her my first letter, addressed to Flag Cadet Org. No postage was needed since it would go through Sea Org mail. I put it on my headboard to drop off in the morning.

10

OVERTS

I raced into the course room and collapsed into my seat as Mr. Morris, the Scientology course supervisor, shouted, "Ten seconds to roll call!"

"That was close!" I whispered to Hallie.

"I know!" Hallie widened her eyes dramatically, and I laughed. Hallie had become my new best friend since Mandy left for Flag. She had arrived recently from the ATA. Everywhere Hallie went, she seemed to be in the automatic good graces of adults and older cadets. Her appearance was a catalog version of what a cute kid should look like, with bright blonde hair, wide hazel eyes, and a tiny figure like a doll. She had a charm that I envied. Everybody liked her.

"Roll call!" Mr. Morris announced. All of us sat at row after row of long brown folding tables. The white walls surrounding us were plastered with posters of Scientology quotes and framed pictures of L. Ron Hubbard. The wide windows at the front and back of the course room flooded it with light.

I doodled as roll call concluded and Mr. Morris segued into talking about our goals for completions to get our stats up. If we got all our course stats up, along with our post stats, we would be rewarded with org awards. Org awards usually meant a movie on Saturday evening.

"Start!" Mr. Morris called out. Students pulled out their materials and began their studies. I watched as Mr. Morris walked to the far corner of the room and reviewed the checksheet targets for each student. While she was occupied, I leaned over to the others at my table.

"Hey," I whispered. "Guess what happened at PE today?" Hallie and Lacy looked over, interested. Lacy and I were the closest in age, so we had been in dorms together pretty much our whole lives, first at the ATA and now again at the Ranch. She was a sweet girl with large green eyes and freckles scattered across her nose.

Beatrice, the final girl at our table, put her finger to her mouth and returned to her checksheet. I rolled my eyes at Hallie and Lacy, and Hallie covered her mouth, her shoulders shaking as she tried not to laugh out loud.

I told them about how I had met up with Derek and two older girls during PE. We had tried to make wine out of the grapes lining the pool by shoving them inside a 7 Up one-liter bottle. We had hiked up the mountain behind the dorms to the large water tanks.

". . . we buried the wine under a rock," I continued.

"Whoa," Hallie whispered. "That's so cool. Aren't you worried about getting caught?"

"As long as no one writes me up I'll be fine," I said as I pointedly glared at Beatrice. Hallie snickered.

"Anyways . . . We're going to go get it in a few w—"

"What's going on here?" A gravelly voice crashed over us, cutting me off. I glanced behind me and saw Mr. Morris towering over our table. Her face was dominated by a bulbous nose. Her graying hair frizzed, and her cigarette breath wafted over me. I surreptitiously covered my nose as I glanced at Hallie. Lacy, meanwhile, pretended to be studiously reading her course pack as if she had not been a part of our conversation.

"I was asking Hallie if she could be my twin on a drill on my checksheet," I said.

"The two of you," Mr. Morris scoffed. "No way. You two goof off too much."

I rolled my eyes at Hallie, aware that Mr. Morris couldn't see me.

"You should clean your black hole," I muttered under my breath. On Mr. Morris's neck there was a tiny black hole that cadets joked about all the time. Was it a hole for storing cigarettes? A hole to the center of the universe? I really didn't know, but it was perfect for teasing her.

"*What* did you say?" Mr. Morris growled.

"I said, 'Can Beatrice give me a check out?'" I looked up at her, wide-eyed.

Mr. Morris stared at me a moment, her eyes boring into mine. "Fine. Beatrice, be quick about it."

Beatrice glared at me as we got up from our table. "Don't worry, it's just a quick checkout, then you can go back on course. Jeez," I said as we walked across the classroom. A checkout was when a person quizzed you on what you had just studied by asking definitions of words and checking to see if you knew the data.

We pulled out chairs at the table in the corner of the room reserved for drills and checkouts. Beatrice slid in and flipped her long hair. Sunlight glanced off the bright strands, as if mocking me. Yeah, Beatrice, I get it. You have gorgeous hair. I resisted the urge to pat my frizzy, brown hair and plopped down.

"We have to do this fast. I want to make my target," she said.

I nodded with a forced smile. Beatrice ran through the motions, and we quickly finished up. As we headed back to our table, I swallowed my annoyance. I really shouldn't dislike her so much for following the rules. A part of me was jealous that it seemed to come so easy to her. How did she always stay in-ethics? Really, I should be following her example. I tapped Beatrice on the shoulder.

"Hey," I whispered.

She glanced back at me.

"Thanks."

"Sure." Beatrice shrugged. I could see she was still annoyed.

"Don't worry," I told her as she neared our table. "I'll study harder now. I'm close to finishing this checksheet, which will help get our stats up."

She gave me a small smile as she slid into her seat. She loved having upstats.

I sat down in my chair. Time to focus. I flipped to the back of my Scientology course. A picture of L. Ron Hubbard looked back at me.

I gazed at the photo. This man was trying to save the world and had created the technology to do it. I felt a pinch in my stomach as his eyes seemed to see right through me. It wasn't Mr. Morris's fault that she had a black hole on her neck. I had committed an overt by teasing her behind her back.

I flipped back to my checksheet, deciding I would make up for my behavior by studying hard. If I wanted to be a good cadet, I needed to knock it off and get on purpose, like Beatrice. I buckled down and began to read.

11

FAMILY MATTERS

Today we were going on a mission. A mission was when you were assigned work to do at PAC Base. I was planning on visiting my dad during the lunch break to hopefully get a couple of bucks from him. I really needed to buy more shampoo and conditioner. My parents still hadn't figured out my Social Security number, so I hadn't been paid in months. I didn't even have enough money to buy essentials during the Sunday trips to Walmart.

We left the Ranch for the hour drive down the mountains, through the sprawling suburbs into LA. The bus pulled into the circular driveway of PAC Base and stopped in front of a set of double doors leading into a seven-story building called the Complex. I followed the other cadets off the bus and lined up.

A Sea Org member led us into the Complex, down a series of hallways and a flight of stairs, ending up in a dusty cavernous room filled with rows of boxes that needed to be sorted and filed. Cadets were divided up and assigned to tables. The Sea Org member turned on Star 98.7 and we all got to work, chatting and listening to music as we went. Every once in a while, the boys would try to change the station to KROQ, and we'd get in arguments until the Sea Org member told us to shut up or he would turn off the radio.

After a couple of hours, the Sea Org member said we could take lunch. I asked for permission to see my dad and rushed out the door as soon as it was granted.

My dad was an OT III supervisor at the Advanced Organization of Los Angeles, or AOLA, just across the street from the Complex. I didn't really know what OT III was, other than that it was an important level for Scientologists to achieve. I walked up to the massive double doors of AOLA, grasped the large handle with both hands, and tugged the door open. I slipped in, walking quickly past the imposing receptionist desk, manned by a pretty young Sea Org member, and made my way across the sparkling clean tile to the elevator up to the second floor.

The elevator doors slid open to an empty lobby. Ahead was a long brightly lit hallway leading to two large doors that I knew from experience were kept locked tight. The technology beyond these doors was top secret. Only qualified Sea Org members had the code to the keypad that unlocked the doors to the OT course room. This was because the information in OT levels was so powerful you could get sick and die if you saw it before you were mentally prepared. Any public training on their OT levels had to be buzzed in and supervised to make sure they trained on the right technology. I had read in the AOLA magazine that OT people developed incredible mental abilities. They were able to do things like change stop lights while rushing through traffic, use mind control on other people, and even change the weather if they wanted too.

I leaned over and pressed the button for the intercom.

"Hello," came a crackly voice.

"Uh, um . . . I'm here to see Allan Spallino. This is Katherine, his daughter."

There was a brief pause. "Okay. Please wait while I look for him." The speaker clicked off.

I leaned against the wall and stared around at the posters lining the hallway. The Bridge to Total Freedom was framed just across from me, and I walked over to peer at it. Two columns of lists ran down the poster, one enumerating the auditing steps and the other the studying steps needed to complete the entire Bridge and achieve OT status. My dad was at a level midway up, at OT III. I wondered when I would get to start moving up the Bridge.

The door creaked open, and I turned and saw my dad peering around it.

"Hi Dad!" I walked over and hugged him, feeling his soft belly give way.

"Hi honey," he said. I peered up at him and wondered how it was that he was OT III. He didn't seem very powerful, with his receding hairline, glasses, and a belly that strained his uniform. There were many other Sea Org members who cut more imposing figures. Maybe OT powers were so subtle that you couldn't tell when a person had them? I had yet to see my dad exercise his, but I knew they had to be there somewhere. Although he had once said he was able to remember a past life he had lived. According to him, he had been a turtle. I laughed when he told me that, because I had expected an elaborate story about being a pirate or a soldier, the types of past lives I normally read about in Scientology magazines. But a turtle matched my dad's personality. He was quiet, calm, and moved slowly. There was no way I had been a turtle in a past life. That would be so lame! I fantasized that maybe I had been a princess, or a strong warrior woman. I was always a female in my imagined past lives because I couldn't picture being a boy. I couldn't wait until I received auditing so I could start discovering my past lives.

"Do you have any money I can have?" I asked my dad. "I don't have any shampoo and conditioner anymore, and I've been using my friend's at the Ranch. Plus, I want to get a snack at the canteen ..."

"Hmmmm," my dad said. He reached into his dark slacks, and I could hear change jingle around. I put out my hands greedily. He dropped some quarters and a few dimes and nickels in my palms.

I stared at the paltry amount. There was no way I would be able to buy shampoo and conditioner.

"Sorry, hon, I haven't been paid yet this week," he said.

I sighed and nodded my understanding. It wasn't my dad's fault he didn't get paid a lot. "It's okay, Dad. I can still go to the canteen. Maybe I have enough to buy a Tiger's Milk bar."

"Sounds good," he said, glancing at his watch. "I've got to get back on the course room floor. The public can't supervise themselves." He chuckled.

"Ha, you're funny." I waved as I turned to go. "Bye, Dad!"

He smiled, then turned and plodded over to the security console. He slid his Sea Org card down the slot and entered his secret code. The light turned green, and he pulled the door open. I was already on my way down the hall, so I didn't see if he turned to wave back. I needed to make it to the canteen before I had to return to work.

I NEVER GOT to see my mom on missions because she was still at the ATA, serving as a dorm mom for the children who had not yet been sent to the Ranch. But a few weeks after seeing my dad, I got a letter from her saying she was planning to come up for my birthday. She even said she would bring me a present!

A week before she was supposed to come, I went down to the main office to call and make sure she hadn't forgotten. When I arrived at the main office, there were only two cadets in front of me. I sat on the curb outside, pulling out my copy of *Goosebumps* to read while I waited. When my turn arrived, I rushed in, plopped down on the chair, and dialed the number for the ATA.

An ATA staff member picked up and I asked for Dolores Spallino. I waited as she put me on hold, my knee bouncing up and down nervously. My mom wasn't always able to make it to the phone, and I worried that this was one of those times.

"This is Dolores. How can I help you?"

"Mom, it's me!"

"Hi, honey."

"Hi." I smiled and settled in my chair. I twirled the phone cord around my fingers as I told her all about my birthday wishes and how excited I was to be turning nine.

"You mean ten?"

"What?" I sat up.

"You're turning ten," my mom repeated.

"No, I'm turning nine," I said determinedly.

"Honey, you were born on August 4th, 1985. That makes you nine, turning ten."

"My birthday is August 5th!" I yelled.

"Oh, yes wait, you're right. About that part at least." Mom went on to tell me about how she went into labor on August 4th, but I wasn't born until early the next morning, so sometimes she got it mixed up.

"So you are saying I was born in 1985? Not 1986?"

"Yes, honey," she sighed. "And I have other news."

Other news, besides me being a completely different age?

"What . . .?"

"I'm afraid my CSW was disapproved. I can't come up to see you this weekend," she said.

I fell back against my chair and closed my eyes. This was the absolute worst.

"I'm sorry, sweetie! I promise to try to come up the next weekend, okay? And I'll bring your present."

I opened my eyes. "Yeah, yeah, okay," I said dully.

"Well, I have to go. My break is almost over, but I hope you have a good birthday!"

"Thanks." I hung up the phone with a solid *thunk*. I sat there dazed until the cadet waiting told me to move.

"Chill out," I snapped at her. I got up and wandered out of the office, up the long road toward my dorm. I went into the bathroom and ran my hands over my face, wiping away the tears that pricked at my eyes.

Who gets their birthday wrong?

I felt so stupid.

AFTER PE MUSTER, I headed up to my dorm with my friends. We flopped on our beds and pulled out some magazines. As I flipped through *Seventeen*, I told them about my phone call with my mom and that she couldn't come up for my birthday.

"Shoot," said Hallie, lying next to me with her *Cosmo Girl*.

"Yeah." I swallowed. I felt tears coming again, so I

quickly turned and rolled onto my back, trying to hold them in.

"Maybe we can have a little party when the Div 6 Secretary makes you a birthday cake," Hallie suggested, nudging me with her leg.

I turned my head and smiled at her. "That would be nice."

"How old are you turning again?" Beatrice asked as she clipped her nails beside her bed, her long hair obscuring her face.

My face reddened. I hadn't told them the part about my mom telling me my real age.

"Ten," I mumbled.

Hallie turned to me, shocked. "I thought you were turning nine?"

I sighed, rolled back onto my belly, and stared at the pattern on the bedspread.

"My mom said I'm actually turning ten," I muttered quietly.

"What?" Hallie nudged me with her shoulder. "I couldn't hear you."

"My mom said I am turning ten!" I forced out, irritated.

"You didn't know your age? Oh my god!" said Isabel, a normally sweet-natured girl lying on the bed across from Hallie and me.

"Wow, so you have no Social Security card, and you don't know your exact age?" Beatrice said. "Do you even exist?"

"Whatever. It doesn't even matter," I replied. "Age is just a consideration." I was paraphrasing a quote by L. Ron Hubbard. Good luck to her in trying to combat that.

"Anyways." I sat up. "I have to go talk to my brother about something," I lied. I walked out of the dorm, aware that no doubt they would start talking about me as soon as the patio door shut.

I still couldn't believe this had happened to me. Hallie was now two years younger than me instead of one. Beatrice was a year younger than me. I was so old! Tears dripped from my cheeks as I walked off into the dirt field behind the schoolhouse, toward the creek where there was no one around. As I walked, I gave myself a locational, looking at different things around me, trying to calm myself down. I wandered along the creek underneath the large oak trees. Sunlight filtered through, leaving circles of light on the dusty ground as my feet crunched on dead weeds and brush. After some time had passed, I felt better.

Who cares how old I am? I told myself. I repeated what I had told the others. *Age is just a consideration. I am a thetan that is trillions of years old. This is just a body.* Besides, I was the same age as Lacy and a bunch of my other friends. And there were still many other cadets older than me at the Ranch. Feeling better, I headed back to the schoolhouse. The bell would be ringing for Scientology studies anyway. Time to get on with it.

12

EXECUTIVE POWERS

I may have lost a year of my life when my mom told me I was turning ten, but that didn't stop me from becoming one of the youngest executives in the Cadet Org. The big news had been delivered at morning muster, after breakfast. An adult staff member announced there would be new posts assigned to all the cadets. As they listed the cadets' names and their new posts, I listened intently for mine. Then, finally:

"Katherine Spallino, Division 6 Secretary."

What?

A few of my friends turns to stare and I did a silent victory dance.

The Div 6 Sec was one of the most coveted posts at the Ranch, and somehow I had gotten it. I felt so lucky. My post duties were simple: make birthday cakes in the galley when it was someone's birthday; gather success stories from cadets; and assign cadets to our various missions. After muster, my friends gathered around, telling me how jealous they were that I had gotten that post. I basked in the attention, telling them I was going to be such a good Division 6 Secretary. The best *ever*.

The next day at muster, I tapped my foot impatiently, waiting for it to end. Today I was going to be making my first cake, and I couldn't wait. Once muster was dismissed, I waved a cheerful goodbye to my friends and rushed into the galley, down the hallway into Mr. Ellis's office. I let her know I needed to bake a cake. Mr. Ellis pushed herself up from her desk and squeezed around it. I followed her as she led me to the large walk-in pantry and pointed to where I could gather the ingredients. The cake was simple to make, since I was following the instructions from a Betty Crocker mix. I only needed to add eggs, milk, and vegetable oil. I quickly gathered the items and set up an area on the stainless steel counter. All the other cadets posted in the galley were cleaning the dishes from lunch. I noticed a few envious looks coming my way, and I reveled in it. I was never the envy of anyone. It felt so good.

That evening, as dinner came to a close, I rushed into the galley to light the candles on the cake, then followed Mr. Ellis through the door of the dining room. She announced that it was Lana's birthday, and the entire Cadet Org sang "Happy Birthday" to Lana, who stared at her hands, embarrassed. I could just make out her smile, though, and my heart felt so full as I set the cake in front of her and stood my ground as her friends pushed and shoved to get close while she blew out the candles.

Immediately everyone clamored for a piece, though the cake would barely have been big enough for a group a quarter this size. I quietly asked Lana if I could have a piece so I could taste it and make sure it was good. I ignored the evil looks I got from her friends as she slid over a slice with a smile.

"Thanks for making my cake," she said.

"You're welcome." I grinned. "It was fun."

I walked away with my slice and slid into a seat at my table. Hallie and Lacy leaned over, asking if they could have a bite, their forks ready.

"Okay, fiiiinnne," I said shoving my plate into the middle.

Within seconds, the cake was gone.

THE NEXT DAY WAS THURSDAY, time for the weekly cadet staff meeting. It was my first staff meeting as an executive, and I couldn't wait to announce that there was a mission this weekend at Malibu. It would involve picking up trash along the beach and learning about Earth Day. Afterward, anyone assigned would get the chance to go swimming in the ocean and stop for pizza before returning to the Ranch. This was pure gold. Everyone would want to go.

That evening I jogged down to the dining room with Hallie and Lacy. We pulled the door open and peered inside. Instead of the long brown tables we ate at, there was a sea of blue plastic chairs, with two of the long dining room tables set up at the front of the room underneath the organization board that hung on the white brick wall. The organization board was about twelve feet long and showed each division of the Cadet Org, along with post titles and the names of the cadet assigned to each post. And there, next to Division 6 Secretary, was my name. It had been on the board for a week, but I still couldn't help smiling when I saw it.

"Bye." I waved to Hallie and Lacy as I made my way over to the executive table. I set up my spot underneath the organization board and gave a shy smile to the current Div 5 Secretary. I couldn't believe I got to sit up here.

The noise level rose as the large room filled with cadets laughing, shouting, and jostling each other. I waved to my brother Judson as he passed me by, and he did a cartoon-exaggerated version of a double-take when he saw me with the executives. I made a face and told him to get in his seat in my bossiest voice. He laughed and waved as he turned away. I chuckled, and the Commanding Officer stood up from his seat.

"Attention!" he shouted.

The cadets nearest the front sat and looked his way, but the rest continued their raucous discourse, laughing and shouting over each other as if we were all just there for a party. There were no adults in the room, so it was up to the cadet execs to keep over a hundred cadets quiet and listening.

"That's it!" The Commanding Officer tried again.

Nothing. The noise continued, roiling, and boiling, cadets pushing and shoving and teasing. Another typical staff meeting of chaos. But this time it felt strange to be on the other side of the noise. Normally I was giggling and laughing with my friends, but now here I was, the one at the executive table. I felt the Commanding Officer's frustration that they wouldn't quiet down. He gestured to the Director of Inspections and Reports, who sighed and got to her feet.

"*Be quiet!*" She screeched so high that cadets covered their ears and groaned. But it worked. The room quieted. Finally, there was silence. *Thank god.* Staff meeting could officially start.

The MAA began roll call. Once that was done, the Division 1 Secretary went over her stats and her battle plan to get them back up the following week. I could already feel my attention drift. Normally I would be writing notes to friends or spacing out during this time of the meeting. But now that I was a big-time exec, I had to pay attention. I lasered my eyes on her and willed myself to focus.

As each executive stood, my heart rate increased. Almost my turn. As the Division 5 secretary spoke, I stared down at my paper, which I had gripped tight, and rehearsed in my head what I was going to say. Suddenly, there was a burst of laughter. I looked up. The Division 5 secretary stood there fuming. What had happened? The mass of cadets in the dining room laughed and jeered and shoved at each other. I looked around bewildered.

"Division 6 Secretary," the Commanding Officer called over the noise. *Shit*. It was my turn. They were moving forward despite the noise from the crowd. I stood up and opened my mouth.

"Uh, today I have an announcement," I said. My words floated and disappeared into the swirling noise.

"Excuuuse me!" I called.

Nothing. I glanced at the CO, hoping for help. But he just sat in his chair, his arms crossed, glaring at the unruly cadets like he wanted to murder them. I felt my body grow hot. Without thinking, I stood on my chair and screamed at the top of my lungs.

"Shut. The. Fuck. Uuuup!"

The room went silent. I looked out at the cadets, feeling a little faint. Had I really just done that? Had I managed to shut the trap of the whole Cadet Org? Me? My eyes caught Judson's. He raised his brows, impressed. It took all I had not to lose my composure.

"Oh my god!" I rolled my eyes. "You, like, take, like, so long to be quiet!"

I cringed at my own valley-girl voice. The energy in the room shifted. Snickers and whispers rose from the crowd. I hurried on before I lost control of the room.

"Annnnywaaaays, I just wanted to say that there is a mission on Saturday. The mission will be at Malibu Beach. We'll be picking up trash for the Way to Happiness campaign."

At the mention of Malibu, the snickers stopped, just like I knew they would.

I cleared my throat. The silence stretched out. I scanned the room. Good. No one was making fun of me now.

I read out the list and watched as my friends faces all lit up when they heard their names. I had only picked my friends for this mission, plus a few randos thrown in for good measure so no one could accuse me of being unfair. After I finished, I sat down, and the rest of staff meeting continued.

Afterward, a few cadets came up to me, mad that they were left off the mission list.

"Sorry, an adult gave me the list," I lied with a bland smile. "I had nothing to do with it."

I loved this post.

Unfortunately, I was only the Div 6 Sec for a few more glorious weeks before being reassigned back to working on the hills deweeding. I was disappointed, but I knew I had to accept my new role and move on. This was just how it was. Every few months you got assigned a new post and that was that.

13

THE CHILDREN

One morning, the Cadet Coordinator announced that the remaining children from the ATA were moving to the Ranch. This meant the dorm moms would be coming with them including my mom! She would be here at the Ranch. With me! I couldn't wait to see her every day.

That afternoon, I watched for the bus as I deweeded the hills behind the woodshop. The sun beat down on my head as I swished the weed wacker back and forth, my heart pumping with excitement.

I stopped and peered out at the road. Here it came, the long yellow school bus pulling up behind the wooden gate. I squinted to make out an adult getting off the bus and pushing the wooden gate open. The bus drove through and down the long asphalt road, then took a right onto the dirt path, pulling up behind the log cabin. I set the weed wacker down and hurried over to the I/C.

"Can I go to the bathroom?"

"You have five minutes," she told me sternly. "Don't take forever."

"I won't," I promised. I ran down the hill, up the road toward the patio as if heading over to the bathrooms beside the canteen, but once I was out of sight, I took a sharp right and trotted down toward where the bus had parked. I stopped and watched as kids clambered down the steps, one after the other. Some looked half my size.

Where in the world will they sleep? I wondered. There were only a few empty beds that I knew of in the girls' dorm, and I was sure it was the same for the boys' dorm.

Finally, my mom exited the bus, ducking her afro so it didn't hit the top of the doorframe as she stepped off. Her face rose back up and a smile wreathed her face as she saw me grinning and waving. I ran over and gave her a hug, melting into her warm embrace. She hugged me back for a couple of seconds, then pulled away.

"Hi, honey!" She rubbed her hand over my hair, which I had scraped into a low ponytail. This was the only thing I could figure out to do with it. It was so rough and coarse, and I didn't like people touching it. My mom didn't know that about me though, so I gave her a pass.

"I'm so excited you're here!" I hugged her again.

"Me too." She gave my shoulder a squeeze and looked past me, scanning the cadets and children milling about. "Where are Judson and Lucas?"

"Oh, I don't know. Probably on post." It hadn't even occurred to me to get my brothers. Whoops.

"Well, I'm sure I'll see them at dinnertime. I must get the children organized, so I'll see you then too."

"Okay." I hugged her again. "See you at dinner!" I felt happy butterflies in my stomach.

I was winding my way through the mess of children when I saw a familiar faced mixed in among them. Ava, an old dormmate of mine from the ATA. What was she doing with all the little kids? Ava was eleven like me, making her the oldest kid coming off the bus. How was she not even a cadet yet?

"Hi, Ava!" I waved at her.

"Hey." Ava grinned up at me through her scraggly, unbrushed blond hair. She crouched down and pulled a skateboard out of the backpack by her feet.

"How in the world are you still a child? Why aren't you a cadet yet?" I asked.

"I guess I don't really want to be a cadet," she shrugged.

This took me aback. "Why not?" I shook my head. "You'll get paid, and you don't have to have an adult watching you all the time. You're basically treated like an adult." I didn't need to tell her that I wasn't currently getting paid, even though it had been over a year. I was a weird case.

"I like being a child," she said as she set her skateboard on the ground and rested a foot on it. "I don't have to work."

I laughed. She had a point there.

"But don't you want to be a Sea Org member eventually?" I asked.

Ava shrugged and looked away, then back at me. "Not really. I guess I just wanna play guitar," she said with a sheepish smile.

"Huh." I had never thought about doing anything but joining the Sea Org. That was our purpose. We had been told this since we were little kids. All of us would one day be the future executives of the Sea Org. "Well, that's cool too, I guess. Maybe you can join the Sea Org band or something?"

"Maybe. I don't know." Ava stepped on the board and skated around me in circles. I turned and watched her for a minute before letting her know I had to get back to work. Her eyes flicked toward me when I said it, and I knew what she was thinking.

See? You have to work, while I can skateboard.

I waved and started walking toward the hillside to continue deweeding. Jeez. I had never thought of anyone not joining the Sea Org. Was that a possibility?

I couldn't imagine it.

Hmmm. It did make me wonder, what else could . . . No . . . There was no point even thinking those thoughts. I bet once Ava studied L. Ron Hubbard's policy, she would change her mind. It was of the utmost importance for us to train to become the future executives of the Sea Org. Once she saw that, she would be back on purpose.

14

MOM

J ust as I predicted, there were not enough beds for the newly arrived children to sleep in. Instead, three-person tents were erected near the dining room patio. After meals, you could see all the little kids milling around. It looked like what I imagined a homeless shelter would. My friends and I were disgusted. Seeing their condition made me even more certain of my place as a cadet. I was glad that I wasn't still a "child" like Ava.

Since my mom was with the children, I was able to catch glimpses of her throughout the day. I savored each time I saw her and always ran over and gave her a hug.

My dad never visited. He had been transferred to Flag in Florida, just like Mandy's mom, to do more supervisor train-ing. I didn't know how long he would be gone for, but a couple of months had already passed. I thought I would be sad that he was gone, but I found that it didn't bother me. I rarely saw him before, so it didn't really change anything. Plus, now I got postcards in the mail from him, which I loved. It was nice looking in my basket in the Communica-tion Center and finding a card from my dad instead of a

Knowledge Report from a cadet tattle-telling on me. I taped my dad's cards on a shelf in my armoire so I could look at them whenever I liked. His cards always had pictures of nature or animals and were pretty to look at. His notes would describe his day a bit and ask if I was being in-ethics. It was nice to be able to connect with my dad through letters. They were probably the lengthiest conversations I ever had with him.

"A TEN HUT!" barked Mr. Hammond, our Cadet Coordinator. Mr. Hammond was a large man, who towered over us. With his chambray buttoned shirt tucked into jeans and his five-o'clock shadow, Mr. Hammond looked like one of those cowboys I had seen in the movies. I stood at attention, watching as he scanned our lines assembled on the patio. I hoped that my division was lined up properly and none of us were fidgeting. I didn't want to be called out in front of everyone and made to do push-ups. Luckily, muster went well, and we were dismissed for post.

Mr. Hammond had made quite the impression the first day he arrived at the Ranch. He made a big show of welcoming himself and gave out root beer floats and let us swim in the pool all afternoon. There had been several Cadet Coordinators since Mandy's mom had left, and they had been okay, but after those root beer floats, I was certain that Mr. Hammond was going to be the best Cadet Coordinator ever.

The next morning, however, we were in for a rude awakening. The bell rang, and I finished my conversation with my friends and walked over to my division. All around me, cadets wandered over to where they needed to be. Meanwhile, Mr. Hammond stood there. Boots planted. Arms crossed. Watching. I assumed he liked what he saw. I mean, it was a bunch of kids mustering themselves. Even I knew that was impressive in the real world.

Attendance was taken.

"At ease!" the CO cadets commanded. I put my arms behind my back and clasped my hands.

"What. Was. That?" Mr. Hammond asked as he glared at us.

"Uhhh . . ." the CO stammered.

I glanced around, wondering what he was so angry about.

"We're going to drill this again! And we are going to make this sharp and snappy! That was way too fucking slow!"

It was?

"We are going to practice this."

I looked around, wondering what we were supposed to do.

"Move it! Walk around. Act like the numbskulls you are," Mr. Hammond demanded.

Okay . . . I walked over to a far corner with Lacy, and we pretended to be talking. This was so weird.

"That's it for muster!"

I ran to my assigned spot as fast as possible.

"A ten-hut!" Mr. Hammond ordered. I stood at attention and tried not let a muscle move. Everyone around me was still. "Dress, right dress!"

I put out my right arm and touched the right shoulder of the person that was directly in front of me. I made sure we were perfectly distanced apart. The Division Heads in the front put their arms out to the right and lightly touched the person to the right of them. Our lines were as straight as a ruler.

"Good. This is how I want you to look at every muster!" Mr. Hammond said, pacing in front of us.

We stood silent.

"What the fuck? Are you deaf? Did you hear me?" he roared.

"Yes sir!" I screamed back along with my fellow cadets.

OVER THE NEXT FEW WEEKS, Mr. Hammond trained the Cadet Org in different marches, how to salute properly, and how to correctly respond to orders. He wanted us to be the best Sea Org members and impress everyone at PAC Base. He challenged us to races to see who was best at following his commands.

"Left face!"

"About face!"

"Right face!"

On and on and on.

Everyone moved in unison. Each command ended with our foot stamping on the ground. Left face. Swivel. Stomp. About face. Every turn. Stomp. Eventually a cadet would stumble. "Out!" Mr. Hammond would shout, and the cadet would sidle out of the group. It was whittled down to a few. This would keep going until everybody was out except one cadet. The last cadet standing was the winner. I wanted to be the winner but would only make it to the last ten or so before I got confused as his orders came faster and faster.

Then we marched. We marched in the field. We marched down the road behind the dorms. We marched around the office. We marched over the entire ranch, stirring up dust clouds as our feet stamped the earth. Our boots pounded down to Mr. Hammond's chants.

"Left, left, left, right, left . . ."

Eventually, I got used to Mr. Hammond's orders and ran through his muster commands like clockwork.

But my mom . . . I wasn't prepared for her to have to deal with this as well.

One of Mr. Hammond's new rules was that whenever you were late to muster, you had to do twenty-five push-ups. I was late all the time, so I became efficient and knocked out my push-ups in thirty seconds or so. I didn't even really mind the rule.

But then one day I was walking to the patio to get a drink from the water fountain when I saw my mom on her hands and knees, her arms trembling, doing push-ups in front of Mr. Hammond. The little children she oversaw had already jumped to their feet, finished with theirs, as my mom struggled on.

Why was she doing push-ups? Maybe she didn't know that she wasn't supposed to?

I hurried over to her and crouched down. "Mom! What are you doing? You don't have to do push-ups! Only the children and cadets do."

My mom stopped and looked up, then put her head down and kept going.

"Mom?"

Why wasn't she answering me?

She stopped at the top of a push-up. "The children were late to muster, so we need to do our push-ups," she answered quietly.

Mr. Hammond peered down at us. I waited for him to say something, but instead he turned away.

Asshole!

"Mom! Only the kids do it. You don't have to!" I said between gritted teeth as she pushed back down.

My mom kept going. How many push-ups was she going

to do? The children had all finished and stood around idly watching. It seemed like it had been an eternity when she finally stopped. I watched her as she heavily pushed herself up from the ground. She glanced at me, then turned away, back to her class of children. Still catching her breath, she instructed them to line up. I stared at her for a second, trying to understand.

Fuck. And now I had to get back on post before I got written up for blowing.

"I have to go, Mom," I called to her. She glanced at me and nodded as she guided her last child into line. I lifted my hand, gave a limp wave, and turned and trudged away. I watched my feet, as if in a daze. I didn't know if I could take this. Am I going to have to watch my mom do this all the time?

THANKFULLY, she was transferred down to PAC a week later. I didn't know why she was sent away. I wouldn't even know who to ask. I was just relieved that she was no longer at the Ranch. I hated seeing the kids yell at her and be brats, and I especially hated that she did push-ups like one of the children. With her leaving, I could just worry about myself. She was no longer my responsibility.

15

METER CHECKS

I sat in the chair with my feet planted a foot apart, lightly holding the two cylindrical silver cans that were plugged into the E-Meter.

The E-Meter is an electronic machine that L. Ron Hubbard invented, that was used to tell what emotions you were having. It was usually used in auditing for Scientologists who were going up the Bridge but I thought it was similar to a lie detector because that's what they seemed to use it for at the Ranch. Every few months Mr. Hammond would order that every cadet get meter-checked to see who had a dirty needle. A dirty needle was an E-Meter response resulting in small, quick jerking motions of the lie-detector-like recording device. If you got a dirty needle, you were forced to write up your overts and withholds, confessing every out-ethics thing you had ever done and ensuring you'd lose privileges the next weekend. But I knew a trick. To prevent myself from getting a dirty needle, I just thought happy thoughts. It seemed to work every time. I don't remember how I learned this, or if I had just figured it out for myself. It was just something I did.

I breathed nice and slow as I held the silver cans that were wired to the E-Meter. The read-out screen faced away from me, and Mr. Williams glanced down at it.

I thought back to the time Derek had been nice to me in front of the entire Cadet Org during a relay race in the pool.

We were all there, the entire Cadet Org. The race was boys against girls, and the boys were kicking our butts. Toward the end, my turn came. I got ready to dive in, but then looked over to the boys' line and found myself pitted against my brother's friend Derek, who I had worked with in the galley. Derek was two years older than me and one of the strongest swimmers at the Ranch. He dove in before I had a chance, but when he came up for air, he just stopped. He turned and treaded water, waiting for me to join him. I jumped in, and he smiled at me. We swam across the pool at the same leisurely speed, the other boys screaming like crazy that Derek was losing their lead. We touched the wall at the same time, tying the race, while a shower of shouts and cuss words rained down on Derek's head. I got out of the pool, and the rest of the girls surrounded me, asking what had happened, were we going out or something? Even the cool older girls craned in to listen to what I had to say. There was nothing really going on between Derek and me, but still, it had made me feel so special.

Mr. William's eyes scanned the E-Meter, and I felt droplets of water on my shoulder, the sun beating down on my skin as I looked at the incredulous faces of girls around me.

In Mr. Williams's examination room, the clock on the wall ticked. I sat still. My mind at the pool. My hands on the cans.

"Thank you." Mr. Williams broke the silence. "Your needle is floating."

Yes. No dirty needle for me, I thought. I set the cans down on the desk. I was a pro at this. To have an examiner say your needle was floating was about the best thing you could get at the end of an E-Meter session. A floating needle meant you were happy and serene. Had Mr. Williams finished this session by saying, "Thank you very much," it likely would have meant I had a "dirty" needle but that she wasn't ready to make it official. First, I would get pulled into the office for further questioning to see just how bad it was.

Even though dirty needles were to be avoided at all costs, they weren't the worst needle responses you could get on an E-meter. That designation went to the "rock slam." In a rock slam, your needle flew back and forth as if going crazy. Anyone who got a rock slam was pure evil and declared a Suppressive Person. I had never heard of anyone getting a rock slam, but it was rumored that people like Hitler would have gotten one for sure. Every time I got meter-checked, there was a small part of me that worried I was about to rock slam. That I'd touch the cans, and my needle would go haywire. They'd kick me off the Ranch, call my parents, let them know I'd been expelled for being evil. But then I'd remind myself that L. Ron Hubbard said a true Suppressive Person didn't worry about being evil; they thought they were good. The fact that I worried about it meant that I couldn't possibly be evil. That would make me feel better.

"Can you send the next cadet in?" Mr. Williams requested. She scribbled on the legal-sized white paper in front of her.

"Yep," I said happily. I headed for the door, glad I was officially off the hook.

16

THE ELUSIVE PHONE CALL

My mom was no longer at PAC Base. She had been sent to Flag in Florida for training. It all must have been decided quickly, because she didn't even say goodbye to me before she left. This was just like when my dad had been sent to Flag.

Ironically, my dad was back in Los Angeles now, just as my mom was being sent to Florida. It seemed like they were always apart.

Now that my mom was at Flag, phone calls from her were less frequent. I used to talk to her once a month at least, but now months would go by without hearing her voice.

One day after lunch, a cadet came and knocked on my door and told me my mom was on the phone at the main office. Yes! I hurried over to where Tory and Lacy lay on their beds, talking about their favorite Sublime songs.

"Tory, can I borrow your bike?" I pleaded. "My mom is on the phone, and I want to make sure I get to the main office in time."

"Yeah sure. Just make sure you bring it back!" Her voice

rose, as I was already running out to the hallway and through the door.

"Okay, I will! Thanks!" I shouted before the door slammed shut behind me. Tory lived in my dorm and was the only one of us who seemed to have an unlimited supply of money. She owned the best Lisa Frank trapper keeper, brand new clothes from places like The Gap, a nice bike, and even a dog. Her mom also owned her own car and visited Tory every other week. I would have been jealous of her, but she was so nice all the time. She always let me borrow stuff, bike included. My bike popped a tire six months earlier. An older cadet offered to fix it if I could scrounge up $20. It took me a week to gather the money. I paid him, and he wound up taking the bike and dismantling it for parts. He denied it, of course, turning the whole thing into a he-said-she-said situation. I wrote a Knowledge Report on him, but nothing came of it. So, my bike was in the garbage, and I was stuck depending on friends' generosity to get around.

I grabbed Tory's bike from the rack in front of the dorm and pedaled down the asphalt road to the main office. I now lived in Dorm 10, at the far end of the Ranch, so I knew I had to rush to the main office to make it in time. I flew past Dorm 9, then Dorm 8, past the galley and down the last hill, standing on the pedals, feeling the wind rush past me, when suddenly a cadet leapt in front of me. He shouted and waved his arms like a maniac.

I startled and the bike flew out from under me, and I slammed hard on to the asphalt. I lay there for a moment in shock. All I could hear was laughter as the bright burst of pain electrified my right side. I raised my head and looked over. It was Eric, the older cadet who had disassembled my bike for parts. He was doubled over, his eyes scrunched, howling at my expense.

"Fucking asshole!" I screamed at him.

Eric continued to shriek with laughter. My outburst didn't seem to faze him one bit. I sat up and gingerly got to my feet, breathing heavily. I lifted my shirt and examined my hip. There was a scrape running all the way up to my ribs, red blood blossoming in the center, where the scrape was the deepest.

"Why did you even do that?!"

"You should have been paying more attention," Eric said with a smirk.

I flipped him off and limped over to Tory's bike, hoping there was no damage. I righted it and breathed a sigh of relief. Nothing was broken. I threw my leg over the bike and pedaled past Eric, ignoring his cheery wave and the stings of pain on my side.

I parked at the main office bike rack and ran inside. Maybe there was a chance my mom hadn't hung up yet. I looked around wildly and saw the phone lying on the side table. I lunged for it.

"Mom!" I said breathlessly.

Beep, beep, beep.

"Shit!" I said under my breath as I slammed the receiver down. She must have had to go back on course. All of that for nothing! I limped out of the office, picked up Tory's bike, and pedaled up the road to the MLO office to clean my scrape. My hip stung as my shirt rubbed against the bloody wound. I gritted my teeth and seethed.

Why the hell did he think it was okay to jump in front of my bike just to scare me? This was yet another overt that Eric committed on top of his pile. He was constantly bullying the little kids and beating them up, he stole money from them and was a liar. L. Ron Hubbard says that if you commit a lot of overts, you pull in bad things. Eric was in for it.

A few weeks later at staff meeting Eric had a seizure. The younger kids were unsympathetic and called him names as he flailed around on the floor. Finally, an adult rushed into the room and escorted Eric out, who had stopped flailing around and now seemed groggy and out of it. As I watched the staff member lead him away, I knew that what L. Ron Hubbard said was true. He had pulled it in for sure.

17

LEGALLY BLIND

I sat in a large black reclining chair and squinted.

"What do you see?" the eye doctor asked. I looked at the dark smudges on a chart up on the wall.

I tried to make it out, but it was no use. "Uh, I can't see what it is," I admitted.

"How about now?" The shapes on the chart seemed to change, but they were still just dark fuzzy marks to me.

"Um . . . no . . ." I trailed off.

"Now?" the doctor said as she clicked again.

"No, sorry." I felt like a failure.

"You can't make out anything on the wall?" she asked. Her voice sounded incredulous.

"Um, no?" Why was she making such a big deal out of this? I squirmed in the chair, uncomfortable under her stare.

"Well, let's try it again with this." The doctor swung over a contraption that had two eye holes to look through. She fiddled with some knobs and then placed it in front of my face. "What can you see?"

I peered through the lenses, and there, plain as day, was the letter *E*.

How had I not been able to see that before? Had this big, obvious *E* been the dark blob all along?

"What is on the wall?" the doctor asked.

"The letter *E*," I told her.

"Good!" she cried out, as if she'd won the lottery. "We're going to go through different lenses and see which are the best for you." She adjusted the lenses. "You are legally blind. I am shocked that you are eleven and went this long without glasses."

She looked over at Mr. Williams, and they chatted about my vision while my mind raced. How could I be legally blind? And what did that even mean? I could see, right? Yeah, sure, I always sat as close as possible to the TV to be able to see the movies during org awards on Saturday nights. And yes, I squinted to read the captions if there were any, but I didn't think it was that bad. This must be why my friends teased me for reading with my books only an inch from my nose. They were able to read from far away because they had normal eyesight! I just thought they liked the books farther from their face.

The doctor prattled on, then turned her attention back to me.

"You are just going to love being able to see." She twisted a dial and a new lens clicked into place. "Okay, what line of letters can you see here on the chart?"

We went through different lenses, A or B, one or two, until the doctor seemed satisfied that she'd found the right combination.

"Thanks," I mumbled. I just wanted to get out of there. I felt so stupid. I was blind and I hadn't even known.

"Okay, because of how farsighted you are and your astigmatism, I would like to dilate your eyes and take a look at your retina in each eye. We are going to put some drops in, and then in twenty minutes, I'll take a peek," she continued.

Astigmatism! What was that? Why couldn't this just be over? Why were my eyes such failures? My mind raced as she administered the eyedrops. Some time passed, and the doctor shone a bright light in my right eye. She directed me to look in different directions. I sighed with relief as she finished the right eye and moved on to my left. Almost done. But then she gasped.

What now?

The doctor turned to Mr. Williams. "She has a tear in her retina," she said. She turned back and shone the light in my eye again. I looked to the left as she continued speaking. "The tear is microscopic, but she will need laser surgery right away, otherwise she runs the risk of her retina fully detaching. She could lose her sight in the left eye."

What? Was this real? I could go blind?

The rest of the eye examination passed in a blur. I didn't get how this was happening to me. Did I pull this in? I was always staying up late past bed time reading books with a flashlight under my blanket when it was lights-out. And there were the times I had snuck out of the course room and hid in my dorm to read. As more of my overts were recalled, I realized that I probably did deserve this. The technician led me over to try on some frames. I tried them on, distracted. I chose a random pair and hoped for the best.

We left the frames at the eye doctor and headed out to the car. Mr. Williams would pick up the glasses when they were ready. As we drove away, Mr. Williams let me know that laser surgery was scheduled for later in the week at a hospital in Los Angeles. I nodded, but inside I was scared. Would they be cutting my eye open?

LASER SURGERY TURNED out to be a painless affair. There were flashes of light shined into my eye from a machine, and everything looked red and orange for a little bit, but that faded away after only thirty minutes, just like I'd been told it would. The technician said they were sealing the hole in my retina closed by burning around the tear. Before the surgery, I had visions of me walking around with a patch on my eye, so it was a huge relief that the procedure was so quick and easy. I was back at the Ranch that afternoon, and later that evening I reported to course.

After course ended, I stacked the blue plastic chairs on the tables, as always. Hallie worked next to me, and I told her all about the laser surgery.

"Wait, you got laser surgery?" a voice interrupted. I looked over and saw Derek standing by a table with his friend Will.

"Yeah," I shrugged. "It wasn't a big deal."

"But can you see through walls now?" Will asked. Derek laughed.

"Nooo. It just fixed a microscopic tear in my eye." I rolled my eyes.

"You have a *hole* in your eye?" Derek said. I felt my cheeks warm.

"Yeah, so?" I shot back.

"Don't worry, the lasers fixed it," Will interrupted. "Now she can see through anything."

"Oh no, everything? Quick, cover your dick!" Derek exclaimed. He cupped his hands over his groin area. Will did the same.

"Shut up guys! I can't see through clothes!" I laughed and grabbed a piece of paper off the table next to me, crumpled it and threw it at them.

"Oh, no—let's get out of here before she sees us naked!" Derek ran for the door, Will following right behind. It shut behind them, but I could still hear their laughter. I shrugged, and Hallie and I gathered the rest of our materials to put away.

They're just kidding, I thought to myself. But still, I felt so pitiful.

A COUPLE OF WEEKS LATER, Mr. Williams brought me my new glasses. I ran to my dorm, opened the package, and put them on. My eyes widened with surprise when I saw my dorm clearly for the first time. The bumps on the ceiling, the grain in the wood of the bunk beds, the speckled brown of the carpet. I'd never noticed these details.

What did outside look like?

I raced through the hallway and left the dorm and stared at my surroundings. I could see the individual leaves on trees! Bugs on the ground. It felt like I was seeing the world for the first time. I understood now why the eye doctor was so rattled. It was like I had been looking out through a foggy window. I couldn't believe it. I went back into my dorm and looked in the mirror.

Wait.

What were those dots all over my nose and cheeks?

I leaned in closer to the mirror and cringed. Blackheads were scattered across my nose and cheeks. I'd read about these in a *Seventeen* magazine but had no idea I had them. Now I could see every one of them.

Another thing was that my frames, which were a thin

black plastic, could barely hold in my lenses which were almost a centimeter thick. With my frizzy brown hair, thick lenses, and face full of blackheads, I had to be the plainest girl at the Ranch.

Oh well. At least I could see. And that was a major relief.

18

PIGS

I stood in the corner of the dumpster area and swallowed my nausea. "This is disgusting," I said.

"This has to be child abuse," Hallie agreed, scrunching up her pert nose.

We were crammed behind the galley along with the entire Cadet Org. The area was barely thirty yards across, so cadets sat on closed dumpster lids, on the wood fence, anywhere they could find a spot. Hallie and I cowered in a corner by the gate, as far as we could get from the metal containers. But the smell still hit me in the face. I pulled my shirt over my nose and tried to breathe lightly through my mouth to avoid smelling the noxious fumes, but it was impossible. There was rotten food underneath the dumpsters, juices of unknown origin streaked on the sides, and flies everywhere.

Mr. Hammond stood at the entrance of the gate and lectured us about how disgusting the dining room was.

"Since you act like pigs, you can eat like pigs," he declared at the end of his lecture.

With that, he gestured to two cadets who came out of the

galley with a gray plastic cart full of bagels and cream cheese. Boys charged to the cart to get their food as if we were at a buffet feast.

"Gross!" I yelled at the guys already stuffing their faces. Derek looked over and laughed.

"You want one?" He held up a blueberry bagel.

"Ew, no!" I wrinkled my nose. "How can you even have an appetite? It smells like rotten eggs—no, worse! Sewage!" I leaned over and pretended to gag.

"Don't be jelly," Derek said through a mouthful of bagel.

"I am totally not jealous!" I laughed despite myself. "You're disgusting." I turned away to join Hallie and my other friends.

FIVE MINUTES LATER, Mr. Hammond blew his whistle. In front of him were plastic gallons of ammonia, mops, push brooms, and dustpans.

Oh shit.

I knew what was coming.

"All of you assholes need to clean this dumpster area to a white glove clean!" Mr. Hammond bellowed. He peered over his aviator sunglasses and scanned the crowd.

"You!" He pointed to Will, the current CO. "Organize the cadets and fix this hellhole!"

Will walked over to the cleaning materials and looked around. It seemed like he didn't know where to start.

"Okay, who wants to sweep?" Several cadets raised their hands, but not enough. "C'mon guys!" Still, no one else volunteered. Will narrowed his eyes as they shrank back into clumps, avoiding his gaze. Hallie and I grabbed each other's hands and slipped back behind the wooden gate hiding from his line of vision.

"Fine. I'll pick myself. You"—he pointed—"you, and you." Each cadet groaned and muttered and sullenly stepped forward. Will continued selecting cadets for different tasks. Some were asked to throw ammonia on the ground, followed by moppers and dustpan duty. Once all the assignments had been given, Hallie and I smiled at each other. We had gotten away with not being assigned work.

We and the other lucky ones watched as cadets ran around everywhere, splashing ammonia in copious amounts. The combination of it mixing with the stench of rotten food was overwhelming. My eyes watered. I pulled my shirt up over my mouth and nose. The cadets had already gone through four gallons, but no matter how much they poured on the cement, the rancid smell would not dissipate.

"Okay, scrubbers," Will commanded. "Start scrubbing!" Cadets sprang into action as I hunkered in the far corner, out of the way. The activity swirled around me as I tried to hold my breath. Soon most of the cement floor had been scrubbed, but the smell still lingered in the air. I wouldn't have been surprised to see green vapor swirling up from the dumpsters.

Mr. Hammond blew his whistle. "All right. You've done enough. This better teach you to keep a cleaner dining room. Go back inside and eat lunch and then show me how clean you can make it."

Cadets scrambled through the gate back into the dining room. I grabbed a plate and a bagel and cream cheese off the cart and headed toward my usual seat.

A FEW WEEKS after the dumpster incident, Mr. Hammond flew into a rage again, but this time I caught the brunt of it.

It was Saturday afternoon, and we had finished lunch. Mr. Hammond appeared at our noon muster. He paced in front of us, ranting about how he'd walked through the galley this morning and seen what a pigsty it was. Why did he have to remind us to keep common areas at Sea Org standards? Once again, a white glove needed to be done.

He gave a booming "Start!" and the cadets rushed into action. I decided to grab dirty pans from the serving line from lunch and bring them to the dishwashing area. I went to get the pots, but as I walked, my head began to spin. *What was going on?* I steadied myself against the wall. I wanted to sit down, but I knew if I stopped, I would get yelled at. I walked carefully with my pans and followed my friend Erica toward the sinks. She looked back at me and stopped so suddenly I almost ran into her.

"What's wrong? Are you okay?"

"I feel strange." I swallowed a wave of nausea.

"Well, let's try to keep moving before Mr. Hammond notices us," Erica said.

We dropped off our pots and she led the way back to the serving area. I trailed behind her and almost ran into Mr. Hammond's large frame. How had I not seen him coming? This guy was a giant and yet I had missed him.

"What are you doing walking so slowly!" he roared down at me.

As I opened my mouth to speak, he reached down and grabbed me by my collar and lifted me until my toes dangled. My shirt caught against my neck. I was at eye level with Mr. Hammond, his whiskery jowls right in sight. I was pretty sure I was about to throw up in his face.

"I don't feel well," I whispered.

Mr. Hammond shook me. "Speak up!"

"I feel sick!" I croaked out.

"Bullshit!" He gave me another shake. "I know you Katherine, and I know the crap you pull. Stop with your excuses and get your ass to work!"

Mr. Hammond let me go. I landed with a stumble and caught myself. I moved away and grabbed more pans and went back into the galley.

What was Mr. Hammond talking about? What crap did he think I was trying to pull?

My head continued to spin. I leaned against the sink. Erica was soaking the pots with water. "Holy shit, your face is white!" she whispered to me.

I opened my mouth to speak, but a hand landed on my shoulder. I jumped.

It was Mr. Ellis, my old dorm mom. My heart settled back into my chest. "Katherine, go to ISO and lie down. I don't want anyone sick in the galley," she murmured in my ear.

I NODDED and set my pots on the counter and trudged toward the back of the galley. ISO was short for isolation. This was where cadets went when they were sick. It was next door to the back galley's entrance, so I didn't have far to go. I focused my gaze on the ground and stretched my hand out against the wall to support me. I pushed open the back door and turned toward ISO. I couldn't wait to lie down on a cot and go to sleep.

I pushed open the ISO door and stared. I couldn't believe what I was seeing. Mr. Stewart, one of the adult staff members, supervising two cadets wiping the linoleum floor with a bucket of soapy water next to them.

"What do you want?" Mr. Stewart barked, her arms crossed over her stocky body.

I felt so tired and worn out. I didn't want to explain. I just wanted to collapse onto a cot.

"I'm sick," I breathed out. "Mr. Ellis said I should go to ISO."

"What, and you expect some sympathy?" Mr. Stewart shook her head. "If you're going to be in here you need to help clean first. Then you can lie down."

I didn't have the energy to argue. I slid down to the floor and grabbed a rag from the bucket of soapy water. I leaned over to start wiping when the floor seemed to shift beneath me. Vomit burst out of my mouth with such force that it sprayed across the floor.

"Goddamn it!"

I looked up at Mr. Stewart, who stared at my mess, disgusted.

"Fine!" She crossed her arms. "Clean up your barf and then you can lay down."

I wiped at it with the help of the other two cadets. Once it was cleaned up, I stumbled into the cot and closed my eyes. I just wanted to feel better and not be such a burden on everyone. Hopefully this feeling would go away after I slept.

When I woke up, I glanced at the clock and saw I had been asleep an hour. Thankfully, I already felt better. It must have been something I ate. I got out of bed and told Mr. Stewart I could help clean.

"Good," she grunted. "We're all done now. Just report back to the galley."

I nodded and headed there. I slipped in through the back door, hoping to avoid Mr. Hammond at all costs. I didn't want to be yelled at again. Cadets seemed to be milling around, and there didn't seem to be any work left to do. I felt a little guilty. I had slacked off while all the other cadets had worked hard. I felt even worse when the Cadet Org was rewarded with popsicles. I decided to have one anyway. I hadn't wanted to barf. It just happened. At least I had cleaned it up.

19

BLACK AND PROUD

After years of frustration with my dark, frizzy hair, I finally decided it was time to embrace being Black by braiding my hair. My friend Mirriam and I sat on the carpeted floor in my dorm as she plaited tiny braids all over my head.

A few days earlier, a bunch of the cadets were talking about movies and actors, and an older cadet teased that I should choose Will Smith as my favorite actor since he was Black and I was half-Black. That I was Black, or even half-Black, had never occurred to me before. Yes, I knew my skin tone was darker than most of the other cadets', my hair a completely different texture, but it never occurred to me to put that in terms of race.

"Mom has to be Black, right?" I asked Judson later that day. "I mean, she's the one who has skin like ours." I held my arm up to Judson's, our skin identical shades of brown.

"Yeah, and she used to have a curly afro." Judson mimed large hair around his head.

"I wonder why she cut it?"

Judson shrugged.

"But Dad is White, right?" I continued.

"I think so."

"Okay, so if Dad is White, then mix it together and I think we are called Mulatto."

I felt an unexpected sense of pride at the realization. It felt good to finally understand this aspect of myself. Being Mulatto explained so much. Like why my hair was coarse and frizzy. All my friends had silky hair so fine it slipped through their fingers like magic when they ran them through it. How was that even possible? I couldn't run my fingers through an inch of my hair if I tried. But now I understood. I needed to do what Black girls do with their hair, just like Alicia Silverstone's best friend in *Clueless*. I needed braids. So, I went and found my friend Mirriam and asked if she would braid my hair over our lunch. These braids would solve everything. No more puffy hair. No more tangles.

"Okay." Mirriam snapped on the last rubber band at the end of a braid. "All done!"

I pushed myself up and trotted into the hallway to look in the mirror. Braids hung down on either side of my face, a little past my shoulders. I swished my head back and forth and watched them swing side to side like ropes.

"I love them. Thank you!"

"You're welcome." Mirriam smiled. "I love your new look!"

I KEPT those braids in for as long as I could. I began "studying" Black people and Black culture as much as I was able, hoping to learn more about myself. I didn't have much to go off, though. Most books at the Ranch only featured White people as the main characters. Instead, I leaned on movies like *Boyz n the Hood*, *Friday*, *White Men Can't Jump*, and of course, *Clueless*. Most of the movies were far outside of my reality, beyond anything I'd experienced before. And they predominantly featured Black males. The only Black character I could kind of relate to was Dionne, Cher's best friend in *Clueless*, a Black girl at a school surrounded by White people. Of course, all the kids in *Clueless* were rich and driving cars around Beverly Hills, while we Ranchers were being barked at by our drill sergeant Cadet Coordinator and fighting over turns to borrow friends' bikes. But she was the closest Black person I could relate to, so I ran with it.

LATER THAT MONTH, Judson and I were both down in LA at PAC for a mission. We got a break over lunch and found a ball to kick around on the grass in front of the blue building that rose seven stories behind us. Judson kicked the ball and I grabbed it. He shouted for me to give it back.

"Da ball? Uh uh," I drawled, adopting the voices of Black people I had seen in the movies.

My brother cracked up.

"You totally sound Black!" he said.

I couldn't help but laugh along with him. Who knew I had this talent? I was getting the hang of my culture.

A FEW WEEKS LATER, I was talking to my mom on the phone. I hadn't seen her in a long time, since she had been at Flag for months. I updated her on my life and told her about braiding my hair.

"Why did you do that?" she asked.

"Because I'm part Black, hellooo." I rolled my eyes, even though she couldn't see me through the phone.

"Wait, what? Why do you think that?"

"Because you're Black and Dad is White," I replied, annoyed that she'd even ask.

My mom laughed.

"What?" I demanded. "Why are you laughing?"

"I'm Puerto Rican, I'm not black." She chuckled. "And Dad is Italian."

"What? Are you kiddi— Wait, what is Puerto Rican?"

"You don't know about Puerto Rico?" my mom asked.

"I don't know. I guess I've heard the name before."

My mom told me that Puerto Rico was an island south of Florida, and it was a commonwealth of the United States. Her parents had been born there and so had she. When she was a little girl, they moved to New York City.

"Don't you remember visiting my sisters and brothers in New York? I think you were around eight," she told me.

Flashes of memories came back to me. I remembered being in New York, surprised to see my mom speak Spanish fluently with my aunts and uncle. I couldn't believe that I'd forgotten that. It was so obvious now that she wasn't Black. I felt so embarrassed—what had I been thinking?

I said goodbye and headed back to my dorm. I needed to get these braids taken out.

20

DATING FRENZY

All at once it seemed the boys and girls at the Ranch were aware of each other in a whole different way. Overnight, any girl who was cool had a boyfriend.

The dating frenzy seemed to start when a new kid named Brett arrived at our school. Brett was fourteen years old, and his family had just moved to the States from Australia.

After only a couple of weeks at the Ranch, Brett asked out Leah, one of the prettiest girls in school. Nobody had really "dated" at the Ranch before, but Brett and Leah set off a chain reaction, and soon it seemed like all the popular girls had a boyfriend. Everywhere you looked, kids were making out. I would be on the bus and look out the window and see a couple behind the bus swapping saliva like no one's business. In the evenings, cadets would be wrapped around each other on the patios of the dorms. The adults would do what they could to break up any kissing when they saw it, but there were so many times when we were unsupervised that it was easy for cadets to sneak away to make out.

With all this action, Hallie and I decided we needed boyfriends ASAP. I knew Hallie could probably land a guy easily, but I worried I wouldn't be able to find one. With my frizzy hair and glasses, I didn't exactly consider myself a catch. The only thing going for me was that I was friends with most of the boys at the Ranch.

One day after lunch, my brother Judson caught up to me as I was heading up to my dorm. He said his friend Antonio liked me and was thinking of asking me out.

"Really?" I said. "You're not just teasing me, right?"

"No, he told me today. I promise." Judson looked down toward the field. "Listen, I gotta go now though. We're gonna go play football over by the schoolhouse. But believe me—he likes you."

With that he waved goodbye. I watched him jog to join the group of guys standing in the middle of the field, jostling each other and laughing. One of his friends shouted for him to hurry up, and Judson picked up his pace.

My thoughts turned to what my brother had said. Was he telling me the truth? I didn't think Judson would lie to me. There was that one time I had been on course and looked up and seen Antonio staring at me. I had made a face at him and resumed my conversation with my friends, assuming he was just being weird. But maybe there was something more? Could that be possible? Sometimes I felt like the ugliest girl at the Ranch besides Susan, who was slovenly and smelled like she never took a shower. Antonio was pretty cute with his Backstreet Boy-style haircut and his floppy brown hair falling in his face. He was two years older than me and was friends with Judson and the older guys. These were all plus points.

But—and this was a big "but"—Antonio was short.

I had never pictured my first boyfriend being level with my nose.

I would just have to disregard that small detail. I decided I would say yes if he asked to be my boyfriend. Hopefully he would work up his nerve to ask me to meet him at the berm by the horses so "we could talk."

A WEEK WENT BY, but I got nothing from Antonio but side glances and shy smiles. Meanwhile, Hallie had been asked out by Liam, Mirriam's younger brother. He was one of our best guy friends, and so it had been easy enough for Hallie to snag him. I couldn't help feeling jealous. Hallie was only ten years old and had already landed a boyfriend. I was twelve! Two years older and I'd never had one. The fire under me was lit. My eyes scanned every guy at the Ranch who remained single. Who could I get?

I decided on Liam's best friend, Ricky. Ricky and I were close. He made me laugh harder than anyone at the Ranch. Yeah, I didn't like him in "that" way, but Antonio was taking too long. I needed a boyfriend *now*.

A WEEK LATER, we rode the bus as it rumbled up the windy roads while cadets sang at the top of their lungs to the radio blaring over the speakers. David, the bus driver, must have been in a good mood, or was too tired to yell at us to be quiet. Usually by this time, he had pulled over and screamed at us to shut our traps, his glasses gleaming, his black beard surrounding his grimacing mouth.

Hallie and I huddled together on the sticky, dark green pleather seat, using the loud noise as cover to plot our next plan. Ricky and Liam sat behind us, whispering as well. Hallie had told Liam the plan to have Ricky ask me out, and now she and I were discussing if he was going to do it now or later. Suddenly, a piece of crumpled paper flew over the seat. I leaned over and grabbed it off the grimy pale green linoleum, which was streaked with dirt and old juice stains. Hallie leaned over my shoulder.

"What does it say?"

"Will you be my girlfriend?" I read out loud through a wide grin. "Yes!"

"We have to write back!" Hallie declared.

I rummaged through my backpack on the floor and found a pencil. I carefully wrote out "yes" and then crumpled the paper.

"Ready?" I looked at Hallie and she nodded. We both popped up and tossed the paper over to the boys, then ducked back down, giggling.

A minute later we heard a loud, "Youlst!" from behind us where Ricky was sitting. I grinned at Hallie. It was official. I now had a boyfriend. As I was basking in my glory, another note came flying over and landed in Hallie's lap.

"What now?" She laughed as she unfolded the paper and read what it said. I leaned in close, smelling her strawberry-scented lip gloss. Ooh, I would need to borrow some of that. But first the matter at hand. I peered down at the scribble. This time it was different handwriting.

Ricky and I will pick you up at 10:00pm from your dorm to take you out on a date. – Liam

. . .

"YAY!" I grabbed Hallie and hugged her. We were going on our first dates!

THAT NIGHT, Ricky and Liam came to the dorm and waited for us on the patio. Hallie and I slipped out to meet them, our lips fresh with rolled-on strawberry lip gloss. We weren't supposed to leave after lights out, but as long as we weren't loud, we would be able to get away with it, since the adults weren't around. Ricky and I decided to walk to the berm while Hallie and Liam headed to the Communication Center at the log cabin.

The berm was the "romantic" spot at the Ranch. It was a long hill with cement down one side, way out on the far side of the Ranch near the horse corral. If you sat on the cement side, people couldn't see you. You faced away from the lights of the Ranch, so that there was an inky darkness, which made the stars extra bright.

Ricky and I sat down on the cold concrete of the berm. As I got comfortable, I wondered what couples were supposed to talk about.

"Wait, what that's sound?" Ricky asked. I stopped moving and strained to listen. It was dark, and I could barely see anything. Suddenly, Ricky grabbed my arm.

"Boo!"

"Ahhh," I shrieked.

Ricky fell over laughing. I kicked him with my foot.

"You asshole. You're supposed to be romantic!" I couldn't hold it together and giggled.

There was another couple farther away on the berm. They glanced over at us.

"Shhhh!" I whispered to Ricky, gesturing at them. I felt bad for ruining their romantic moment. I couldn't see who it was, but their presence reminded me of why we were there in the first place.

"Okay, we need to be serious now," I said. "Let's look at the stars." We stared up at the sky and pointed out constellations, but we knew of only a few names, so we made the rest up. There was the rope. Over there was the square. Within minutes we were doubled over, hands over our mouths trying to contain our mirth.

After a minute of laughing, I calmed down. I had come here for my first kiss. I needed to take this seriously. I took a deep breath.

"Should we kiss?" I whispered to Ricky.

Ricky nodded. He looked like he was facing the death penalty. I almost lost it again.

"We can do this." I smiled encouragingly. I shifted my body to face Ricky and took a deep breath.

We both leaned in at the same time.

Crack! Our foreheads thudded together.

We burst out laughing.

"Shit! Okay, okay, okay," I said. I wiped my eyes. "We have to get this done. Are you ready to try again?"

Ricky put his hand on his face and tried to wipe the silliness away.

"Okay, we got this." Ricky nodded.

I leaned in with my eyes closed. I opened them slightly to see if Ricky was going in for a kiss. His eyes were wide open, staring into my face.

"What the hell!" I shoved him away. A chuckle escaped. "Don't look at me while we're trying to kiss."

"Sorry, sorry," Ricky whispered back. He looked like he was struggling not to crack up. "I didn't know that was against the rules!"

We tried to kiss a few more times, but each time we couldn't manage to keep it together.

In the end I told him we should just try again tomorrow. We headed back, holding hands. I smiled. At least we had gotten that part right.

When I arrived at my dorm, I whispered good night to Ricky, pulled the patio door open, and slipped inside. The lights were off. The bathroom to the left creaked open, sending a beam of light into the hallway. Hallie gestured me over. I slid in and shut the door quietly behind me.

"How did it go for you?" I whispered to Hallie.

"We haven't frenched yet." She shrugged. "But we will tomorrow."

I was relieved. Since Hallie was only ten and I was twelve, there was no way I was going to let her be the first to be kissed. I told her we hadn't either, but we would on our next date as well. With that plan in mind, we slipped off to our dorms. That night I laid in bed and plotted how I would kiss Ricky until I fell asleep.

THE NEXT EVENING, Ricky and Liam came back to pick us up. We had about twenty minutes until lights out. We had decided earlier in the day that the Communication Center at the log cabin was where we were going to hang out this evening. The Comm Center was where you went to receive any communications sent to you, like Knowledge Reports or Commendations. At this time of night, no one would be there, and it would give us the privacy we needed. We had a mission to accomplish, and that was getting frenched.

First, we had to get past the log cabin where the adults slept. We passed Dorm 9, Dorm 8, and then skirted the patio to remain hidden behind the short brick wall that surrounded it. The lights from the adult dorms streamed out from the windows in the doors. We darted across the dirt to the cement patio to the left of the log cabin and ran across it to the Comm Center. We raced up the short flight of concrete stairs into the room and shut the door.

"Youlst," I whispered. "We made it!"

"There were no adults even around," Ricky rolled his eyes. "They're probably all at the main office."

I shoved him. "Whatever. We're still safe!"

Liam laughed and strolled past us to the exec room connected to the Comm Center. He waved for Hallie to join. She giggled nervously and followed him in.

"Bye." Liam grinned, then shut the door.

Ricky and I stood in the middle of the Comm Center and stared at each other. The only light in the room came from the small window by the door from the lamppost outside. The room smelled musty from all the papers stacked on tables and inside the inboxes. This was not very romantic, but we had to make the best of it.

I took a deep breath and reached for Ricky's hands.

He leaned in, his lips puckered, his eyes closed like we agreed. I closed mine and leaned forward.

Crack!

Our foreheads slammed together again.

"Ow! Fuck!" I rubbed my forehead and smiled through my teary eyes. "Why do we keep doing this?"

"We just really suck," Ricky joked.

"No kidding." I laughed. "Okay, let's try again."

We tried a few more times, but each time we ended up busting out laughing.

Knock, knock.

We stopped and turned.

Hallie opened the exec office door and walked in with Liam, holding hands.

"We frenched," she said with a Cheshire cat smile. "What are you guys doing?"

Damn it, she beat me.

"Oh my god. Good for you guys!" I forced a smile. "We're just messing around. Why don't you guys go wait outside. We'll be there in a sec."

They left and shut the door.

I turned to Ricky. This was it. No more messing around. We leaned in slowly, and I closed my eyes until I felt his lips touch mine. I opened my eyes a sliver to see what he was doing and saw that he had his open a little too. I quickly shut mine to stop myself from laughing again. We needed to do this!

I concentrated on sticking out my tongue. I touched it to his, and we rubbed them against each other. His was rough on mine and slippery with saliva. I wanted to recoil, but I was determined to kiss him for at least a minute. We moved our mouths against each other like in the movies with our tongues battling it out. When mine began to tire, I pulled away.

"We did it," I said grimly. That kiss was slimy, but who cared. We had made out. I grabbed Ricky's hand and we headed out of the Comm Center.

Liam and Hallie jumped up from the steps that lead outside.

"We frenched too," I told them.

"Cool," Hallie said.

We grinned at each other. I felt like we had accomplished something big. We were growing up.

21

SOURCE

Every Monday evening, all the cadets were sent down to the art room for Source night. I don't know why it was called that, since we never did art in there. It was a large room in a cabin with floor-to-ceiling mirrors and a linoleum floor. Source night was an evening spent devoted to L. Ron Hubbard's works, listening to lectures or watching videos about Dianetics or Scientology. I dreaded Source night because most nights it was incredibly boring. Of course, I didn't tell anyone that, since I didn't want to get in trouble, but I was pretty sure that's what everyone else thought.

Source night wasn't so bad if we watched videos that taught us important Scientology processes like how auditing worked and how important it was to get rid of your reactive mind. There were also videos about The Way to Happiness campaign and how to behave well. One of my favorites was a video called "Say No to Drugs," which was unintentionally hilarious because the acting was so bad.

It was the L. Ron Hubbard lectures that bored me to tears. These lectures were over two hours long, and I'd spend the entire time trying my best to not fall asleep. To make the hours pass I would slip notes to friends, but usually there was an adult present, watching us like a hawk. Sometimes I felt guilty that I didn't pay enough attention. To make up for this, I clapped extra hard when we did our "hip hip hoorays" to L. Ron Hubbard's portrait at the end.

TODAY WAS A MONDAY, and Hallie and I decided that we would sneak a note to Ricky and Liam at course time telling them to meet us at the berm right before Source night. Then we would sneak out back onto Department of Water and Power property on the other side of the horse corral. Hallie and I scribbled our notes down in our dorms, then headed to roll call. She split from me to go into the 3Rs course room, which is where you did regular school subjects such as reading, writing and arithmetic, while I headed into the Scientology course room. Hallie was lucky, because both Liam and Ricky were in 3Rs with her, so it would be easy for her to slip Liam his note. I would need to make up an excuse to leave the Scientology course room, but I was confident that I could do it. I was a pro at making up excuses.

During roll call I scanned the room, thinking of a reason to leave. I noticed there were no more dictionaries on the shelf. Perfect. As soon as attendance had been taken, I raised my hand. Mr. Morris came over, and I asked if I could go to the 3Rs course room to get a dictionary. She sighed and grumbled for me to move quickly. I agreed and scurried out the door. I walked to the 3Rs course room and opened the door. As I stepped inside, I spotted Ricky immediately by the tables toward the front. I sauntered over and dropped the note onto his lap. He looked up and grinned, his hand moving quickly to cover it. I moved past him to the bookshelf and grabbed a dictionary, doing my best to look natural. I made my way back to my room and I plopped into my seat. Success!

I was studying when I noticed the MAA of the Cadet Org come in. If you were in trouble, you were summoned by the MAA. I pretended to be reading while keeping an eye on what was going on. I peered over my course pack and watched as the MAA whispered something to Mr. Morris. Mr. Morris scanned the course room until her eyes caught mine and zeroed in on me.

Uh oh.

She crooked her finger and beckoned me over. I pushed my chair back and trudged over to her, my feet dragging on the carpet. This couldn't be good.

"What's the meaning of this?" Mr. Morris said, holding the note I had written to Ricky.

"I didn't write that," I immediately responded.

"Yes, you did." The MAA sneered. "Ricky told us."

What a rat! I thought. I couldn't believe he had reported me.

The MAA told me to go down to see Mr. Hammond.

Oh shit.

My heart thumped in my chest. I gathered my course materials, put them away, and followed the MAA down the path to the office, doom hanging over my head.

WHEN I WALKED IN, I saw Hallie standing there with Mr. Hammond and his assistant Mr. Smith. Mr. Hammond looked over and pinned me with his hard glare.

"Hallie, you can go back on course now," he told her. Hallie avoided my gaze as she walked past me. What was going on? Why was she acting like she didn't know me? I stood there awkwardly as the MAA handed my note to Mr. Hammond. The silence seemed to last forever as he read over my message. Finally, he looked up. "What the fuck is this?"

"I don't know," I muttered. I knew that it was the wrong thing to say as soon as it came out of my mouth. Mr. Hammond hated when cadets responded with that answer.

"I DON'T KNOW?" Mr. Hammond bellowed.

I flinched.

"What kind of bullshit is that? You are trying to blow from Source? This is not the behavior of a cadet who is going to be a future executive in the Sea Org," he spat out.

I stared at the ground, my stomach in knots.

"You are going straight to the ECG."

I looked up in shock. The Ethics Correction Group! All because of a stupid note? This was the worst punishment I could get. The ECG was the Ranch's version of the RPF, or Rehabilitation Force, which is what adult Sea Org members were assigned to when they got in trouble. On the ECG, you were assigned hard labor, no one was allowed to talk to you, and you had no privileges. No libs, no desserts at dinner, no free time. I tried to swallow, but it felt like a rock was lodged in my throat.

Pull yourself together, Katherine, I told myself. I straightened my spine and crossed my arms. I hoped my face showed that I didn't care, even if my insides were a mess.

Meanwhile, Mr. Smith stood behind Mr. Hammond and smiled a fake smile at me. Mr. Smith was sixteen, with freckles and a snub nose that made her look even younger, but her age meant she was considered a full adult and was not a cadet at the Ranch. She had been assigned to this post as Deputy Cadet Coordinator not long after Mr. Hammond arrived. Looking at Mr. Smith and her smug face made me want to tell her off so bad. But I held my tongue. I stood there as Mr. Hammond continued to berate me.

"You will be given Scientology policies to study and work on your lower conditions. You are now assigned a condition of Treason."

"Conditions" were states of existence that L. Ron Hubbard had written about, which every human being existed in. The lowest condition was Confusion, then Treason, Enemy, Doubt, Liability, Non-Existence, Danger, Normal, Affluence, Power Change, and Power. I would have to work through each condition starting with Treason, all the way up until I was in good standing with the group. Then, I would need to make amends for what I'd done, which meant hard labor for hours. And on top of that, I would have to walk around the Ranch and have cadets sign a paper asking if I could rejoin the group. It would be so humiliating.

Mr. Hammond turned away and sat at his desk. He told the MAA to take me to the ECG trailer to start on my conditions. The MAA gestured for me to follow her. I numbly trailed her out of the main office, up the back road toward the trailers.

"Is Hallie going on the ECG too?" I asked the MAA hopefully. Maybe at least we would be together.

"Not that it's any of your business, but no she is not." The MAA strode ahead of me. "She has ethics protection."

I stopped in my tracks.

"What ethics protection?" I protested. "She did the same thing as me!"

"No, she didn't." She gestured at me to keep moving. "There was no note."

I started walking again, my thoughts racing. No note? Had Liam managed to hide the note in time? And what did the MAA mean about Hallie having ethics protection? L. Ron Hubbard policy declared that anyone who is upstat has ethics protection and is protected from getting in trouble. But how could Hallie have it and not me? We were always together and up to the same mischief. She wasn't any more in-ethics than I was.

We arrived at the ECG trailers. I trudged up the three metal steps leading to the flimsy door. The trailers were parked in the open field next to the log cabin, across the road from the workshop and laundry. They were double wide, longer than a school bus, with thin walls, dark brown trim, and windows spaced every six feet. The MAA opened the door and I stepped inside.

Two cadets sat by the long wooden table inside the trailer. There was Janice, an older girl who was friends with my brother Judson, and my friend Lilly. They looked over at the sound of the door. Lilly smiled when she saw it was me, while Janice returned to whatever she was scribbling. Lilly and I had shared a dorm back at the ATA, but I hadn't realized she was on the ECG. I gave her a small smile and plopped down next to her. The MAA told me to unpack and work on my conditions. The door banged shut behind her as she walked out.

"Hey." Lilly smiled. "Welcome to our shitty trailer."

Janice ignored me, her curly black hair falling over her face, hiding her expression.

"So. . ." Lilly tilted her head. "Are you allowed to tell us what happened?"

That was all the encouragement I needed to relay the whole story, including how unfair it was that Hallie wasn't even assigned to the ECG. It felt good to get it all off my chest. Even Janice joined in on the conversation, saying it was bullshit that Hallie wasn't in trouble too.

"Why are you guys on the ECG?" I inquired once there was nothing left to add to my story.

Janice acted like she didn't hear me and returned to her drawing.

Lilly shrugged.

"Are you not allowed to say?"

Again, they stayed quiet. Silence hung over us like a blanket.

"I just have to work on my conditions," Lilly murmured. She bent her head as if she was studying the ethics conditions. I peered at what she was reading, and the word "Doubt" jumped off the page at me.

Huh. I wondered if they wanted to leave the Ranch. It was considered entheta to talk about wanting to leave, and you could get in trouble for it. That was probably the reason why they couldn't tell me what they were on the ECG for. While a part of me wanted to ask more questions, I felt it was best not to. I didn't want to get in any more trouble than I already was.

"What's the ECG schedule?" I asked instead.

Lilly slid a paper from her manilla folder toward me.

I peered down at it, resigned to my fate of being a reject with these two on the ECG.

THE DAYS on the ECG were filled with work from morning to night, doing miscellaneous projects around the Ranch, like deweeding and shoveling horse manure. The evenings were spent in the trailer doing lower conditions or writing up overts and withholds. There was no regular school, which frustrated me. I liked school. I loved to read. I liked to discover new things. I did well in both Scientology studies and 3Rs, but 3Rs was my favorite since it was regular school, like reading, spelling, and math. But instead, we had to work to make up the damage we had done. Our meals were also in the trailer after the rest of the Cadet Org had eaten. Sometimes the food would run out and we would just have to have PB and J sandwiches. Although PB and J was delicious, I liked my chicken and hamburgers too, goddammit.

The worst part of it all was that cadets could not speak to you. My friends would walk by and ignore me, as if I were a ghost. Even Hallie did this. I felt so alone. I knew they weren't allowed to, but still—I didn't like them acting like they didn't know me just because I was in ethics trouble.

NOT BEING able to talk to my friends was the incentive I needed to get off the ECG. I sped through my re-entry program in two weeks' time. My last step was to read and get star-rated on a policy written by L. Ron Hubbard called "Responsibility." I opened the large adult textbook to the correct page and felt a zing of excitement. I felt so smart reading a policy meant for grown-ups. It was a page and a half long, crammed with tiny text, but I zipped through it quickly. I grinned to myself. I was only twelve and reading adult stuff.

I now had to report to Mr. Smith. I was nervous about the star-rate from her even though I understood the policy. She was probably one of those horrible star raters who ask all the small words that are impossible to define just so that they can flunk you. When I arrived at the main office and peered inside, I saw her at her desk talking to another cadet. I strode over and waited for her to acknowledge me. She finally looked over.

"What is it?" Mr. Smith asked.

"I need a star-rate," I said.

She sighed and rolled her eyes.

"Fine. Hold on while I finish my first cycle." She didn't wait for me to respond. Instead, she continued talking to the cadet. In my head I was calling her names while I took a seat in the chair by her desk. I sat with my arms crossed while she chatted for another twenty minutes.

She is totally meaning to keep me waiting, I thought to myself. I gritted my teeth.

Finally, Mr. Smith turned to me. "Okay, ready?"

"Sure." I gave her my sweetest, fakest smile—all teeth, lips curved—while I mentally shot daggers at her with my eyes. She looked at me for a second and seemed about to say something, but shook her head and looked down at the bulletin.

"Okay, start of star-rate." Mr. Smith scanned the page. "What's the definition of *treason*?"

"It's when you do something to betray the group," I said.

"Flunk, there is more to it than that." She reached over and grabbed the red Scientology technical dictionary and flipped it open and found the word *treason* and read it out to me. "Treason is defined as betrayal after trust."

"That's basically what I said!" I glared at her.

"No, you didn't, otherwise I wouldn't flunk you. Now go restudy the bulletin and only come back when you're ready."

This was bullshit.

I snatched *Vol o* from her and stomped out of the main office. No *way* was I going to restudy. I knew what the policy meant. Instead, I went and hung out with Lilly for a while and played cards. When I felt like enough time had passed, I strolled back down to the main office and told Mr. Smith I was done restudying.

Mr. Smith took *Vol o* out of my hands.

"That was fast," she said.

"Yeah." I shrugged. "I'm a fast reader."

"Sure you are," she deadpanned. "Whatever. Okay, start of checkout. What's the definition of *treason*?"

This time I gave her the definition verbatim, since that seemed to be what she wanted. Mr. Smith went through the rest of the policy. She then asked me to demonstrate a few of the key points in it. She passed me, which was a surprise. I thought for sure she would make it harder. Maybe she had better things to do than torture me.

I was almost out of the ECG. Now all I needed to do was petition the cadets to sign my Liability papers, agreeing to let me rejoin the group. Then I would be out of lower conditions and be in good standing again.

But the next day I was called down to see Mr. Hammond. What did he want?

22

DOUBLE TROUBLE

I walked slowly down the path, my heart racing, wondering what was going on.

I arrived at the office and opened the door. My eyes widened when I saw how many cadets were crammed into the room. I saw my brother Judson in the corner, and I squeezed through cadets over to him.

"What's going on?" I whispered.

"They found out that my friends and I were taking quarters from the laundromat at PAC."

"Oh shit. That's sucks," I said. I knew about Judson and his friends stealing quarters. But what did that have to do with me?

Mr. Hammond berated the cadets. He said that all of them would be going on the ECG so they could do their conditions and get back in good standing with the group. Protests rang out.

"Shut the fuck up!" Mr. Hammond roared. "The next cadet I hear backflashing will be running laps around the Ranch until I say they can stop."

The room went silent. Everyone hated running laps. Mr.

Hammond told everyone to report to the ECG trailer and their ethics programs would be brought to us shortly. As the room emptied, I stayed behind to find out why I had been called to the office. After everyone left Mr. Hammond noticed me standing there.

"What?"

"Uh, I was sent to the office. Someone needed me," I stammered.

"I already made the announcement. Weren't you listening, you bimbo?" Mr. Hammond said as he turned away from me toward his desk.

Great. Now Mr. Hammond was calling me a bimbo just like the boys at the Ranch. I chose to ignore it.

"You mean the stealing quarters thing? I wasn't a part of that."

Mr. Hammond turned back. "Did you know about it when it was happening?" he asked.

I stared at him and didn't reply.

Mr. Hammond carried on as if I wasn't there.

"You were an accessory to the crime. LRH says, 'An accessory to a crime receives the same punishment, if not even more for not reporting it.'"

"But I'm already almost done with the ECG. I have one checkout left and then I only need signatures for my Liability," I protested.

"Not anymore," Mr. Hammond responded. "You will have a new program. And let me tell you, this one will whip you into shape." With that, he turned away.

I wanted to scream at Mr. Hammond, but I couldn't work up the nerve. Instead, I turned and stormed out of the office. This was so unfair. I gritted my teeth as I made my way back up the road to the trailer and let myself in. Lilly looked over as the door slammed shut behind me.

"Can you believe it?" she said to me. I realized that she had been in the office too, which meant she must also have been an accessory. She would be having her program extended too. I slumped down next to her at the table. We spent the rest of the evening nattering about how unfair it was and how much Mr. Hammond sucked.

THE FIRST MUSTER with the much larger ECG was different. We even had an ECG I/C who would make sure we were working hard and staying on task. I perked up a little when I saw that it was Tom, one of the last remaining older cadets at the Ranch. Tom was seventeen, and though he was much older, he never acted like he was too cool to talk to me. On top of that, he was attractive, with golden brown hair, broad shoulders, and slim hips, just like the men in the romance novels I loved to read.

"Okay guys," Tom said with a loud sigh. He did not look like he was enjoying his new post. I couldn't blame him. Trying to keep this group under control wouldn't be easy.

"This is the schedule," he said. "Morning will be set aside for projects around the Ranch. In the afternoons, some of you will go out back and dig up compost for the gardens and some of you will do renovations. In the evening, you will work on your programs in the trailer. And you know the drill—no talking to the other cadets. You are the out-ethics group, and you need to stay separate until you are done with your conditions."

With that he sent us up to the horses to shovel manure. We started up the path at a leisurely pace. "Guys, can you even pretend to run?" Tom asked.

No one responded, but I smiled at him and began to jog.

"Thanks Katherine." Tom grinned at me.

I grinned back. What a cutie.

"Hey, Katherine." Jonathan came jogging up alongside me. I glanced over, surprised. Jonathan was one of the coolest guys in the whole school.

"Yeah?"

"I didn't know you were a quarter thief too." He chuckled.

"Oh." I laughed. "No, I'm not. Judson told me about it though, so I got caught as an accessory. It's so stupid."

"Yeah, that sucks," he said. "But hey, thanks for not ratting us out."

"Yep," I smiled. Out of the corner of my eye, I saw Hallie and Beatrice walking down the grass hill from Dorm 10 to the main mess. I felt their eyes on me. This time I was the one ignoring them. Instead, I made sure I laughed extra loud at Jonathan's next comment. The ECG was horrible, but at least I was surrounded by hot guys. If I could make Hallie and Beatrice a teensy bit jealous, all the better. It still bothered me that Hallie had never gotten in trouble for writing notes. What made her so special that she didn't have to deal with the same consequences?

BEING on the ECG with the cool kids was different. Whenever the ECG group moved from project to project, we would always sing as loud as we could, especially when we were passing the other cadets. It was unspoken, but I think we all wanted to make the other cadets think we were having more fun than them. Instead of the ECG being the worst place to be, we were trying to make it the "hot" group.

"Isn't this supposed to be a punishment?" I imagined my friends would mutter as we passed, singing with gusto as we carried our deweeding tools to the next hill. It was even better when we all piled into the Ranch pickup truck to be taken out back to dig for rotten leaves for compost in the gardens. As Tom drove the truck up the field, we would scream and laugh, speeding across the dirt as the other cadets looked on from their muster on the patio. I loved that part of it.

The guys teased me a lot on the ECG, and most of the time I laughed and enjoyed all the attention coming my way. But Alexander, Ricky's older brother, always took it too far. He liked to call me "The Bean," after the ugly scar on my shoulder, or "rat," his favorite nickname for people he considered annoying and beneath him. One time he had even chased me across the patio and squirted ketchup all over my white tank top, all because I squirted a tiny bit of ketchup on his hand at lunch as a joke. Yet no matter how horrible he was to me, I was drawn to him. Why did he have to be so good looking? He looked like a Spanish conquistador with his brown skin, handsome features and his goatee that he was already growing at fifteen years old.

ONE DAY I was joking around on the dried patch of earth next to the trailers. I was surrounded by the guys as I marched around, mimicking Alexander's walk, when suddenly someone farted loudly. Laughter erupted around me.

"You farted!"

"Wow, go to the bathroom, Katherine."

"Judson, I didn't know your sister farted so well!"

"That wasn't me," I protested. "This is bullshit! One of you assholes farted just to blame it on me!"

"C'mon, just admit it." Alexander smirked. "We all know it was you."

"You guys are such dicks!" I flipped them off, walked into the trailer, and slammed the door behind me. I slumped down on a chair and laid my head on the table. Why were guys always picking on me? I was going to be remembered as "The Farter" forever. Tears dripped down my cheeks. I had to face it: I hated the ECG no matter how much I tried to pretend that I liked it. I was cut off from my friends. I had to do hard labor, which I despised. No regular school. No privileges. And all of the guys teasing me all the time. My life sucked.

23

THE SEWAGE PROJECT

The next day, we were assigned a new project. The septic tank that was buried in the lawn in front of the office was leaking and needed to be fixed. Mr. Hammond ordered us to dig trenches around it so that the hole could be located. The problem was it had been raining heavily the past few days, so the area around the tank was flooded. The septic tank was twelve feet long and six feet wide, and we were to dig four feet deep on all sides of it.

The long gray tank was barely visible beneath the muck and water. We gathered around and stared. No one wanted to be the first to step into the murky water, which was most likely mixed with shit. The worst part was the fumes. It stank like rotten eggs.

"This is so disgusting," I muttered to Judson as he stepped forward. I followed his lead into the septic water. It immediately filled my sneakers. "Oh, gross!"

"Ew!"

"What the hell!"

Complaints rose around me as I gripped my shovel, looking for where to dig.

"Guys, just get to work and stop complaining so we can get through this," said Alicia, our new ECG I/C. She had taken over this post from Tom only yesterday, and we did not get along. She was a few years older than me, and I thought she so uptight. She even looked uptight, with her brown hair pulled back from her face and her black glasses framing her large nose, which always seemed to be turned up at me. I didn't know why Tom was no longer in charge. It bummed me out that he was gone. The other day he had been helping me load the back of the truck with shovels, and we'd spent the time joking and laughing. No way would Alicia ever joke around with me.

I sighed and pushed my shovel into the mud, lifting a soupy, brown mess of sludge. Within minutes my feet were freezing. It was a cold day, with the sky the color of slate. Time passed slowly. I shoveled methodically. This was the worst.

"Move over, Rat," Alexander said as he stepped next to me and began to dig.

"Don't call me that," I retorted. I threw a load of sewage, dirt, and water over the trench that was now over two feet deep. It was getting hard to reach down low with the shovel, and even more difficult as the trench filled up with dark brown water mixed with who knows what. "You don't like being called a rat?" Alexander chuckled.

"No, and you know that," I said. The water made a gross slurping sound as I continued to dig.

"But it suits you so well." Alexander grinned as he flung a pile of the watery mess a little too close to me.

"Hey, watch it!" I exclaimed.

"Whoops," Alexander said.

"Yeah, right."

"Stop flirting, Katherine, and get to work!"

I turned and saw Alicia standing on the other side of the sewage tank, her arms crossed, glaring at me.

"I'm not flirting. I'm working while I talk." I glared at her. "What's wrong with that?"

"Yeah, right." She rolled her eyes and turned away. I stabbed my shovel into the slop with great force. Why was she accusing me of being a flirt? All I was doing was talking!

"So, do you think this is actual sewage?" I asked Alexander.

"I don't fucking know. But it smells like it," Alexander said.

"Don't you think that—"

"Katherine!" Alicia shouted, interrupting my next question. "Stop talking and focus on work!"

I turned around to face her.

"Why are you only yelling at me? I'm not the only one here, you know!"

I turned back to continue shoveling, but as I turned, my foot missed the edge of the sewage tank and I stumbled. I grasped at air as I fell over into the trench. *Splash.* The cold, rancid, brown water enveloped me and covered my head. I reached up and grasped the sewage tank and tried to catch my breath as the dirty water streamed down my face. All around me the ECGers were laughing, doubled over, including Alicia. I tried to hoist myself back up, but my hands were too slippery, and I slid back in. They all laughed harder. I couldn't believe this was happening to me. I was submerged in sewage! My brother leaned over and grabbed me and pulled me up. Even he was grinning.

"You guys are such assholes!" I pushed away from Judson. I jumped over the trench and started walking away. I had to get out of there.

"Where do you think you're going?" Alicia called out.

"Where the fuck do you think? I have to take a shower before I get sick from all of this shit all over me!" I shouted over my shoulder as I continued up across the lawn. I stepped onto the road and glanced back. The ECG group stood like a ragtag group of bums with shovels, wet and muddy, surrounding the septic tank. My insides burned. How was this even allowed? This had to be against some child abuse laws. I never read about children shoveling shit in books!

Alicia said nothing back, so I turned back in my squishy sneakers and squeaked up the road, water trailing behind me like piss.

I threw open the door to my dorm and headed straight for the bathroom. I peeled my wet clothes off and stepped into the shower stall. As I scrubbed my hair, tears ran down my face. I was so pathetic. Who falls in sewage?

Knock, knock. Someone rapped on the bathroom door.

It had better not be Alicia getting me to come back to work.

"What?" I screamed.

"Are you okay?"

From the sound of voice, I could tell it was Susan, who was also on the ECG. It was rumored she was being disciplined for wanting to commit suicide. She was constantly locking herself in the bathroom crying. I found it to be annoying. *Stop crying and move on with your life*, I used to think.

"Do you need help?" Susan's voice came through the door.

"No, I'm just washing off. I'm upset about what happened, but I'll survive," I said. "I'll be out in a minute."

When I came out a few minutes later, Susan was sitting

on a bed, seemingly waiting for me. She hefted herself up and lumbered over.

"What is it?" I muttered. I just wanted to lie on my bed and close my eyes.

"I want to show you some photos I have." Susan held up a stack of Kodak prints.

I perked up at that. I loved photos. I followed her back into her dorm and sat next to her, with my towel wrapped around me, clamped under my armpits.

"Where did you get these?" I asked as I flipped through the pictures. There were ones of cadets doing work all over the Ranch. Painting walls, digging up garden beds, weeding on the hills.

"Oh, I stole them from the office," she told me casually. "They were taken for compliance reports and the doubles get stored in the filing cabinet."

"Oh. Wow, that's cool." I grinned in surprise. There were photos of cadets at muster, cadets painting dorms, and even a few photos of Judson with Patrick, Antonio, and Alexander doing work out in the field. Susan was nice enough to give me those pictures and even told me where the photos were kept at the office in case I ever wanted to steal some on my own, which I knew I would do the first chance I got.

"Thanks, Susan. I better get back now," I said. I handed her the rest of the photos and walked into my dorm to get dressed.

Once I was cleaned up and ready, I put on flip flops since my sneakers were so disgusting and made my way back down to the ECG group. They were just wrapping up the sewage project. My brother saw me and walked over.

"Are you okay, sister?" he asked.

"Not really. But thanks for asking." I gave him a small smile. "I can't believe I was covered in sewage."

"Yeah, that was crazy," Judson said.

Alexander strode over and patted me on the shoulder. I looked at him, surprised.

"Sorry that happened to you," he said.

"Thanks," I answered with a shrug. It cheered me up a bit that he cared enough to say something nice.

The ECG was dismissed to head up to the trailers for dinner. As I walked back with Judson and his friends, the guys cracked jokes to make me laugh. I felt a little better. The sewage smell still seemed to permeate my body, but at least the guys were being nice to me.

24

HIGH SCHOOL DREAMING

My feet thudded on the dusty ground as I jogged with the other ECGers along the creek bed. Sweat glistened on my forehead and strands of my hair stuck to my face. Mr. Hammond had ordered the ECG to do twenty laps around the Ranch because he felt we were slacking off too much. I didn't know how far each lap was, but it felt like a mile. The first one hadn't bothered me, but by the second I was starting to get mad. As each foot hit the ground, I thought about how unfair this all was. Why was this our punishment? My brother was running a little bit ahead of me, and I picked up my pace to catch up with him.

"Hey," I puffed.

"Hey, sister," Judson said.

"This sucks," I grumbled. "I feel like this would be considered child abuse."

I glanced around to make sure no one was directly behind me. If they heard me, they might write a Knowledge Report on me, and then I would be in even more trouble.

The only person I could complain to was Judson. I wouldn't dare say it to anyone else.

"I just feel like we aren't treated fairly," I said as I kept pace with him. "We would never have to do something like this if we were in regular school."

"Yeah, I know," Judson agreed. "I would love to go to high school and be able to play football on a real team and compete instead of running laps."

"Yeah! That would be so fun," I said. I felt my mood brighten. "And I could be a cheerleader."

Okay, I wasn't athletic or pretty, but at least I was good at making friends. It would be so fun to be at a real school with Judson. It would be like the books I read about with the twin sisters in the Sweet Valley High book series. Judson would fit right in, and he could help me be popular too. My brother and I continued fantasizing about high school as we passed the schoolhouse and jogged toward the horse corral. Maybe we could stay with our family in New York. We knew there was no way our parents would leave the Sea Org. Our mom was at Flag in Florida now, and our dad down at PAC. We never saw our parents anyway, so it wouldn't be a big deal to live in a different state. I was close to thirteen, almost old enough to start high school, and Judson was fifteen and could enroll straight away. This was the time to do it. We just needed to tell Mr. Hammond.

As we jogged up the dusty field, we came up with a plan. The next time we ran by the main office, we would stop and go inside and ask to speak with Mr. Hammond. As we circled back around and thudded down the long main road, I wiped sweat off my forehead with my forearm. Butterflies grew in my stomach as the office drew closer and closer.

"Okay." I tried to take a breath as we approached. "You go first."

"I can't." Judson glanced at me. "I'm too scared."

I rolled my eyes and he grinned. My brother was not confrontational, so I could see why he didn't want to go in. But I was scared too. To tell Mr. Hammond that we wanted to leave would create a lot of Dev-T. Dev-T is developed traffic, which L. Ron Hubbard defined as anything that deviated from the task of clearing the world. We would be put in isolation, as well as on twenty-four-hour watch. A cadet would have to sit and watch us to make sure we didn't try to sneak off the Ranch. Our parents would be notified and would be upset that we wanted to leave. Just thinking of what my mom's face would look like when she heard the news made my heart hurt. Maybe one more lap would be best to build up our nerve before we broke the news.

"Yeah, I'm scared too," I told Judson. "How about we go around one more time and plan this a little better?"

"Okay," he said. The office disappeared behind us as we jogged past.

A few laps later, we still hadn't gotten up the nerve to go in. After the ninth lap, Alicia, the ECG I/C, said we could stop to have dinner even though we hadn't even come close to the twenty laps. I was worn out but relieved.

"Maybe we should just try to get off the ECG," I mused aloud. "Maybe then things will be better. I don't want to create problems for Mom and Dad. Plus, don't we want to clear the planet? It's important that we become executives in the Sea Org, right?"

"Yeah," Judson agreed. "I don't think Mom and Dad would be happy if we left."

With that decision in place, we followed the others up to the trailers for whatever measly leftovers were our dinner. I had a sour taste in my mouth, but what else could we do? Being cadets was our purpose. We were meant to clear the planet, and we were being selfish for wanting something other than this.

25

THINGS THAT SHOULDN'T BE

I t was an unusually cold day for April. I was in the ECG trailer shivering, attempting to work on my lower conditions. The trailer only had one tiny space heater and the wind outside seemed to blow through any crack it could find. My metal chair was as close to the heater as I could get it.

I hunched over the table and wrote, "Life sucks, I hate this, I'm the worst, I'm pathetic," over and over. I could not bring myself to do any work on my conditions. The thoughts that I tried to suppress last week with Judson had bloomed and enveloped my whole mind.

I hated it here. I kept trying to like being at the Ranch, but I couldn't force it anymore. Why should I work on my lower conditions when I didn't even want to be here? Wouldn't it be better for the group if I left since I was so out-ethics anyways? I should just be with the wogs. Wogs were people who knew nothing about Scientology and just went about their daily lives with no idea of how to live. From how L. Ron Hubbard described wogs, they sounded stupid. But still. They weren't bad. They just didn't know better. And honestly, the wog world looked way more fun. I could just envision having nothing to worry about but going to school and hanging out. No post to do. No orders to follow. No Scientology studies.

I sat up. An idea formed in my head. I would write a *Things That Shouldn't Be* report. I leaned over and grabbed a fresh sheet of paper from the wire basket in the middle of the table. Each word made deep imprints into the paper as I pressed down hard with my pencil, writing feverishly.

CADET COORDINATOR—MR. *Hammond*
Katherine Spallino
Pac Ranch Cadet

Things That Shouldn't Be

I DO NOT WANT to be at the Ranch anymore. No matter how hard I try to be upstat, I keep on getting into trouble. I was almost done with my ECG program when I was assigned a new, longer program because I knew of something my brother and his friends did. It's like I can't stop myself from getting myself into these situations. At this point, I think it is best that I leave the Ranch. I don't help or contribute to the group in any way. I understand that my parents will not want to leave the Sea Org, but I have aunts and uncles in New York that I can stay with. Can you please let me call my mom so I can let her know and she can contact my aunts or uncle?

· · ·

This is true,

Katherine Spallino

I took a deep breath and stared at my report. I felt as if I was floating on a cloud. It was nice to get all that out on paper. Now I just needed to deliver it to Mr. Hammond's inbox. This was much easier than talking to Mr. Hammond in person. I folded up the report and walked out of the ECG trailer. The door swung shut behind me. I held the report carefully in my right hand so it wouldn't wrinkle as I hurried to the main office.

When I arrived, I stopped and put my ear to the door to make sure there wasn't an adult muster going on. It sounded quiet. I opened the door and looked inside. It was just Mr. Stewart, one of the adults, sitting at the long table studying a book holding L. Ron Hubbards policies.

Good. Mr. Hammond wasn't there.

Mr. Stewart looked up as I walked in and quickly slid the letter into Mr. Hammond's inbox. I waved at her as I walked out, and she nodded and returned to her studies.

I ran up the road back to the ECG trailer, my heart thumping, my mind racing. I didn't want to be anywhere in sight when Mr. Hammond read my letter. This was going to be a whole new beginning to my life. I couldn't wait to go to school and maybe become a cheerleader. Maybe I could somehow become pretty and even date one of the guys on the football team. I knew I wasn't doing what was the greatest good for the greatest number of dynamics, but maybe in the future, when I was rich, I could help Scientology in another way. I could donate a ton of money and go up the Bridge and win awards like those top Scientologists at the International Association of Scientologists events that were held each year.

An hour later, I was in the trailer daydreaming about my new life when a cadet appeared in the doorway.

"Katherine, Mr. Hammond wants to see you."

This was it. I stood up and walked down to the main office. My palms felt clammy. I didn't care though. I was ready.

I arrived at the main office and cracked the door open. Mr. Hammond was sitting at his desk poring over some papers, but he swiveled in his chair towards me.

"Hello, Katherine," he said.

"Hi," I muttered. I looked down, then back up, trying to keep my TRs in and maintain eye contact.

"Did you write this?" Mr. Hammond held up the letter.

"Uh, yes." I shifted my feet.

"No one helped you?"

"Um, no." Now I was confused. Where was he going with this?

"Well, I gotta tell you, I'm impressed," Mr. Hammond said. He glanced at the paper and then back at me.

"This is very well-written. In fact, it's the best piece of writing I've seen by a cadet."

"It is?" My mind raced. Was he messing with me? Was he going to say something like, "No, you dumb ass, this is the lousiest excuse for a cadet to try to walk away from her responsibility to clear the Earth."

"Yes." Mr. Hammond nodded. "This letter is concise and to the point. You're sure no one helped you with this?"

"Um . . . no. I just wrote it down," I said. I couldn't believe this. He wasn't joking. But he had to be. I hadn't put much effort into the letter. I just scribbled it down.

There was a deep silence as I tried to not fidget under Mr. Hammond's gaze.

"Here's what I'm thinking," he said. "I am going to take you off of the ECG and let you rejoin the cadets."

My heart jumped. I was going to be off the ECG? Mr. Hammond continued talking while my mind raced. I could barely pay attention to what he was saying.

"You can finish your ECG program during Scientology studies time. This way, you're still with the group. Once you are finished with the program, we can talk and see if you still want to leave the Ranch. Does that sound good?" He leaned back in his chair and surveyed me.

I stood there dumbly for a second.

"Oh, uh . . . yeah." I shook my head. "I mean, yes sir!"

"Good. Your new dorm is going to be at the apartments. Go ahead and pack your stuff. The bus leaves in thirty minutes."

"Okay, um . . . thank you," I said. I floated out of the office in a daze. Not only was I off the ECG, but I got to live at the apartments now! Had this just happened? The apartments were in Valencia, a town thirty minutes away. They had been rented out for cadets to stay in around six months ago so that the children could move out of the tents and into actual beds. Around thirty cadets were bused to the apartments after evening course and bused back in the morning. Mainly older cadets were chosen to live at the apartments, but a few of my friends lived there. And now I was one of them!

But wait . . . didn't I want to leave the Ranch?

Well, really, this could be just what I needed. A fresh start in the Cadet Org did sound nice. Maybe things would be better this time around. On top of that, my parents would be upset if I left, so really I would be making everyone happy by staying. And besides, I would be living at the apartments! That would be almost like living a regular life.

I took off at a run to get to the ECG trailer and tell my brother Judson the news. It was too bad he couldn't join me, but maybe he could write a report too.

26

THE REALITY

I boarded the school bus at 9:30 p.m, ready to head out to the apartments. After a thirty-minute drive down the windy roads, we arrived. I peered out the window, excited for my first look. All I saw was a two-story brown apartment building with a courtyard. It didn't look too exciting on the outside, but it was dark out. Maybe it was really nice inside. We departed the bus and headed up a flight of stairs that led to a second floor overlooking the pool. I couldn't stop staring.

"Do we ever get to swim?" I asked my friend Erica.

"No," Erica said. "We always have to leave straight away in the morning."

"Oh," I said, my spirits dampened.

"Here's our apartment." Erica opened a door. I peered inside, my eyes scanning my new home.

There wasn't much to look at. It had bunk beds in both the bedroom and the living room, and that was about it. There was a small kitchenette, but it didn't seem to be used for anything except tea, since we had all our meals at the

Ranch. The tea was kind of cool though, but then I found out that was just for Mr. Ellis, the dorm mom.

Bo-ring. Nothing new here then.

I climbed up into my bunk bed and drifted off to sleep. Maybe the morning would be more exciting.

The alarm went off at 7 a.m. I groaned as I pushed down the covers. That was earlier than the cadets who lived at the dorms at the Ranch. They didn't have to wake up until eight o'clock! I hadn't thought of that when I so happily agreed to move to the apartments. I got out of bed and got dressed. Before I knew it, I was on the bus headed back to the Ranch. As we drove away in the early morning light, all I saw were similar apartment buildings with faded stucco walls, then a series of chain department stores—Sears, Walmart, and all the rest.

The apartments were a disappointment. All you did was arrive, sleep, wake up, and go back to the Ranch. Big whoop.

Now that I was off the ECG, Ricky and I were back together again as boyfriend and girlfriend. Ricky sat with me on the way to and from the apartments. At first, I thought I would love to be with him again, but our conversations became stilted and forced. Why couldn't we be like how we were before? I think a part of me was a little irritated that he never got in trouble for being caught with my note, although it had landed me in the ECG. *But it wasn't his fault*, I told myself. *What could he have said*? Still. Something was off. After a few days of this, I decided it was no good. We would be better off as friends. That evening I had to break up with him. I just needed a good excuse.

·   ·   ·

"Soooo," I turned my head to Ricky and leaned my cheek against the cool, green pleather seat as the bus rumbled up the road toward the Ranch. "I was thinking . . ."

"Yeah?"

"Maybe we should just be friends, you know, instead of 'boyfriend' and 'girlfriend.'" I used my fingers for quotation marks.

"What?" Ricky furrowed his brow. "Why?"

"I mean, it's not like we have passion for each other or anything," I said.

Ricky gave me the side-eye.

"Look, we don't even like kissing." I lowered my voice. "Let's just go back to how we were when we could just joke around."

He shrugged.

"C'mon Ricky." I nudged him. "You know that you are the only one who can make me pee from laughing so hard. Don't you want to do that again?"

"Only you would say that as a compliment, Katherine," Ricky said, chuckling.

"What?" I laughed. "It's true!"

And that was that. We were back to being friends. My resentment or whatever I was holding on to seemed to disappear.

27

THE CHOSEN ONES

The bell rang as I lay on my belly, my book in my hands. It was dinnertime, and I was devouring a Julie Garwood romance novel before Scientology studies that was starting in fifteen minutes. I glanced over at Tory, who was lying in the bed next to mine reading a magazine.

"That's weird," she commented. "It's not even seven yet."

"Yeah," I sat up. "I guess we have to go." I looked around and spotted a pair of Tory's sandals. "Um . . . can I borrow your sandals again?"

"Sure," Tory said.

"Thanks." I slipped them on, and followed her out the door. My shoes were so old they had worn down, with large holes in the toes and soles that were falling apart. They hadn't been wearable in a month. I had promised Tory that my mom was going to bring me new ones as soon as she came up to visit, so for now she was fine with me borrowing hers. My mom had been in Florida for training but had recently been transferred back to PAC. Hopefully she would come visit me soon. I didn't even remember the last time I had seen my mom. I linked arms with Tory as we walked down the little path.

"Hey!" Hallie called as she and Lacy joined up with us. She linked her arm through my free one, and Lacy linked her arm with Tory. "What do you think this is about?"

"I don't know. I wonder if there is a mission at PAC or something," I said.

"Huh. Why is everyone walking to the field?" Lacy pointed with her free arm. I could see cadets gathering in the field behind the pool. This was strange. We never mustered there.

"Muster in the field," Cody, one of the older cadets, called out.

"Yeah, we kind of guessed," I said.

He flipped us off, and we giggled as we passed.

We joined the other cadets mingling on the field. I could see three executives from PAC standing in front with Mr. Hammond. You could tell they were execs from their Sea Org uniforms, styled like those of naval officers. Usually when execs came from PAC, they gave us lectures about the Sea Org and how we were the future executives and so on. But this seemed different. There was an air of excitement as I separated from Hallie and Tory and trotted to my division for muster.

"Attention!" Mr. Hammond roared. I straightened up, eyes straight ahead.

Attendance was taken.

"At ease," he commanded. I shifted into a more relaxed stance with my hands clasped behind my back.

"This is Mr. Greilor, from RTC," Mr. Hammond said. One of the execs stepped forward and nodded. He was a nondescript man with a uniform I hadn't seen before. His crisp button-down had many bars of accomplishments pinned to his right breast. He seemed to exude power in the way he stood. This made sense. RTC was the top executive organization in the entire Sea Org. They were the most powerful and respected members. I swallowed and gripped my hands tighter, my heart thumping in my chest. Something big was about to happen. I could feel it.

"And this is Mr. Cartor, the HAS of CLO. And Mr. Feldman, L. Ron Hubbard's Communicator," Mr. Hammond continued, gesturing to the two women beside him. They looked almost identical, with hair parted down the middle and pulled back in sharp ponytails, young but serious faces, and full Sea Org regalia. Their black blazers displayed their ranks, paired with black skirts that ended at the perfect point at their knees. I thought they might be close to my sister's age of twenty, but I wasn't sure.

Mr. Cartor stepped forward. "Good evening," she began.

Crickets.

"She said, 'good evening!'" Mr. Hammond bellowed.

"Good evening," I shouted along with the other cadets, our voices like a cannon across the darkening sky. The executives stood silhouetted by the setting sun.

"Thank you." Mr. Cartor held up a clipboard and squinted down. "If I call out your name, line up over here to the left of me." She gestured with her hand next to Mr. Hammond, then began reading out names from a list pinned to her clipboard. My heart beat loudly in my ears as I listened for mine. Cadets trickled from their stations and walked to the front. I didn't know what being called meant, but I wanted it. It felt like something special was about to happen.

"Jonathan."

I looked over and saw Jonathan leave the ECG group and walk over. Huh. I didn't think anyone from the ECG would be called, since they were the out-ethics group. So, was being on the list bad then? Soon, about thirty cadets were standing beside Mr. Hammond. I looked around and saw large gaps in the Cadet Org remaining. The cadets who had been chosen looked back at us, some of them making funny faces, others looking worried. I stared at them, trying to figure out the qualifiers. Most of the older cadets had been selected, but there were a few sprinkled in who were twelve like me, or even younger. A murmur rose as we all wondered aloud what was going on.

"That's it!" Mr. Hammond said before the murmurs could rise to a cacophony.

The field fell silent. The sun had set, and the sky had turned deep blue, almost purple. Mr. Cartor cleared her throat.

"The cadets that were called have been assigned to a special mission. They will be reporting to PAC Base and training to be Class V auditors. We—" Before she could finish her sentence, cries of shock rang out.

"Tonight?"

"Does this mean they are going into the Sea Org?"

"Wait, we're leaving?"

"What?"

I turned to Ricky, who was standing behind me. "This is so crazy!"

Ricky nodded his agreement, but before he could speak, Mr. Hammond's gravelly voice interrupted. "That's it!" He stepped forward; his jowly jaws clenched. Arms crossed.

I turned back to face the front before I could get yelled at. The whispers around me subsided.

Mr. Cartor scanned the cadets, then continued. "We have chosen these cadets to be the top auditors in the Sea Org." She directed her gaze at the group in the front. "You should be honored to receive this training. You will be called the Technical Training Corp."

The chosen cadets glanced around at each other. They looked as surprised as the rest of us. Just like that, their lives were going to change.

What about the cadet training lineup that had been issued this year, I wondered? There was a long list of courses you had to complete before joining the Sea Org, and it was a long-running joke among cadets that it would take forever to get through. I guess the lineup didn't matter anymore. These cadets were joining the Sea Org anyway.

My thoughts turned to myself. I wondered why I hadn't been chosen. I was one of the top students at the Ranch and was ahead for my grade level per the tests the adults had us take each year. Well, except for math, but who cared about math. You didn't need math to be an auditor. If this new group was dedicated to studying full time, you would think I would have been picked for that.

My stomach pinched as it dawned on me that I obviously wasn't good enough. I glanced over to the left and spotted my best friends, all remaining at the Ranch. Well, at least Hallie, Lacy, and Tory were still here too. They hadn't been picked either. The knot in my stomach loosened.

". . . all of you chosen need to pack one suitcase of your essentials. Leave everything else here. It will be shipped to you at a later date. Right now, it is of the utmost importance to get you all down to PAC and on study. You guys are the future auditors for the Sea Org and have been chosen for this important mission. Now behave like it. Start!" Mr. Cartor ordered.

At that, they scattered to their dorms or to get on the bus to the apartments to pack their bags. The rest of us remained standing, bewildered at what just happened.

"Okay, all of you," Mr. Hammond addressed the rest of the Cadet Org, "we'll be reorganizing the org board. This will be announced tomorrow. In the meantime, report to your current post or go on study as you would normally do on your schedule. Tomorrow we will be arranging the new dorms. The apartments will no longer be needed."

And that was it. There was no big farewell. No party to celebrate their graduation into the Sea Org. They were gone.

FOR A FEW WEEKS, the Ranch felt deserted. With so many cadets gone, everyone was moved back into dorms at the Ranch, including me. I had only spent a month at the apartments but was happy to move back into my old dorm. I ended up in Dorm 10D with Tory. I wished I was in the dorm with Hallie and Lacy, but at least they were also in Dorm 10, just down the hall.

In June, we were told we would be going on a summer schedule. We would have extra time for arts and crafts and days when we could go to the beach, as long as we had enough course completions. It was like we were getting an actual summer vacation, like kids in the real world.

I told myself that it was a good thing I wasn't on the TTC. Training to be an auditor all day versus having fun activities at the Ranch. This was so much better. I'd lucked out by not being selected.

I did my best to ignore the tiny part of me that whispered reasons why I wasn't chosen. That I wasn't good enough. I was a reject. Over time, I squashed that voice like an annoying bug and convinced myself that being at the Ranch was *way* better than being in the Sea Org.

When we went down to PAC for missions, we would sometimes see the cadets who had been pulled away for the

TTC. I used this opportunity to talk about all the awesome things we were doing at the Ranch. The camping trip, the cherry festival, the all-you-can-eat buffet when we got our stats up, the beach. The former cadets would exclaim how unfair it all was, how jealous they were of us who had remained at the Ranch. When I heard that, I felt vindicated. Good. Sucks to be them. I didn't want to join the Sea Org yet anyway.

28

THE BEST GIFT IS SHOES

My mom had returned from Flag a month earlier, but she still hadn't come up to see my brothers and me. I waited, hoping to hear from her, then finally got a letter saying she was coming to visit. I was so excited. My dad couldn't come, which was too bad since she would be here on Father's Day. I had a card for him that I would give to her, so maybe he would enjoy that.

When the bus pulled up the road, I waited on the tips of my toes for my mom to disembark. As soon as she stepped off the bus, I raced over and gave her a big hug. I was so happy to see her, but I was even more happy when I saw the plastic bag with a shoe box inside that she had brought along. She'd remembered to bring me shoes! I snatched the bag from her hands and raced up to the patio to open it up as she followed behind with my brothers at a slower pace.

I sat down on the brick wall surrounding the patio and cracked the box open. Plain black tennis shoes nestled in the paper. They were not Skechers, which I had been hoping for, but oh well. These weren't ugly and they were *shoes*. I would take it. Now I could stop borrowing Tory's sandals. Recently, she had told me that her mom said to stop letting me borrow things from her. I was so embarrassed that her mom thought I was only friends with Tory so I could use her stuff. I had stopped asking to borrow her shoes, and instead usually walked around the Ranch barefoot. I joked to friends that I would have the most calloused feet and soon I'd be able to walk on anything, but really I felt like a bum.

"Do you like them?" Mom asked. She sat down next to me, and I reached over and hugged her, inhaling her soft scent.

"Yes! Thanks, Mom." I tugged the sneakers over my bare feet and swiveled them back and forth. They would do just fine.

Judson, Lucas, and I spent the next hour regaling our mom with stories about our lives. Well, I did most of the talking, but my brothers didn't seem to mind. I brought them all up to my dorm and showed my mom my bed, and how I had my headboard set up, and the CDs I borrowed from dad the last time I was at PAC. Blondie, Paul Simon, and more.

Before I knew it, my mom's one-hour visit had come to an end. We walked her back down to the school bus. After I hugged her, I asked her for some money. She rifled through her purse and pulled out a couple of dollars.

"Thanks, Mom! And remember—as soon as you get me a Social Security number, I can get paid, then I won't have to ask you for money."

"Okay, I will get working on it," she said.

"Thanks, Mom." I waved goodbye as she got on the bus with the other Sea Org members. It rumbled away down the long road and through the wooden gate. My brothers and I turned to walk up to the patio for Sunday afternoon muster. I sighed happily as I watched my black sneakers make dusty footprints in the sand. New shoes, and a couple of bucks!

29

RUNAWAY

Lately Hallie and I were constantly trying to one-up each other. It was exhausting. Sometimes I felt like she wasn't even my friend. Last week she had stolen my diary and read it with Lacy. When she returned it, she laughed it off as if it didn't matter, but it made me not want to write in it anymore. But after a few days I needed somewhere to vent so began writing again, hiding it in a better spot underneath my mattress.

ONE MORNING, I walked into my dorm during Scientology studies break time and saw Hallie and Lacy with two younger girls whispering near my dresser.

"What are you guys doing?" I crossed my arms.

Hallie turned to me with a sly smile. "Do you change your underwear every day?" she asked, ignoring my question.

"What?" I said, caught off guard. "Yeah!"

This wasn't true. I had only one pair of underwear because I couldn't afford to buy more. No way was I admitting that. As long as they didn't smell, I wore them every day.

"Oh really?" She snickered.

"Yeah, *really*!" I crossed my arms and glared at her.

"Well, how come you don't have any underwear in your drawer?" she asked.

"Um . . . because they are all getting washed."

"I don't think so. I asked Tory, and she said she never sees underwear in your basket." Tory was the laundry I/C and was in charge of doing everyone's laundry at the Ranch.

"Well, maybe she shouldn't be paying so much attention to my underwear," I said. "Can you guys get out of my dorm now?"

"Oh. My. God. You totally don't change your underwear!" Hallie exclaimed. All the girls laughed.

"Don't be stupid. Of course I do." I walked over to my bed and sprawled on it as if I didn't have a care in the world. "Are we done? Because I want to read my book now."

I picked it up and stared at the pages, the words a blur. I wanted to shut them out, hearing them whisper behind me as they walked out into the other dorm. Hallie and Lacy knew that I didn't have any money. It had been several years now since I had last gotten paid, and my parents rarely sent me money. These girls were supposed to be my friends, yet here they were snooping in my stuff, making fun of me. I squeezed my eyes tight as I heard a burst of laughter from the dorm next door. Thoughts raced through my mind.

Fuck them! I hate it here! No one even likes me. I should just leave!

Another burst of laughter from the dorm next door probably at my expense. This made me more determined. I could hitch a ride from a stranger and get driven to PAC. From there, I would find my mom and tell her that I didn't want to be at the Ranch anymore. I wanted to go to a regular school and be with normal people in the wog world. I decided the best time to go would be PE time. After lunch muster, I would walk down to the main gate, and once I saw that no one was looking, I would climb over and walk along the road until I could hitch a ride. I would be wearing a cadet uniform, but I didn't think anyone who saw me on the road would know what it meant. Our uniform was a plain, dark green cotton shirt. It didn't have a symbol on it like some of our uniforms in the past. With my plan set, I headed down to finish Scientology studies and bided my time.

At lunchtime I sat down and ate methodically. My supposed friends chatted around me as if everything was normal, even though they knew I was mad at them. I stewed as I chewed and swallowed.

On my way out of the dining room, I grabbed an apple from the buffet line and put it in my pocket. I slipped out the side door and waited for lunch muster by myself under the shade of the large oak tree. I ignored the boys and Ava skating on their skateboards and stared at my shoes. Just muster to go, then I was gone.

Mr. Hammond called us to muster. I went through the motions, hardly aware of what was going on around me. Once we were dismissed, cadets dispersed to their different activities. I followed a group who were headed to the field to play kickball. When they reached the field, I peeled away toward the creek that led straight to the driveway out. It was dry right now and perfect for me to walk in since I would be barely visible from the field.

As I descended into the creek bed, the sun filtered down through the oak tree branches that loomed overhead. Weeds scratched at my calves as I trampled through the overgrown brush that had cropped up in the dry season. Within minutes I was at the culvert in the road that the water ran through during heavy rains. The gate was thirty yards away. For me to get to it, I would have to climb up the side of the creek unnoticed. While sometimes cadets left the Ranch to rollerblade down the road, it was always in buddy pairs. Being by myself could raise the alarm, so I needed to not be seen.

I took a deep breath, then scrambled up and walked as casually as possible toward the gate. I reached it and slipped through, my heart pounding in my ears. I resisted the urge to sprint. Running could alert someone if they happened to look out the main office windows that faced the gate. Instead, I continued at my even pace until I reached the road. I took a sharp right and continued walking. I kept waiting to hear someone shout out at me, but all I heard were the faint shouts and cries from the kickball game. A car came around the curve up ahead and sped by. A few minutes later, another car rushed past. I rounded the curve that led past Spunky Canyon Road, then let out the breath that I hadn't realized I was holding. I had made it.

I grinned to myself. Now all I needed to do was walk until a kind person gave me a ride to LA. I plodded along for a while until I came to the reservoir. There was a metal guardrail that protected cars from careening down the mountain into the water. I leaned over and admired the Bouquet Reservoir spread out below me. The sun reflected off the water. I always loved this view. There was something so calming about it.

I pushed off the fence and continued my journey. As I walked, I wondered whether I should stick out my thumb. Not many cars had passed, but I knew I should try to catch a ride. I decided to keep walking and try in a little while. I walked and walked and walked. The sun began to dip closer and closer to the horizon. The reservoir was now far behind me. I needed to get a ride before it got dark.

I worked up my nerve and stuck my thumb out. A car whizzed past. I saw another car coming and put out my thumb again. It zoomed by. After several vehicles had passed, I put my arm down. I felt stupid. Maybe I was doing it wrong. Or maybe there was a better spot to hitchhike. I would try again when I was closer to the biker bar that should be coming up soon. I rounded the curve and saw the falls ahead. I had come here a few times with the Cadet Org whenever our pool was out of service. There was a deep grotto nestled in the mountains with small waterfalls. When you climbed down, you could find rocks to slide down into the water on, like nature-made slides. I loved coming here, but today seeing the falls worried me. They were only fifteen minutes away by bus, and I had only just arrived. I had a long way to go before I even got off this mountain. The biker bar was farther down the road, which could be another hour of walking. The sun could be down by then.

I felt discouraged and decided I needed a break. I walked over to the edge and sat down in the dirt and peered down. Down below I saw a family playing in the water. The parents were sitting on the bank watching as two little girls splashed around. I wondered what it was like to be with a family like that. Maybe my parents could leave the Sea Org and we could be like a real family? With that thought, I decided I needed to get moving again. I stood up and brushed the dust off my shorts.

But after a long while of trudging along, I grew discouraged again. I thought I would have made it to the biker bar by now. Finally, I rounded a corner and saw the bar up ahead. Thank goodness. It being a Tuesday, there were only a few bikes out front and no cars. I was getting hungry, so I decided to have a snack. I saw a nice boulder that would make the perfect bench for me. I sat down and munched on my apple. I ate the apple down to the core, then tossed it in the bushes. The sun was low and cast long shadows. A breeze caressed my face and arms. I wrapped my arms around me and shivered. I hadn't thought to bring a sweater because I'd expected to be in LA by now. I needed a ride. I was going to have to suck it up and stick out my thumb until I got one, because there was no way I was making it to the city on foot.

I was about to do so when a dark blue car pulled over from the road and slowed to a stop in front of me. A small part of me wondered if I was about to be raped or murdered, but I pushed the thought away and watched as the door opened and a cowboy boot stepped out, followed by jeans and then the hefty body of a large man with a mustache.

"Hey there, you need a lift?" he asked. I stared for a second as I decided what to say. His face seemed too kind to be a rapist's.

"Uh, yeah. Thanks," I answered. I got up from the rock and dusted the sand off my shorts as I walked over.

"Where ya headed?" he said as we settled in our seats.

I buckled my seat belt and looked over. "Um, can you take me to LA?"

"LA?" He raised his eyebrows. "What's over there?"

"Oh, my mom and dad live there."

"Huh. Then what are you doing way out here?"

I glanced at him and decided to tell the truth.

"I'm running away from my boarding school. I don't want to be there anymore."

"Where's your school at?" he asked. I pointed in the direction from where I had come.

"What's the name of it?"

"The Canyon Oaks Ranch," I replied.

"Oh yeah, I've seen that school." He scratched his beard. "Huh."

The driver was quiet for a moment. He glanced at me and seemed to come to a decision.

"Well, I gotta be honest with you. I can't take you all the way to LA. But how about this? Why don't I take you back to your school and you can give your folks a call and maybe they can come pick you up?"

I sat silently for a moment and thought about it. After all that walking, I didn't think it was likely I would make it to LA. Going back to the Ranch wasn't what I had planned, but I didn't want to be stuck outside on the mountain. It would be cold. Not to mention the cougars and bears that had been sighted over the years. I slumped back in my seat.

"I guess that's fine." I shrugged.

He put the car in drive and pulled onto the road. I watched as trees and brush flashed by. I wondered if anyone had noticed I was missing. Would I be in big trouble? Could I make up an excuse for why I was gone?

"So, they treat you okay over there?" The man's gravelly voice interrupted my thoughts.

I glanced at him. I wondered if he was thinking the school abused me. I didn't want him to judge Scientology based off this interaction with me. He could decide to never become a Scientologist and I would be taking away his chance for total freedom.

"Oh, no. They are very nice." I gave him what I hoped was a genuine-looking smile. "I actually really like it there. I just thought it would be nice to see my mom and dad. But I'll call them instead."

"Hm." He kept his hands on the wheel and eyes on the road. "Well, we'll be there in a couple minutes here."

The car fell silent as we sped along. Before I knew it, we were pulling into the driveway.

"Uh, thanks," I said as I unbuckled my seat belt and opened the door.

"Hey," he said.

"Yeah?" I looked back at him.

"Next time you want to run away, maybe you talk to one of your teachers first. It's dangerous, and you wouldn't want to be picked up by the wrong sort." He nodded his head in agreement with himself.

"Okay, yeah. I will. Thanks," I said. I shut the car door and waved goodbye as he reversed out the drive and pulled away. It was dusk, with the sun sinking behind the mountains as I watched his taillights disappear down the road. I took a deep breath, turned around, and started up the driveway. I could see someone come out of the main office and stand silhouetted on the front lawn. I squinted. It was Bryan, the security guard. When I got within ten feet, he called out.

"Where the hell were you? Who dropped you off?"

"Uh, it was just some guy giving me a ride," I responded.

"Are you joking? Just some random guy?" Bryan said.

"Weeeell, I decided to go for a walk during PE, but then I walked too far and lost track of time," I said.

Bryan stared at me as if trying to read my mind. "Yeah right. But whatever. I don't have time for this crap. Go to the main mess for dinner," he ordered. He turned and strode back inside the main office.

I stared after him, speechless. That was it? No being yelled at? I wasn't assigned lower conditions or put on twenty-four-hour watch? That's normally what happened if a cadet blew. I was somehow off the hook.

I hurried up the back road toward the main mess. When I walked inside, I expected my friends to at least ask where I had been, but no one commented as I sat down. Instead, Hallie chatted happily to Lacy and didn't even look over when I took my seat next to her. I ate my dinner slowly, letting the conversations roll over my head. I was in a mix of emotions. Was I relieved or angry that no one had noticed that I was gone? Did anyone even care? What was I, chopped liver?

Suddenly, Hallie turned to me and asked where I had been during course time. At least she had noticed. I shrugged. Hallie seemed to accept my shrug as permission to talk to me and launched into a story about something that happened at course time. I listened, and couldn't help but laugh at the funny parts. I felt my resentment drain away. As Hallie chattered on, she leaned in and grabbed my hand and squeezed. I smiled at her and squeezed back. She was so cheerful and happy talking to me that it caused me to doubt myself. Maybe I had blown the whole underwear thing out of proportion. Hallie was my friend. She probably hadn't meant to hurt my feelings. I laughed at the end of her story and leaned in and hugged her. Hallie hugged me back, then got up and grabbed her plate.

"Do you want to go up to the dorm with Lacy and I and read my new *Seventeen* magazine that my mom sent me?"

"Yeah, sounds fun!" I pushed up from the table. The three of us bussed our plates and headed off to the dorms.

30

MY NEW FRIEND

Early in the spring, two new cadets arrived at the Ranch. Allison and Kayla were sisters from Austin, Texas. Before the Ranch, they had gone to an actual, normal school. They had a regular family and lived in a house, just like kids in the books I read. Then their mother joined the Sea Org and they were sent to live with us at the Ranch. Allison was my age, and I wanted to know everything about her. I loved hearing about her life back in Austin. Their school, how they got to have friends over to their houses, what kind of music they listened to. *Everything.*

Allison seemed bemused by the attention.

"Yeah, we lived in a house," she'd say with a shrug and a smile. "It was all right."

"So, you guys like, cooked meals in a kitchen and sat together and had dinner?" one of us would ask.

"Uh, yeah."

"But what was it like being a Scientologist? Did you have to study all day?"

"No, we only went to the church every once in a while."

I took that in. Not having to study Scientology every day

sounded nice. I was ahead in Scientology studies at the Ranch, but I didn't love the subject. I knew that was bad, so I never said it out loud, but I preferred to read fiction or learn geography or history. Those were my favorite subjects. I wished we had more of that here at the Ranch.

"But my mom went on course every day," Allison added.

"Yeah," said Kayla. "She is really dedicated."

We nodded approvingly.

Learning about life outside of the Sea Org fascinated me. And Allison was such an easy person to be friends with. She had a calm, sweet aura and didn't have a mean bone in her body. This friendship was a nice break from the constant tug-of-war I had with Hallie. Hallie and I were still thick as thieves, but I sometimes felt an undercurrent of something rippling beneath the surface. Would she betray me again and go rifling through my things? Was she talking about me behind my back? Having Allison, a girl I knew I could trust, was a welcome relief. I was determined to make her one of my closest friends.

Allison had only been at the Ranch a few weeks when the apple tree project was announced at muster one day. Mr. Hammond pointed to the dusty field behind the schoolhouse and informed us that the Ranch was going to have an apple orchard there, and we were going to plant them.

"That's where we play football!"

"What the hell!"

"This sucks!"

As exclamations rose in the air, I joined in. "Boooo!"

I certainly didn't want to plant apple trees all day.

"Shut the fuck up!" Mr. Hammond shouted.

Silence.

I knew that complaining wouldn't change anything. I wondered what Allison thought about having to do hard labor. I was sure this wasn't something she was used to. I glanced at her, but she seemed unfazed.

THE FIRST SHIPMENT of trees arrived after dinner. The bell rang, summoning us from our dorms. The CO cadets organized us into units with specific jobs. I made sure to stand next to Allison so that I had a friend to work with. We were assigned to dig holes in the field for the trees to be planted in. I grabbed a shovel and shivered. It was cold out and I was freezing under my thin sweater. I wanted to complain, but Allison seemed happy, and I didn't want to seem like a whiner.

We began making a hole where an adult had tapped a small stake to show where we needed to dig. Soon my breath was misting my face as I warmed up from working so hard. Allison and I talked about the movie *Titanic* as we worked, and how much we loved Jack. I was surprised at how much I was enjoying myself. It's not every day that you have to plant trees. It was surprisingly fun. We worked for three hours and planted around thirty trees. An orange cooler was set up on the pickup truck with something called panther piss, a disgusting mix of apple cider vinegar, water, lemon, and a little bit of molasses. Whenever I took a sip, I gagged as the liquid burned down my throat. Luckily, there was a cooler of just water next to it, so I switched to drinking that. By the time we were finished digging, it was 10 p.m. The good news was that Mr. Hammond told us we could sleep in the next morning, which drew cheers from everyone.

. . .

A FEW DAYS LATER, the tree shipment didn't come until late in the evening, after we were in our dorms about to get ready for bed. Mr. Hammond told us that because the temperatures were dropping, we needed to get all of the trees in the ground so they didn't die. There was a lot of grumbling until he yelled at us to be quiet. He had some news. We all went silent. Mr. Hammond proceeded to tell us that if we got the work done, he would set up a trip for us to head to Santa Monica beach the next day.

We cheered. That night we stayed up until past midnight planting trees. But I didn't care. We were headed to the beach! The next day I had so much fun riding the rides on Santa Monica Pier with Allison and our friends.

OUR BEACH REWARD didn't mean the project was over. Within a week the large field was crowded with trees, but Mr. Hammond chose a new area past the horse corral for the project to continue. One week after the trip to Santa Monica, we were digging well past sundown. The headlights of a pickup truck parked fifteen feet away illuminated our work. Other cadets dug in the trenches nearby. I was tired of digging and decided it would be a good time to take a bathroom break. I asked Allison if she wanted to join me.

"Sure," she said.

"C'mon, let's go ask Cody." Cody was an older cadet and the current Commanding Officer. He stood tall with his muscled arms crossed as he supervised those of us in the trenches. With his tousled black hair and chiseled face, Cody looked like he could be a lead actor in a teenage movie. Unfortunately, he didn't have the personality to match it. He was a bit of a dick. We pushed our shovels into the dirt and walked over.

We stopped in front of him, and he stared at us.

"What?"

"We need to go to the bathroom," I told him.

"No," Cody scoffed. "You guys are just trying to slack."

Shoot. I had thought having the new girl with me would make him a little nicer, but apparently not.

"No." I put my arm around Allison. "We really have to go! We promise to come back. Right Allison?"

Allison looked uncomfortable but nodded her agreement anyway. She probably wasn't used to lying, but soon she would see that it was the only way to get some time to yourself at the Ranch.

Cody's eyes flicked at Allison, and then he flung his hands up to the sky.

"Fiiiine," he groaned. "But you better not take forever."

"We won't! Jeez. It's just the bathroom." I turned to go before Cody changed his mind, pulling Allison along with me.

"He's so dramatic," I whispered to Allison, rolling my eyes. She giggled and leaned in closer as we walked along the dirt path leading through the trees and brush. A half-moon hung in the sky and shined a soft glow on everything, but once we were beyond the reach of the truck's headlights, I had to squint to see. The soft murmur of the cadets faded behind us as we crunched down the path.

"It's a little spooky," I whispered to Allison.

"I know." She grabbed my arm tighter. "It's like a scary movie."

Suddenly, I heard rustling in the bushes and edged closer to her. I looked behind me but couldn't see anything. My heart thumped. Cadets had spotted a black bear roaming at the Ranch a few times. There was even a bear trap cage by the dumpsters, but we'd yet to catch the bear.

Maybe it was tracking us? Suddenly something jumped out of the bushes ahead of us.

Allison and I shrieked, holding onto each other.

We gathered ourselves and looked, seeing Alexander and Antonio, clutching each other and laughing their heads off.

"Oh my god, you guys are so annoying!" I laughed and swatted at Alexander's arm. "We're going to get you back!"

"Yeah, sure you are," he drawled. They turned to walk up the path toward the other cadets, chuckling over how clever they were.

"We have to get them back," I told Allison.

"For sure," she agreed. We walked the rest of the way to the dorm as we plotted how we would scare them. After arriving, we decided to stay there instead of returning to the apple tree project. I convinced Allison it was more important to plan how we would take Alexander and Antonio down. With it being so dark, I was pretty sure we wouldn't be missed and get any punishment.

31

SO IT GOES

I received a call from my mom during lunch. She was requesting Sunday off from work. It had been seven months since she had taken a Sunday off, so I was excited. L. Ron Hubbard policy said Sea Org members could request the day off every other week if their production was higher than the week before, but my mom and dad never seemed to do it. I don't know if they hadn't worked hard enough that week and so weren't allowed to, or if they just didn't ask for time off. It didn't make sense to me, and I had been bugging my mom about it for months. And now it was finally happening.

It was now up to me to get Sunday off so we could spend the day together. To get approval, I was going to need to work hard on my studies and make sure I had enough student points and completions earned.

On Thursday, I learned that my production points were going to be high enough. I turned in my statistics and then ran up to the course room to write my CSW report requesting Sunday off. I made sure to mention that I hadn't had the day off with my mom in forever, and I attached my student stat graphs showing my production. I strode to the Comm Center and slid my CSW into my senior's basket. It would take a day to go through the lines. I would check on it on Friday.

The next day, I walked down to the Communication Center and jogged up the three steps, opened the door, and headed straight to the wooden communication shelf filled with cubby holes labeled with each cadets name and post. I could already see the few sheets of paper sitting in my cubby hole. I reached in and grabbed them, certain my CSW would be approved.

Fuck.

My request had been sent back to me with a disapproved signature from Cody, the Commanding Officer. I wanted to crumple up the paper and throw it away, but I resisted the urge. I had to calm down and see if I could change Cody's mind. Just then, his laugh floated in from the executive office next door. I gritted my teeth, then walked over and poked my head in the doorway.

There he sat, leaning back, not a care in the world. His black hair ruffled just so. His handsome face grinning at whatever the other two cadets who sat across from him were telling him. I wanted to push him out of his office chair so badly.

"Hey, can I talk to Cody about something?" I interrupted with a forced smile.

"What?" he said.

I walked over and thrust the papers at him. "How come you disapproved my CSW?"

"Because . . ." He crossed his arms, ignoring my papers. "You slack all the time." With that, he let his chair fall back with a thud and turned back to the other execs in the room, ignoring me.

"What are you even talking about?" I grabbed his chair and gave it a nudge so he had to swivel back to me. "I haven't been slacking. I've been on full-time study. My stats are up."

"Yeah, right," Cody said. "You slack off all the time. You don't work hard when we are doing the apple tree project. You goof off and blow to your dorm."

"So? Everyone does that. I'm not the only one!" I took a deep breath. "I want to see my mom. I haven't seen her in seven months."

"Well, that's too bad. You should have thought of that before you blew. Your CSW is disapproved, and I'm not changing my mind."

He turned his chair away from me again. One of the executive cadets watching this confrontation snickered.

"Well, screw you guys," I said. I turned and left.

"What did I do?" I heard someone say behind me. Laughter erupted.

I slammed the door hard and walked through the Comm Center, down the steps.

I headed toward my dorm to mope, but as I passed the boys' dorm, I thought of Judson. Had he gotten his CSW approved? I swerved onto the path leading to his dorm and walked up. I knocked on the door until a boy answered.

"Yeah?" he asked.

"I need my brother," I said. "It's important. Can you get him?"

"Okay." He turned and shouted, "Judson! Your sister is here!"

I was tempted to go in after him and look for my brother myself, but girls weren't allowed in the boys' dorm, and I didn't want to prove Cody right by getting in trouble right after yelling at him that I wasn't out-ethics. Instead, I slouched against the wall and waited, letting the sunlight warm my face. The door opened and Judson came out.

"Hey, what's up?" he asked.

"My CSW got disapproved," I told him. I blinked hard. I could feel my eyes start to water.

"Shoot. Mine did too." Judson tossed a tennis ball he was holding into the air.

"I wonder if Lucas will at least get libs," he said as he caught it.

"Yeah, me too." Silence fell as Judson continued tossing the ball up and down.

"Aren't you mad?"

"I guess. But there's not anything we can do about it. You know how it is," Judson said.

"Well, I'm mad." I kicked the back of the wall behind me. "It sucks!"

I watched the ball as it went up and down a few more times, almost mesmerized. My anger waned. My brother was so chill and laid back. I needed more of his attitude. He was always like this, which made him very popular with both boys and girls. There were rumors that Judson was gay, because he got along so well with the girls, and even participated in the dances the older girls made up on the patio during break times. But because he was so athletic and played a lot of sports, those rumors were swatted aside. There was no way he was gay. L. Ron Hubbard said homosexuals were perverted and the most covert individuals who would stab you in the back in a second. Judson would never do that.

"I'll call Mom and let her know that we can't come because our CSW's were disapproved," I said as I pushed away from the wall and began walking back toward my dorm.

"K." Judson caught his ball. "See ya later."

He headed back in. I guess that was that. Who knew the next time I would get to have libs with my mom?

That evening I tried to call her but couldn't reach her. Instead, I left a message with the receptionist saying Judson and I were both not allowed to take liberty to see her this Sunday. Hopefully she wasn't sad when she read the message, but there was nothing I could do about it. It was out of my control. I thought she would understand. She undoubtedly went through the same thing all the time. It was probably why she never visited.

LIFE WENT ON, though. Day after day. The same routine. Then something happened. In March, about a month after my mom was supposed to have visited, my dad called me. I hadn't heard from him in awhile, but it turned out he had good news. He told me he had received my Social Security number. I was finally going to get paid.

Thank god. I was sick of being broke.

It had been years since my last paycheck and it had been so hard.

When that first one came a week later, I headed right to the bus that took cadets to Walmart on Sundays. I got myself some socks and underwear, which had become a top priority since I'd had so few of them for the past year. Having a little money gave me a sense of relief. In his own way, my dad had come through and taken care of me.

. . .

Weeks later I heard some news. My brothers were leaving the Ranch. They had been chosen along with fourteen other cadets for a rushed study program to get them into the Sea Org ASAP. Alexander and Antonio were also chosen, along with Cody, the current cadet CO. That was the one silver lining. I wouldn't have to deal with that asshole anymore.

Starting immediately, the chosen cadets were tasked with additional study sessions with a special tutor to help them pass their GED exam as soon as possible. This way, they could be full-time Sea Org members and not have to go to school. Judson was fifteen and Lucas sixteen, so I could see that they were old enough to join, but still. I was going to miss my brothers. Especially Judson, since we were so close.

I was also sad that Alexander and Antonio were leaving, because Allison and I had been involved in a prank war with the two of them for the past few weeks. Just last night I had been lying in my bed in my dorm with Allison reading a magazine when we heard something hit the window. We ran over and opened the curtain, but no one was there. Then, *Boo!* They jumped up and scared us. I laughed so hard. I would miss stuff like that. Who would prank us now?

Well, at least I had Patrick. Patrick had not been chosen to go and was upset about it but I was relieved. Patrick had been Judson's friend since the ATA, along with Alexander and Antonio. The four of them were a tight group, and now for the first time in his life he was going to be separated from them. I commiserated with him, but I was relieved he wasn't going. Patrick and I had been hanging out together often, even if we spent most of the time arguing. We debated about everything from who was smarter, to what was the best movie. Patrick also explained his list of the most attractive girls at school. I told him off for being a sexist but was then taken aback when I came in at number ten on the list.

Me? On the pretty list? I couldn't help feeling secretly pleased, but I still let him know he was pathetic for judging us like that. My friends were always teasing me, saying that we liked each other, which I denied up and down. But there was a tiny part of me that was wondering if maybe that was true. Regardless, at least he was still at the Ranch and not leaving.

32

LRH'S BIRTHDAY EVENT

Every year in March, the Sea Org threw a big event to celebrate L. Ron Hubbard's birthday. It was held in Los Angeles at the Shrine Auditorium, the same place that the Grammys and Oscars were held. To me, this proved how important Scientology was to the world. We were in the same auditorium as the stars.

I loved being with all the public and Sea Org members who supported Scientology and hearing what steps were being taken to make the world a better place. Also, I really liked dressing up.

I boarded the bus with the cadets after lunch. We headed to the Shrine several hours before it started to help prep food and décor, like we did for most events. There was the New Year's Event in late December, L. Ron Hubbard's birthday in March, the Dianetics event in May, the Auditor's Day event in September and the International Association for Scientologists event in October—each one proclaiming the wonders of Scientology and our many accomplishments over the last few months.

We arrived at the Shrine and worked for a couple of hours. When we were done, we were dismissed to go change in the bathrooms upstairs. My friends and I raced up the elegant staircase clutching our bags that held our dresses.

The bathrooms at the Shrine were spectacular. The women's room was massive and covered wall-to-wall in plush maroon carpet. Floor to ceiling mirrors without a smudge on them. Marble counters, magenta velvet cushions to sit on while you put on makeup or waited for your friends to get dressed. You could picture famous actresses in this very room, touching up their makeup just like us.

I claimed a corner of the room with Allison, Hallie, and our other friends. Allison had lent me a gauzy blue dress that floated down to my knees, and I couldn't wait to put it on. We rushed into the stalls to change. I shut my door and pulled off my clothes and tugged on my dress. Hallie and Allison did the same in the stalls beside me. When I was done, I darted over to the full-length mirror and smiled at my reflection. I actually looked decent. I had recently switched to contacts and was still getting used to the sight of my face without glasses. My hair was long enough to part down the middle and scrape into a long puffy ponytail. The dress was a little snug around my chest area because my boobs had gotten bigger, but I didn't think it was too bad. I swiveled my hips a little, and the fabric swayed softly from the waist down to my knees. I turned to the side. It was so nice to be in a dress instead of in our same old cadet uniform.

"You look so pretty," Allison exclaimed as she stood next to me.

"Really?" I blushed.

"Yeah, totally." She smiled.

"Thanks." I turned toward her. "Oh my god, I love your dress! You're the prettiest one here for sure."

Allison laughed and shook her head, then said she needed to go find her shoes.

I stayed by the mirror and studied my reflection. Maybe I really was okay looking? It was hard to believe when I compared myself to my friends with their long, silky hair and blue and hazel eyes. I was just brown, brown, brown. But maybe that didn't matter anymore? I shook my head at myself in the Shrine bathroom mirror. I was way over-thinking things. Besides, even if I was pretty, I was too loud for any boys to like me. I was always being told I needed to simmer down. I walked away from the mirror and over to my friends to admire all the other girls' dresses.

ONCE WE WERE READY, we filed out of the bathroom and trotted up the stairs to the top balcony, which is where we sat at every event. The floor seats were for the public Scientologists only, but I didn't mind being way up. The view was worth it. It was breathtaking to look around the huge auditorium and the thousands of Scientologists milling below. The stage was lit up. There was an elaborate podium in the middle of the stage for the speakers to stand at. Large gold curtains were tied off to the side, and of course, there was a massive portrait of L. Ron Hubbard hanging above the stage, looking over the whole room.

"There's the Int Ranchers!" Hallie said. She nudged me and pointed to a group of cadets one section over. Int stood for International. The Int Ranch was for cadets whose parents were in the management orgs of Scientology. I peered over, trying to catch a glimpse of them. It was rare to see the Int Ranch cadets at these events. Their Ranch was at a top secret location. It was a secret because they didn't want Suppressive People to find them. I was always so curious about what it was like at the Int Ranch. It's like they were us, but more important or mysterious. Living at a top secret ranch doing who knows what, rarely ever appearing at these public events. We had heard stories from cadets who had transferred between ranches that the Int Ranch was super strict. They weren't allowed any music that was considered degrading, rarely went on field trips, and couldn't wear any perfume or eat sugar. The list went on and on. Sometimes the PAC Ranch got strict on those rules, but this was rare and never lasted long. At the Int Ranch, they weren't even allowed to have boyfriends or girlfriends.

A booming voice emanated from the speakers all around us and brought me back to the present. The voice expounded on the wonderful attributes of our founder L. Ron Hubbard. He then announced the first speaker, Mr. David Miscavige. The current leader of the Sea Org.

Mr. Miscavige walked onto the stage, and the auditorium filled with applause. The noise reverberated around me.

"Thank you very much!" he cried out over the screams and claps of adoration. The cheering continued. Mr. Miscavige's face filled the large screen as he beamed at the audience. I cheered louder, impressed with this handsome young man, with his carefully slicked back hair, stiff military uniform, and strong presence. He raised his hand for silence. Slowly the cheers faded.

"Welcome to L. Ron Hubbard's birthday celebration!" he declared.

The auditorium erupted in cheers again. This went on for several minutes, and I cheered with gusto along with everyone else. Finally, the auditorium quieted, and Mr. Miscavige spoke again. He told of the many accomplishments of L. Ron Hubbard. At first, I listened intently, but soon my attention began to drift. I pinched my fingers one by one to try to force my focus back to the stage but kept getting distracted by fantasies of this extravagant ballroom and the fancy events it hosted on other nights.

After what felt like hours, the next speaker was introduced. I groaned. It was L. Ron Hubbard's autobiographer. Every year he spoke at the event, and I swear, he won the award for the most boring speaker. He was an old man with gray hair and an English accent that was impossible to decipher at times. I don't know how the audience didn't fall asleep, because I could feel myself start to nod off within minutes.

"Wanna come with me to the bathroom?" I whispered to Hallie. She nodded and nudged Lacy, who was sitting beside her. Lacy whispered to Tory, and down the row the whispers went. Only Hallie and Lacy wanted to come, so we squeezed down the aisle and headed out into the hallway. Mr. Morris stopped us on our way out and hissed at us to get back to our seats. We told her we had to go to the bathroom.

"Fine," she said. "Be back in five minutes. No hanging out in the hallway."

"Five minutes?" I protested. "It'll take us that long just to walk there."

"Then you better walk fast," she said, peering at us from underneath her bushy gray eyebrows.

I rolled my eyes and turned away to jog down the stairs toward the exit with Hallie and Lacy following behind.

After a quick restroom break, we hung out in the hallway looking for Scientologist public boys who might be goofing off in the hall. It was always fun at these events to scout out boys we didn't know. We'd speculate about which school they went to, and which one of them we would go out with if we went to their school.

Next, we decided to go to the childcare rooms set up for the Scientologist public. I would get to see my mom, who was assigned to work in childcare at every event, but mostly I just wanted to spend the rest of the time holding the babies. I loved babies. They were so soft and warm and melted into my arms. My heart softened like butter when I held them, their chubby fingers grabbing my face. As a future Sea Org member, I would never have children of my own. My parents' generation was the last one that was allowed to have families. In the late '80s, a policy letter was issued that prohibited Sea Org members from having children. I didn't know why—maybe they decided that raising us and setting up these ranches wasn't worth the trouble. Regardless, I really hoped they'd eventually change the rule. I really wanted a family of my own one day.

After thirty minutes of cuddling the babies, we decided to sneak back into the event. Reluctantly, I put down the chubby baby I was holding into her baby rocker and said goodbye to my mom, and we headed back to the auditorium. We chose to go down the aisle opposite from Mr. Morris and made sure to avoid looking her way. There was no way for her to yell at us since we were twenty seats away and she wouldn't want to make a scene. I also figured she wouldn't care all that much. Turns out I was right. After a quick glance in our direction, she turned back to watching the event. We were back, and that was what mattered. The event ended fifteen minutes later, and we clapped enthusiastically.

"Hip hip hooray!" The auditorium cheered for L. Ron Hubbard. The lights went on and the public flowed out to head down to the ballroom.

It took forever to get through the crowd, but finally we made it. The ballroom was a long hall the size of a football field. On each end were large buffet tables piled with appetizers, small sandwiches and deserts. Throughout the room were different display tables and booths from each org, along with whatever new Scientology product they were selling. At every event, there was always some newly released book or course, and there was a big push on all the Sea Org members to get the public to buy it. I always thought LRH was a genius to have created so much that there were still new releases of his work coming out even though he dropped his body over ten years ago.

Walking into the ballroom after the event was like walking into a packed pen. It was hard to squeeze through the adults and get to the buffet, but my friends and I managed to do it. After gorging ourselves on food, we spent the next couple of hours walking around and finding our parents at whatever booths they had been assigned. My dad was at AOLA's booth, and I made sure to say hello. My sister was busy racing around, monitoring each org's production. I ran into her on the way to get some more cake. We hugged and chatted briefly before she had to get back to work. She looked so important with her clipboard, dressed all in black, ready to go yell at the Sea Org members who weren't making their targets.

At 10 p.m., the cadets gathered outside the ballroom to get back on the bus to go to the Ranch. As I was waiting, I heard someone mention that they were staying the night with their parents instead. She had worked it out with Mr. Smith. She'd stay with her parents at PAC and the bus would come back and pick up cadets tomorrow. All you had to do was ask.

Excited by the opportunity to possibly spend a night

with my parents, I raced back into the crowd in the ballroom and squirmed my way toward my dad's booth.

There he was, standing by the AOLA booth, seemingly staring into space.

"Dad!" I called out.

My dad turned and lifted his clipboard and gave a lazy wave.

"Hi, hon."

"Some of the cadets are staying the night with their parents. A bus will take them back to the Ranch in the morning. I haven't had a sleepover with you and Mom in forever. Can I please stay with you guys?"

"Oh," he said. He looked surprised. I couldn't blame him. I couldn't remember the last time I had stayed in their room at PAC.

"Pleeease!"

"Uh, yeah, sure."

"Great! You just have to go tell Mr. Smith that I can stay with you guys," I said.

My dad nodded, set his clipboard down at the booth, and followed me through the crowded ballroom back outside. As we stepped out onto the dark sidewalk, I spotted Mr. Smith standing inside the bus next to the driver's seat.

"Wait here," I said.

I trotted up the three steps onto the bus.

"Take a seat," she said without looking at me.

"Actually, my dad said I can spend the night with him and my—"

"No," Mr. Smith interrupted. "No more cadets are spending the night."

"Wait, why?" I protested.

"Don't backflash, Katherine." Mr. Smith glared at me.

I glared back. Urgggh. Why did she seem to hate me so much?

Mr. Smith didn't back down, her gaze like ice. My eyes dropped as I made a sound of frustration.

"Whatever," I muttered. I turned and stomped down the bus steps.

I realized I'd just have to have my dad ask her. She wouldn't have the nerve to say "no" to a grown-up.

But as I looked at my dad, again staring off in the distance with his hands in his slacks, his bald head reflecting the streetlight between the strands of hair he had combed over, I felt a twinge of doubt. I had never seen my dad stand up to anyone. Even my mom bossed him around the few times we were all together. Did he have it in him? I sighed. It was worth a try.

"Dad?" I said. "Can you tell Mr. Smith that you want me to have time with you and Mom?"

"Sure," he answered.

He plodded to the bus and gripped the handrail as he climbed the steps, each foot landing with a heavy thud. I peered up from the sidewalk and watched as he chatted with Mr. Smith. I couldn't hear what they were saying, but it didn't look like this was going to work. He had already turned away from Mr. Smith and was now plodding down the steps.

My heart raced. Maybe, just maybe . . . ?

"Sorry, Katherine," he said as he put his hand on my shoulder. "She said they can't let any more cadets stay in LA. The bus tomorrow is too full."

Disappointment flooded me. Why couldn't my dad be one of those parents who demanded to see their kid every Sunday no matter what? Like Tory's mom. It seemed like she always had to see Tory every weekend, or else.

"It's fine," I muttered. "Thanks for trying."

I gave my dad a limp hug. As I stepped on the bus, I avoided looking at Mr. Smith. I had a feeling she would be smirking, and I couldn't take it right now. I slumped down into an empty seat and leaned my head against the window and closed my eyes. The excitement of the day was gone.

33

MY FOURTEENTH BIRTHDAY

On my fourteenth birthday, we headed down to Los Angeles, even though it was a Thursday. The cadets were all going to PAC to do backlog filing for a mission. I hoped I would see my dad and brothers. I wouldn't be able to see my mom though, because she was in South America. They had her traveling frequently these days trying to recruit new Sea Org members from Spanish-speaking countries.

Our mission consisted of going through parishioner notes to sort and file the paperwork. We worked hard all day except for our lunch break, when they ordered pizza. I didn't mind the work because Mr. Hammond and Mr. Smith let us listen to K-ROQ and Star 98.7, our favorite radio stations. They didn't even seem to mind that we sang along at the top of our lungs to every song we knew. All in all, this was turning out to be a fun birthday. Usually, I would just get a birthday card from my parents in the mail a few weeks late with some money, so being off the Ranch was a treat.

At dinnertime, Mr. Hammond told us we would be eating in the dining room with all the Sea Org members. We didn't eat there often, so this was exciting. We all filed down the stairs to the first floor, chatting and bumping into each other. We quieted as we entered the large dining hall filled with Sea Org members already midway through their meal. It was a bright, airy room, with tables, that sat eight to ten people each. It was cool to see all the Sea Org members in the uniforms of their respective orgs. After a quick scan, I didn't see my dad or brothers' orgs, but I wasn't too bothered. I had my friends.

I headed to the buffet line, filled my plate, and grabbed a table with Hallie, Allison, Beatrice, and Lacy. While we chatted, I heard clapping, as if someone was trying to get everyone's attention. It was Sean, the Galley I/C, standing next to a cart with a cake on it.

"Today it is a cadet's birthday," he announced. "Let's all sing 'Happy Birthday' to Katherine!"

Sean led the whole dining room, three hundred or so Sea Org members and all the cadets, in singing "Happy Birthday" to *me*. I couldn't believe it. My face felt hot. Was this real? My birthday being announced in front of everyone at PAC Base? I could feel all eyes on me. I covered my mouth behind my hands to hide my wide grin.

Sean brought over a small cake to share with my table. Tory was with him and shoved a card in my hand.

"This is for you! We wanted to surprise you," she said. Hallie, Lacy, and Allison nodded, their faces beaming. It dawned on me that they had done this in secret. They had arranged all of this during the day while I was busy filing. I had no idea! I hadn't realized that they cared about me that much. I swallowed and smiled, feeling my eyes water.

"How surprised were you?" Hallie asked. "Be honest! Did you have any idea?"

"No, I didn't." I looked down at the card and opened it.

There were notes and signatures from many cadets, including former cadets that were now on the TTC!

My jaw dropped.

"Wow, how did you guys do this?"

"Tory asked one of the adults if she could get the TTCers to sign the card while we were working. We distracted you while she did it." Hallie smiled.

I took a deep breath and gazed around. I had known most of these girls since I was a baby, and here we all were, now teenagers. These friends and I were going to be together forever, proud members of the Sea Org, clearing the world. I was so lucky.

PART II

THE SEA ORG

EXCERPT OF SEA ORG CONTRACT

I, _____ DO HEREBY AGREE to enter into employment with the SEA ORGANIZATION and, being of sound mind, do fully realize and agree to abide by its purpose which is to get ETHICS IN on this PLANET AND UNIVERSE and, fully and without reservation, subscribe to the discipline, mores and conditions of this group and pledge to abide by them.

THEREFORE, I CONTRACT MYSELF TO THE SEA ORGANIZATION FOR THE NEXT BILLION YEARS.

34

THE TIME HAD COME

This was it.

I was joining the Sea Org.

I sat in the passenger seat as Mr. Williams drove down the windy road toward PAC Base, my fingers curled tight in my lap. My whole life had built toward this moment. A few weeks ago, I'd had no idea this was in store, but after my birthday I had been put on full-time study. Mr. Hammond said it was of the utmost importance that I get my A, B, and C Certs. These were the three certificates that would qualify me for the Sea Org. The C cert was doing a grade 5 math test, the A cert, an 8th grade vocabulary test and the B cert was the easiest; I had to write 500 words in cursive under a time constraint.

Mr. Williams had called me to the main office and informed me that I was joining the Sea Org only this morning. And here I was, in the car headed to PAC. I would be assigned to the Estates Project Force, or EPF, which was a program like a military boot camp. Every Sea Org member needed to complete the EPF before formally joining.

"Today?" I had asked. "Like, now?"

"Yes," Mr. Williams said with a smile. I had always had the feeling that I was a cadet that Mr. Williams was proud of. She thought I was smart and had told me so a few times. She was pretty much the only adult I had ever known who seemed to believe in me, and it gave me some confidence.

"Wow." I smiled. "Do we know what org I am going to?"

"No, but they will assign one to you when you finish," Mr. Williams said. "I am sure you will speed through the EPF as long as you stay on purpose."

I nodded, resolving to not let any of my silliness distract me. A few weeks ago I had been reprimanded for being too loud and out of valence. For some reason it bothered the adults and other cadets when I danced around, singing the Christina Aguilera song "Genie in a Bottle," or whatever else happened to be in my head at the time. I was always told to calm down and be quieter and more focused and not create distractions. This is what she meant by being "on purpose." In the Sea Org, there would be no more dancing at random, loudness, or silliness of any kind.

But it was fine, I told myself. It was time I got on purpose. I could always be silly on days off.

In the office, Mr. Williams had me sign the EPF routing form and the billion-year Sea Org contract. I wrote my name on each with a flourish. This wasn't the first time I had signed the billion-year contract. They had us do it every now and then, I think even back at the ATA. But this time felt different.

"Now, hurry up to your dorm and pack only what you need. Any nonessential items can be put in the storage unit in the log cabin. I want to get you routed on the EPF today," Mr. Williams said, interrupting my thoughts.

"Okay." I gave her a wave before I raced out of the main office and sprinted to my dorm. It was important that I help get the stats up, so I had to be routed on the EPF before 2 p.m. to count toward the stats for this week.

I had shoved all my items in a large backpack quickly. I didn't have much so it hadn't taken long.

Hallie wandered in after lunch and helped me pack. When I was done, she gave me a big hug, promising to write me every day.

"Bye," I had called with a wave. I opened the door and started down the path toward the office. I couldn't believe I was leaving. I was so proud that I was joining the Sea Org before them. I had been chosen! It was so rare to be singled out. Usually, I was the last one picked compared to them, even going back to the ATA days, when Hallie was chosen for every promotional video shoot for Scientology. Or even the times when I got in ethics trouble and Hallie didn't. But finally, I had beat her at something. I had finished the A, B, and C Certs before her, Lacy and Tory. I wasn't the first of our friends to go but I was still proud. Allison had left a week before and was already slated to join a management org. And no wonder. She was the total package for the Sea Org: hard working, sweet, and in-ethics. That was going to be me now. I would follow her example.

The car pulled into the parking lot on Catalina Street across from PAC Base. I jerked out of my reverie as Mr. Williams unbuckled. I grabbed the backpack that I had between my feet and slung it over my shoulders as I got out. The strap dug into me from the weight of the two photo albums I had stuffed in there at the Ranch. Mr. Williams had said to leave personal items behind, but there was no way I was leaving my albums. My friends and I loved buying disposable Kodak cameras and taking pictures of our lives. There were photos of us at Santa Monica Beach, on our camping trips, and silly ones of us lounging in our dorms.

The albums contained my whole life and I couldn't risk leaving them behind in the moldy storage at the log cabin at the Ranch. Cadets were always goofing off in that storage room and who knew if they were going through bags. I wouldn't put it past them. Plus, there were still bags in there from the cadets that got sent to the TTC and it had been over a year. It seemed like they were never going to go back to get them. So yeah, my albums were staying with me.

Mr. Williams heaved herself out of the car and gestured for me to follow her into the Complex. She led me through the double doors down the shiny white-tiled hallway to the EPF office and opened the door. I peered around her and saw Allison sitting in a small office with another Sea Org member. She gave me an excited wave.

"Allison!" I squeezed past Mr. Williams and rushed over to give her a big hug.

"Shhh," Allison hushed after hugging me back. I looked around and realized I had distracted some of the EPFers from their studies. Whoops.

As I looked around at the scowling faces of the EPFers I had interrupted, I couldn't help but notice that a lot of them were . . . kind of hot? What was going on here? There were a ton of good-looking guys on the EPF. A few of them were staring right back at me. I looked behind me, but no one else was there. Maybe they were looking at Allison? I felt my cheeks warm regardless.

"Guess what?" Allison said in a whisper. "I am going to be your buddy."

"Oh good!" I said, relieved she would show me the ropes.

Mr. Williams had been conversing with the EPF I/C, but now turned to me. "Katherine, this is Mr. Valentino, the EPF I/C," she said.

"You can call me Mr. V for short," he said.

"Okay," I said. I smiled shyly.

Mr. V cut an impressive figure. He was clean-cut and fit, perhaps twenty-five years old, with his white button-down shirt with the Sea Org logo tucked into crisp black pants. His patrician face looked like an English lord. My stomach fluttered but I tried to calm myself down. He was my senior officer! My mind kept racing despite my effort to stay focused. All those EPFers, and now Mr. V too. I glanced back into the course room and started to count how many hot guys there were in my head.

"Allison will be your buddy for today and help you get set up with your uniform and show you where your bunk bed is," Mr. V said, interrupting my thoughts. "After that, you can come back and join the other EPFers on study. Be quick, Allison."

"Yes sir," Allison replied. She turned and gestured for me to follow her. As I turned to walk away, I felt Mr. V's eyes travel the length of my tan legs. Maybe he thought my shorts were too short? I glanced back. My eyes met his, and I saw something that shot a bolt of warmth down my belly. I turned away quickly, and jogged after Allison.

Great.

Day one, and I was already crushing on Mr. V, who was a decade older than me. And married. I had seen the band around his finger. So much for being focused and in-ethics.

After grabbing my uniform, we took the elevator up to the sixth floor, where the EPF dorms were.

The EPF girls' dorm was like a dorm at the Ranch, except the bunk beds were three high to pack more of us into each room. Each bed's blanket was military tight. The carpet was plain beige, the walls white, no adornments at all. Allison showed me an empty bunk and a drawer where I could put my belongings. I stowed my backpack underneath the bed and quickly pulled on my uniform, a cotton blue T-shirt in a size small with the EPF logo emblazoned on the front. I tucked my shirt into dark navy shorts and tightened my belt. I was ready to go. We jogged down three flights of stairs to join the EPFers at muster.

The course room was packed with EPFers lined up between the long brown tables. I followed Allison to her line, and Mr. V called attention. After attendance was taken, Mr. V ran us through marching drills, doing left face, right face, and about face. I easily followed Mr. V's instructions and saw I was better than even some of the other EPFers.

Once drilling was complete, Mr. V assigned each unit to their work around PAC Base, jobs like mopping hallways, cleaning bathrooms at the church orgs, and washing windows. This was called Decks time, similar to the Ranch. My unit was assigned to cleaning the main mess.

After muster, we headed out. I started walking but the others jogged ahead. The I/C turned and saw me and said that on the EPF you always had to run everywhere. This was like when I was on the ethics correction group at the Ranch, but I didn't complain. I picked up my pace and caught up to the others.

When we arrived at the dining room, the I/C gave orders. Allison and I were instructed to clear all the tables and bring the dirty dishes downstairs. We got to work cleaning, and after an hour we were done.

Next, we headed into a tiny hallway that led out of the dining room. There was a door with a round window trimmed in elaborate gold that you could peek though. The word "Officers" written in cursive script above. Allison opened the door and walked in with me following behind. My jaw dropped when I saw how fancy the officers' dining room was. The main dining room was nice compared to what I was used to, but it was nothing compared to this. There were tables covered in thick white tablecloths with upholstered chairs. My older sister was an officer, so she ate here every day. Meanwhile, my mom and dad ate with the masses in the main dining room. I wondered if it bothered my parents. Probably not. They understood that even though Darcy was their daughter, she was an important person in the Sea Org, and so it was right that she ate here in accordance with her status.

"Here," Allison said, interrupting my thoughts. She had pushed the gray cart over and started loading the dirty plates. I followed her lead and began to lift the heavy, white formal plates onto the cart. We cleared each table, one by one. Once we finished, we moved on to cleaning the hallways. After what felt like hours of work, we were finally done for the day.

We went back into the large dining room, where about two hundred Sea Org members had gathered to eat. Although I was tired, I immediately perked up. It was hamburger night, and I could smell the French fries. Allison and I got in line at the buffet and filled our plates, then sat at one of the five round tables on the west side of the room.

"Yum!" I exclaimed as the cook walked by pushing a gray cart piled with large gallons of several flavors of ice cream. At the Ranch you couldn't have sugar unless it was an org award.

"We can't have any," Allison said.

"What?"

She went on to explain that there was no sugar allowed on the EPF. My mouth dropped. I was tempted to complain, but I reminded myself that I was an all-new Katherine. Instead, I kept these thoughts to myself as we bussed our plates. There would be no point in whining. I also didn't want to risk another EPFer overhearing me and writing me up. No way was I getting a Knowledge Report on my first day. I just needed to graduate fast so I could have dessert.

After dinner, Allison and I jogged down to the EPF course rooms, which were located on the ground floor. Before heading in, I was told by an EPFer to go to security so I could get my ID card. Every Sea Org member was issued one. You used the cards to get inside the doors in the main building. There were security touchpads beside each door that led into the Complex, and you slid the card and entered a four-number code to unlock the door. This system was in place throughout all of PAC and was a way to keep Suppressive People from sneaking into the church. Every time I had come down from the Ranch on a mission with cadets, we had to wait outside these doors until a Sea Org member let us in. Now I couldn't wait for the other cadets to come down from the Ranch so I could let them in the door when they were stuck outside. I would look so cool.

After getting my picture taken and filling out a form with my height, weight, and eye color, I went back to the EPF course room. I was assigned my first course and studied in silence along with the other EPFers.

At 10 p.m., we were dismissed from the course room. Many of the EPFers headed to the EPF office to spend the last few minutes before bedtime writing letters to family, so I took the opportunity to write to Hallie, telling her all about my first day. I signed off saying that Allison said hello. A part of me hoped that Hallie would be jealous that I was here on the EPF while she was still at the Ranch.

THE EPF EXPANDS

I had been on the EPF only a couple of weeks when Allison graduated and joined the Sea Org. By then I had many new friends and was comfortable on the EPF. I was already at the end of the Introduction to Scientology Ethics Course, which was the longest course, so I knew I would be joining her in the Sea Org soon.

With Allison gone, I had three friends that I began to hang out with more: Leslie, Casey, and Jamie. They were tough, sturdy-looking girls with permanent scowls on their faces. They didn't wear makeup, and only wore sports bras. This struck me as funny. What did they have against bras? I was surprised by how little they cared about how they looked. At the Ranch, my friends and I were always trying to look pretty, and sometimes we wore makeup even though it wasn't allowed. But these three could not care less about girly stuff.

I was fourteen, and Leslie and Casey seemed much older even though they were just fifteen years old. Jamie was young at only twelve but seemed wise beyond her years. The three of them were from the Int Ranch, where the children of top Sea Org executives went. One hot afternoon, I was walking with Leslie across the street to the parking structure for muster, and I asked how they'd been told they were joining the EPF.

"They just told us we were going," Leslie said with a shrug.

"But did they announce it?"

"Yeah, they called a muster and told us which orgs we were assigned to."

"Wow," I said. *All* the Int Ranch cadets had been told to join the Sea Org. Just like that.

"Is there anyone left at the Int Ranch?" I asked.

"No, they shut it down." Leslie led the way to where the EPFers were milling around on the blacktop. She leaned against the concrete wall, and I followed suit.

"It's closed! Whoa. I wonder if that is going to happen to the PAC Ranch?"

"Probably."

Jamie walked over and joined.

"What's up?" She nodded her head at us.

"Leslie was just telling me how you guys were told you were coming to the EPF."

"Yeah." Jamie laughed derisively as she hefted her body up onto the small concrete wall. "They sent all the rejects to PAC."

"Wait," I said. "What do you mean?"

Leslie rolled her eyes.

"All of the Int Ranch cadets who were sent to Flag were cadets that were upstat and never got into trouble. We're the losers who didn't qualify," she said.

"Really?" I couldn't help snickering. "They told you that? That's so mean!"

"Well, they didn't say that exactly, but we could tell by just looking at who went to Flag and who went to PAC."

"Yup," said Jamie.

"Muster!" Mr. V shouted, putting an end to our conversation. We jogged to our places in line on the blacktop. As I followed instructions to dress right dress and come to attention, my mind was elsewhere. Was the PAC Ranch going to be emptied too? Were Allison and I the first of the rest of the cadets?

It turned out that it was true. I wasn't "special" for being one of the first of my friends to arrive. The PAC Ranch sent several cadets to join the EPF that week, then another van load of cadets the following week. Every week there were more cadets. After a month, the EPF had doubled in size and was filled with PAC Ranchers, including my friends Lacy, Tory, and Ricky. They had emptied at least a quarter of the cadets from the Ranch by now.

Because of how many new EPFers arrived, the EPF was arranged into new units. I had been there longer, so I was assigned as an I/C for the first time. Since I was rarely ever put in charge of groups, I was excited to prove myself. That day at muster I stood at attention, my eyes shining with purpose. I was going to show everyone that I could command others. That I was worthy. Maybe if Mr. V noticed what a good job I did, he would mention it to someone at CMO, and I could get assigned to the management org when I graduated the EPF. That would be so cool. I would be able to eat in the officer dining room and everyone would have to call me sir. My head filled with these fantasies until Mr. V dismissed the units to get to work. Time to prove my worth!

. . .

I LED my unit to the pots area on the ground floor of the Complex, directly underneath the main mess. The pots were cleaned in a tiny room in the far corner of the large galley. The room was hot and steamy with walls of maroon tile that dripped with condensation.

I began to assign each EPFer a job.

My old boyfriend, Ricky, had joined a week ago and was in my unit, so I figured I'd start with him.

"Ricky, you'll be in charge of rinsing," I ordered.

"Yes sir," Ricky responded with a salute. I swallowed my laugh. I could tell he thought it was crazy that I was in charge, but thankfully he went to his position and the other EPFers followed suit once I told them what to do. Within minutes we were working, getting the pots off the dirty rack and down the line, scrubbing till they were cleaned. I felt proud of myself. Look at me, running a unit!

Ten minutes later I was holding the hose, spraying pots. But I needed more room. I asked Ricky to scoot over. Ricky ignored me and continued talking to Justin, a lanky teenager from Orange County whose parents were Scientologists.

I repeated my request. Ricky kept talking to Justin as if I had said nothing.

Oh yeah? You think you can ignore me? I lifted my hose and sprayed him.

"Katherine! What the fuck?" Ricky looked down at his soaked shirt.

"I needed to get your attention," I told him calmly. Ricky narrowed his eyes at me. He then glanced toward the wall where the second hose was hanging.

"Don't do it, Ricky," I warned. "I was just trying to get your attention. We have a lot of pots to wash."

Ricky tilted his head and grinned. Then, quick as a

snake, he lunged for the hose, turned, and sprayed me full in the face.

"Aaah! Asshole!"

I squeezed my hose handle and sprayed him back.

Justin laughed and grabbed a bucket and dunked it in the sink filled with soapy water and dumped it on me. The other two EPFers in my unit ran out of the room as Ricky, Justin, and I tried to soak each other as much as possible.

"Knock. It. Off!"

The baker was standing in the doorway, red in the face, his belly heaving.

"What is going on here?" he bellowed. "This place is a mess. You are creating Dev-T! I'm bringing you to Mr. V! Follow me right now."

I made a face at Ricky as we hung up our dripping green rubber aprons and meekly followed the baker out the door, through the galley to the EPF office. My feet squelched with each step I took.

He opened the door to the EPF office and gestured for us to go inside. We walked in, and Mr. V looked up. We stood there, soaking wet, with puddles forming around our feet. Mr. V's face said it all. I knew I had blown it. No more being an I/C for me.

36

STOP LAUGHING

"What is the definition of 'heavy petting?'"

"Are you serious?" I laughed. I was getting a checkout on a policy letter about the Second Dynamic rules in the Sea Org. The Second Dynamic is one of the seven dynamics that L. Ron Hubbard defines. This dynamic had to do with sex, children, and family. There were many rules about the Second Dynamic in the Sea Org, such as no fondling each other (referred to as heavy petting) and no sex outside of marriage.

Jack nodded with a smirk, his long body slouched in his seat, one eyebrow quirked up. He was my age and also from the Ranch, but he had been on the TTC the past year. We hadn't hung out at the Ranch, so I didn't really know him well. A few TTCers had been assigned to help give checkouts to get cadets through the EPF faster. I stared at Jack, knowing he was probably messing with me but not completely sure.

"It's when you do sexual stuff that is not allowed," I whispered fiercely, feeling my face warm.

Jack pursed his lips, then shook his head.

"I need more details, or I'll have to flunk you," he said.

"Jack!" I exclaimed. Heads turned our way. Mr. James, the course supervisor, must have heard me from the other room, because suddenly he was towering over us.

"What's going on?" he demanded.

"Jack wants me to explain the definition of heavy petting. He knows I know what it means!" I was trying not to laugh as I looked at Jack, who was working hard to keep a straight face.

"I need to make sure she understands the word fully," he told Mr. James neutrally.

Mr. James crossed his arms. "Knock it off, Jack, and just give her the checkout."

"What?" Jack raised his hands up innocently. "I'm supposed to ask her definitions of words in a checkout, right? That's all I'm doing."

"Give her a proper checkout, Jack," Mr. James repeated.

"Fiiine," he said with a drawn-out sigh. I muffled my laugh as Mr. James walked away. Once he was out of earshot, Jack turned his gaze back to me.

"Please demonstrate to me what heavy petting looks like using these blocks." Jack pushed a pile of blocks kept in the middle of the table for the purpose of demonstrating in front of me.

My mouth dropped opened in disbelief.

"You dork. No way!" I whispered fiercely.

"You have to. Or I'm going to flunk you." Jack grinned from ear to ear.

No way was I letting him win this battle. I picked up two blocks.

"Here's a guy and here's a girl. They're kissing."

I pushed the two blocks together and made smooching noises.

"He begins to put his arm lower." I added a block to the other block and moved it toward the bottom of the "girl" piece.

Jack and I broke into laughter.

"That's it!"

I looked up, and Mr. James was at our table looking cross.

"Jack, go back to your org. You're done for the day," he said. "Katherine, come with me."

I stood up and followed Mr. James but smacked Jack on the head as I passed by. "Dickhead," I mouthed over my shoulder as I walked out. Jack grinned and shrugged.

Mr. James brought me over to Mr. V's office and laid out what had happened.

"She is not to come back in the classroom until she completes her ethics routing form," Mr. James finished.

Mr. V glared at me. I sighed and slumped down in the seat in front of his desk. The walls in his tiny office seemed to close in around me. Mr. James left.

"So, this is how it's going to be?" Mr. V asked.

"Jack was making me laugh. I don't see what the big deal is," I said as I avoided his gaze, looking at the blue carpet beneath my sneakers.

"It's goofing off and not staying on purpose," Mr. V said. "I want you to read this policy letter by L. Ron Hubbard." He reached behind his desk and pulled out a green textbook and flipped to a tabbed page. He slid it over to me. I took the large book and stood.

"You can do your work over there." Mr. V gestured to the long table set up in the hallway in front of his office. I nodded, trudged over, slumped down into my seat, and began to read the L. Ron Hubbard policy about ethics.

37

UNIT LOSER

Many weeks passed. I was still on the EPF, stuck on the ethics routing form that Mr. James had put me on. Mr. V created a unit called "Unit L," and anyone on ethics lines was assigned to this unit. I was picked along with three others. There was Jamie, who I had befriended at the beginning of the EPF, and another Int Rancher, Tasha, a snub-nosed girl who had a habit of mouthing off. The last girl who rounded out the group had joined the EPF a few weeks ago. Her name was Nicole. She was twelve, two years younger than me. Nicole and I were often told that we looked like sisters. Nicole was half Black with light-tan skin the same shade as mine, frizzy hair like me, and a sassy attitude. She and I became friends the first day she joined the EPF. She happily participated in my out-ethics activities, like sneaking away to buy treats at the store a couple blocks away. So here she was in our little special group, "Unit L."

. . .

ONE WARM DECEMBER MORNING, our unit was brought to the VRU, a large cement courtyard between the Complex and Lebanon Hall with a chain link gate covered in blue tarp surrounding it. This was where Sea Org cars and the bus got repaired. The trash compactor for PAC Base was in a court-yard along the Complex wall. Mr. V brought our group of misfits to the compactor and told us that he wanted us to climb in and scrub the insides with bleach and water. Its smell enveloped us in a putrid bubble.

"Are you fucking kidding me?" I crossed my arms and shook my head. "It stinks!"

"Of course it stinks." Mr. V laughed. "That's why I want you to get in there and scrub the leftover food. Then it'll smell like rainbows."

"Ha!" Tasha kicked the side of the compactor. "Yeah right."

"Gross!" Nicole scrunched her nose.

Jamie stood there resigned, as if this was her lot in life.

"I'm not getting in there. I seriously feel like I am going to puke." I pinched my nostrils. "Isn't this child abuse?"

"Just get some jumpsuits on and you'll be fine." Mr. V grinned.

"I'm not doing it." I turned and began to walk away.

"Get back here," Mr. V ordered. "Or you'll be in for it."

I looked back over my shoulder.

"Oh yeah?"

My stare met Mr. V's. Was there a glint in his eye? Was he enjoying this? I stifled a grin, then took off at a run.

"Damn it!" I heard Mr. V exclaim from behind me as Nicole, Jamie, and Tasha laughed and cheered me on.

"Go Katherine!"

"He's coming after you!"

I raced around the bus and screamed as I felt Mr. V's

hand brush my shoulder. I ducked out of his reach, ran to the stairs leading to the laundry room, and took them two at a time. I felt him right behind me. Adrenaline rushed through my body as I pushed to go faster.

"Gotcha!" Mr. V grabbed my arm, and pulled me toward him. My back fell against his chest as he wrapped his other arm around my waist. He lifted me as he carried me up the last four steps. There was a chair in the corner of the landing. Mr. V turned and sat down, pulling me down with him, onto his lap. I wriggled to get free, straining against his strong arms. Mr. V pulled me closer, and I leaned back against his chest. Warmth pooled in my stomach.

"Knock it off, Katherine," Mr. V ordered as he tightened his arms around me. I relaxed into his body.

I leaned into him half listening, distracted by his legs beneath my thighs, his arms around my waist.

"You need to stop backflashing and just do as you are told," Mr. V continued. "This work is meant to help you make up for all of the out-ethics you have done this past month. You can make up the damage. Do you understand?"

"Yeah, okay."

Mr. V loosened his arms, and I reluctantly slipped off his lap. He stood up and walked down the stairs. I followed him down, admiring his broad shoulders, which stretched against his white uniform polo.

So, there we were, all of us Unit L, the Loser Ladies, in blue jumpsuits as if we were about to go to jail. Equipped with mops and soapy buckets of water, we looked like an army of janitors. We wore long blue coveralls, our hair pulled back, and rubber gloves snapped on to our elbows.

We climbed into the dumpster in shifts. One of us would

go in, move the brush back and forth once or twice, then climb out shrieking. When it was my turn to climb inside, I scrambled in the four-by-four-foot hole that trash was thrown into and pushed the mop around a couple of times, trying not to breathe through my nose. The air was so rancid it felt like it was sinking into every pore of my face. As I pushed the mop around, I began to worry that someone would turn on the trash compactor while I was in it. Suddenly I felt certain of it. I turned toward the square of light and threw my mop out and heaved myself out and over and jumped to the ground.

"What the hell," the EPF I/C who was sent to supervise us yelled. "You were only in there for thirty seconds."

"I didn't want to get crushed!" I crossed my arms. "I'm not dying in a dumpster!"

The EPF I/C rolled his eyes but didn't argue with me. He gestured at Jamie to go in next, and she grudgingly began to climb in. I noticed Sea Org members that passed by on the way to CTO, the Continental Training Organization, give us the stink eye. I wanted to flip them all off. It's not like we'd chosen to do this. I didn't want to be diving in a fucking dumpster.

After about thirty minutes of half-heartedly moving the mop around in the dumpster's innards, we declared it "clean," even though it still stank. Luckily, the EPF I/C agreed to let us go inside to take showers. We walked back to our dorm, dragging our mops and buckets. Any Sea Org member who was within five feet of us face blanched at the smell emanating from our nasty crew. We laughed as we saw their faces. At least they could get a taste of we went through.

38

THE NEW MILLENNIUM

There was going to be a big Scientology event at PAC Base to celebrate the New Year. This one was going to be extra special because it was the beginning of the new millennium, the year 2000. This was one of several events that Scientology was throwing. An event had already been held at the LA Sports Arena, on December 28th, but PAC was throwing their own event and it seemed like it was going to be awesome. There was even supposed to be a live band and dancing.

PAC had made it clear that the event would go on despite all the stories and conspiracy theories on the radio that the world was going to end, or that all the computers would break, and our society wouldn't know how to function. PAC had prepared for an emergency by buying two massive storage containers and parking them in the VRU next to the dumpsters. Rumor had it they were packed full of canned food and water and other essential items. Just in case.

I had hoped that I'd have graduated the EPF by then so I could go, but I wasn't even close. EPFers did get to attend events if they were assigned catering duty, but I wasn't assigned since I was too out-ethics. Instead, I was sent to bed with the remaining EPFers at 10 p.m.

While getting dressed for bed, Jamie, Nicole, and I whispered about how unfair it was that we weren't picked to go. We decided we'd sneak out of the dorm and go to at least peak inside the tent.

After lights out, we waited ten minutes to ensure the coast was clear. Then one by one we left the dorm, meeting up in the stairwell at the end of the hall. We ran down the six flights and outside onto Catalina Street. Dressed in PJs and sticking to the shadows, we jogged toward the large public parking lot off Sunset Boulevard, where the event was in full swing. We could see the large white tent peeking out from between the buildings. Mr. Miscavige finished his speech and the crowd cheered and shouted, "Hip hip hooray, hip hip hooray!"

"Good! They're just finishing cheering LRH. Now the party is about to start!" I told Jamie and Nicole as we trotted up the sidewalk. We could see two bright beams from the event spotlight shining up in the sky, twisting and turning. I bet you could've seen those rays of light from anywhere in LA. They were so bright, the night seemed almost like day.

"What should we do?" Nicole whispered.

"Let's peek in the tent." I headed over to the far corner and pulled back the flap carefully.

"Whoa, it looks so nice in there!"

"Let us see!"

Nicole shoved my arm so she could squeeze in front of me.

"Hold on!" I put my arm out and scanned the crowd to make sure it was safe. My eyes locked with Mr. V's. He stood there as if on guard, wearing his full Sea Org uniform instead of his EPF standard shorts and white polo shirt.

Shit.

Of all the places he could have been standing, of course he was right there.

"Uh oh," I whispered to the girls.

"What?" Nicole demanded. Before I could say anything, Mr. V was there, yanking the flap back.

"What the fuck are you guys doing here?"

"We just wanted to see the event! Can we please watch, and then we promise to go back to bed?" I pleaded.

"Are you fucking kidding me?" He turned and waved a security guard over.

"Escort these EPFers back to their dorm and don't let them out of your sight," Mr. V told the guard.

"You guys will be doing some hard deck work tomorrow," he informed us before striding off. As I watched him walk away, I had a feeling that this time I had gone too far.

39

FITNESS BOARD

I sat at the ethics table doodling on a blank piece of paper. I had no energy to work on the overts and with-holds that I was supposed to be writing up. It felt like a heavy blanket was sitting on me, making it difficult for me to even lift my head. The past few weeks at the EPF had been hard. Mr. V treated me like a piece of dirt under his shoe. He wouldn't make eye contact and engage when I made jokes. It was business only. I hadn't realized how silly and fun Mr. V had let me be until now. Even though I was usually in trouble, I had always gotten the feeling that he liked my spunk. But now, ever since I had snuck away for the event, that was over with. I hated it.

On top of it all, my friends were gone too. Jamie had been kicked off the EPF and sent to the Ranch. A week later the same had happen to Tasha, then finally Nicole. I was the only one left. The EPF had returned to its normal size, as most of the other cadets, including Lacy and Ricky, had graduated to the Sea Org. Somehow, I was the reject left behind. I shouldn't have been surprised, since I hadn't done any work on the EPF courses in weeks, yet I was.

"Katherine!"

I jerked up and craned my head toward Mr. V's office. He raised his hand and beckoned me with his finger.

I sighed. What now?

"We are sending you back to the Ranch," he said without preamble.

"Wait, what?" But I only had one course left on the EPF! I was so close!

Mr. V signed a piece of paper in front of him as he continued.

"Your ride is leaving in one hour. Go pack your things and go to the horseshoe driveway."

"Uh, okay." I stood there waiting for anything more from him, but Mr. V continued scribbling away. "Well, bye I guess."

Mr. V nodded, barely lifting his head to meet my eyes. I turned and walked away.

How could I go back to the Ranch and face the other Ranchers? It was embarrassing that I wasn't able to finish the EPF. At least I would see Hallie again since she was still at the Ranch. There would be so much to catch up on. Plus, Jamie, Tasha, and Nicole were there. Hmmm...this could actually be fun.

I arrived at the Ranch later that afternoon. I stepped out of the car and took in the bright blue sky, the scattered brown buildings with the mountains towering overhead. A smile crept over my face. I had missed it more than I thought.

I was sent to Dorm 10 to unpack my bag. I felt déjà vu as I walked up the asphalt road past the dining room and the boys' dorms. It was strange to be back as I stepped in and threw my bag on an unclaimed bed. The room was empty—everyone was probably cleaning the common areas since it was a Saturday. I abandoned my bag and stepped over to the bed next to mine and peered at the photos taped to the headboard. It was my friend's Sally. I smiled. That girl had always made me laugh. I walked over to each of the other four beds and examined their photos on display. I was back home.

I started unpacking my bag when Hallie burst into the dorm.

"Oh my god, you're back!" Hallie squealed as she hugged me tight.

"Yup," I said and hugged her back, my cheek resting against the top of her little head.

"So, what happened?" Hallie said. She plopped on my bed.

"Ugh." I collapsed next to her. "So much. You won't believe it." I began to recount the past weeks to her. The good and the bad, everything flooded out. "We had to climb inside a dumpster and clean it!"

"Oh gross!"

"I know! But it was really funny. I ran away, and Mr. V chased me all the way through the VRU, and when he caught me, he pulled me on his lap!"

"That's so hot."

"Yeah," I said. "It made climbing in the dumpster worth it."

Hallie and I chattered on while I finished unpacking until the bell rang. I ran down the path and onto the patio and was immediately surrounded by my friends.

The rest of the day passed in a happy blur. That evening they showed a movie in the art room. With half the Ranch now on the EPF or graduated into the Sea Org, the room was no longer cramped and it was easy enough to get a good seat. I was surprised when no adult commented, saying I was too out-ethics for org awards. Nope, instead I was allowed to watch front and center, with Hallie. I would never have been able to do that on the EPF. No movies for EPFers until they graduated into the Sea Org.

On Sunday, the bus took the cadets to the mall in Antelope Valley. Again, I was allowed to join them. I loved that I wasn't in any trouble and was able to rejoin the group. It was strange but I wasn't going to question it.

A few days later, I was called down to the office.

"You can go back on the EPF," Mr. Williams told me. "You just need to promise to be in-ethics by signing this promissory note.

Huh. What had been the point of sending me back to the Ranch then?

"All I need to do is sign a note?" I asked skeptically.

"That's right." Mr. Williams nodded. "I know you can succeed on the EPF if you put some effort into it."

"Okay." I took the pen Mr. Williams was holding out to me. The Ranch was fun, but I missed flirting. There were no older cadet boys at the Ranch anymore, since they were all at PAC now. And no Mr. V. I had to admit it to myself. I had a crush on him, and these few days away had been hard. Yeah, Mr. V was married and in his twenties. Way too old for me. But still. I leaned over and scrawled my signature, agreeing to be in-ethics.

ARRIVING BACK on the EPF the second time around wasn't the same. Mr. V was strict from the get-go and wouldn't joke around with me at all. I wondered if he was still angry about the event stunt I had pulled. But then why was I allowed back on the EPF in the first place? Since he didn't seem to care about me at all, I fell back into my old habits and was back to being out-ethics. Within weeks I was kicked off the EPF again and sent back to the Ranch a second time. Soon I was served a notice called a fitness board, declaring me unfit for the Sea Org due to numerous Knowledge Reports and taking too long to get through the EPF.

I didn't know what to expect back at the Ranch. The whole purpose of the Ranch was to train future Sea Org executives. Getting kicked off the EPF the first time had turned out to be no big deal. But twice?

40

ROUND TWO

The Ranch car bumped up the asphalt drive leading to the main office. I slouched in the passenger seat, gazing out the window. I couldn't believe I was really back here again. We parked, and I slid out of my seat and followed the Sea Org member into the main office.

A new staff member recently posted at the Ranch was waiting for me at the Deputy Cadet Coordinator's desk. Mr. Hammond's desk was empty. I breathed a sigh of relief.

Mr. Barlowe introduced herself and informed me that I would be on twenty-four-hour watch while here. She directed a cadet to follow me to my new quarters in Dorm 9.

I trudged up the asphalt road with the cadet following close behind. When I opened the door to the dorm, I was surprised to see all the bunk beds had been disassembled and removed. It was just empty rooms—brown carpet, curtains hanging off bronze rods, and in one room, a single mattress all alone in a corner. With the Ranch now half the size it had been before they started shipping everyone off to the EPF, Dorm 9 was vacant. Well, not anymore. I was here, plus the lucky cadet assigned to sit outside the dorm. I didn't get why they thought I needed to be on watch. Were they that concerned I was going to blow the Ranch?

THE NEXT DAY I walked down to the main office. I creaked open the door, and Mr. Barlowe looked up.

"Um . . . is there something I should be doing besides staying in Dorm 9?" I asked as politely as I could muster.

"Mr. Hammond is going to decide the next step, and he is at PAC right now. Please stay in your dorm and don't talk to any of the other cadets. You are no longer on twenty-four-hour watch if you can agree to do that."

I nodded my agreement. "But what am I supposed to do all day?"

"You can figure it out," Mr. Barlowe said before swiveling back to her desk in her office chair.

I sighed, but Mr. Barlowe ignored me. I could see the conversation was over. I turned and shuffled out of the office.

"I guess I can go," said the cadet who was watching me.

I turned to my former jailer and shrugged. He jogged off to join his buddies for PE time, and I trudged back to the dorm.

I spent the rest of the day reading comics. None of my old friends were allowed to talk to me and they followed the rules and stayed away. Even Hallie hadn't bothered to come wave hello through the window. The only one who deigned to say hello was Leslie's younger brother. He was the one who lent me the comics.

So, I was alone. Just me and my thoughts. Hours passed. I lay on my mattress, eventually bored even of reading, my favorite thing to do in the world. Instead, I stared at the ceiling and fantasized about what it would be like if I left the Ranch. I knew our purpose was to save the world, but I couldn't seem to keep my act together. Wouldn't it be better for everyone if I just left?

Or was that thought just me being selfish? How come I didn't want to try to get into the Sea Org and help Scientology? Shouldn't I be a better person?

A loud knock interrupted my thoughts.

"Yeah," I called out.

"Mr. Hammond wants to see you!" a cadet's voice yelled through the door of the patio.

Finally. At least something was happening. At this point, I was so bored that I was looking forward to hearing from Mr. Hammond to find out where I stood. Was I a cadet again? Or was I being kicked off the Ranch? What was going to happen?

I jogged down to the office and entered to find Mr. Hammond at his desk doing his work.

"Katherine," he said as he flicked a glance my way. "I need you to go rake the front lawn. When I am ready to have a conversation, I will have someone get you."

Seriously? Rake the lawn? The lawn in front of the office was huge. This would take ages.

"Yes sir," I said instead. I trudged up the road to the workshop and got a rake, then walked back. I started raking in front of the main office so that Mr. Hammond could see I was working. As I kept going, frustration boiled. After I had four large piles of leaves, I flung the rake down. Break time, I decided. I glanced at the main office. Mr. Hammond wasn't even at his desk. Good. I marched off toward my dorm. Once inside, I flopped down on my mattress on the floor and closed my eyes.

A few minutes later, before I'd even had a chance to relax, a knock on the door startled me. I sat up.

"Katherine?" a voice called out.

"What?" I said.

"Mr. Hammond said you need to get back to raking right now."

I groaned.

"Let's go!" the voice called again through the door.

"Fiiiine! I'll go back to the child abuse!" I screamed.

There was silence. I rolled my eyes and pushed myself off the bed. I opened the door and brushed past the cadet standing there. I trudged back to my slave work with him trailing me a few paces back.

I surveyed the lawn when I arrived. I was only about halfway done. I gritted my teeth as I leaned over and grabbed the rake I had dropped earlier. I started up again, banging it unnecessarily hard against the ground. I kicked the pile of leaves. This was stupid! I had been here all afternoon, yet Mr. Hammond continued to ignore me. It was past dusk now. How many hours had I put into this? It was dark enough outside now that I couldn't even see my own work. I squinted at the ground and tried to see where my pile was but couldn't make it out.

I flung my rake to the ground. Fuck this! This was pointless!

I strode over to the office and banged on the sliding glass windows that faced out on the lawn. Mr. Hammond heaved out of his chair.

"What?" he harrumphed as he slid open the door.

"It's too dark out to see," I said.

"You can plug in the flood lights over there. Go get an extension cord from the workshop. You need to complete this cycle of action," Mr. Hammond ordered.

Really? He wanted me to keep fucking going? Why couldn't I just go back to my dorm?

"Well?" He waved one of his hands as if to shoo me away.

I pivoted and turned away, my back stiff as a board. My legs ate up the ground as I strode past the workshop. I didn't even pause as I passed it. I was done. This was making me more certain of what had always been in the back of my mind. I wanted to get the hell off the Ranch and be in the real world where I didn't have to do shit like this. I could go to school and be a regular teenager. I was fourteen. I should be in high school right now. I threw the door to Dorm 9 open, slamming it against the wall, marched to my bed, and fell face forward on it. "Argghhhhh!" I screamed into the mattress.

TIME PASSED. I was lying on the mattress reading another comic book when someone banged on the door once more.

"Katherine!"

Here we go again.

I got up and opened the door. The CO cadets stood there glaring at me. He was a younger boy who would never have been promoted to this position if all the older guys were still at the Ranch instead of in the Sea Org. Now I had to take orders from this kid. I resisted the urge to tell him to fuck off.

"Mr. Hammond wants you at the main office right now," the CO said.

"Oh, does he?" I said sarcastically.

The CO stared at me.

"Fine," I said, giving in for now. I followed the kid down to the office.

When we arrived, I opened the door and found the adult staff sitting at the long brown table, gathered for muster. Mr. Hammond barked at me to wait outside until they were done.

"Are you serious?" I protested. "It's freezing!"

"Knock off the backflash!" Mr. Hammond roared.

I didn't even flinch. The old Katherine would have been intimidated by him. Instead, I swiveled on my foot and stormed out, slamming the door behind me. I sat on the cold curb and rested my head on my arms. I shivered. My arms were covered in goosebumps.

A few minutes later, the door creaked open. Adults filed out one by one. They ignored me as they passed. Even Mr. Williams, who had always been kind to me before. Their disregard for me cemented what I had come to understand. These people did not care about me. I was too out-ethics for the Sea Org. I needed to leave.

When they were gone, I opened the door, strode over to Mr. Hammond's desk, and glared at him, waiting for his "plan." He leaned back in his chair and crossed his arms.

"Katherine, you need to go and finish the job you started. Go get the light from the workshop," he said.

I stared back at him and said nothing. There was no way I was raking that fucking lawn.

Mr. Hammond repeated his command.

I said nothing. He repeated himself two more times.

I didn't move.

"If you are not willing to do the work assigned like all other cadets, then you don't belong at the Ranch."

"You're right." I crossed my arms. "I don't deserve to be here. I am a Degraded Being and should leave. I should go live with my mom's family in New York."

There, I said it.

Now it was Mr. Hammond's turn to stare at me.

Good. I seemed to have shocked him.

"You're right. Go pack your things. I am getting you off the Ranch by tomorrow morning," he said.

"Okay." I suppressed a smile and turned and walked out of the office. As soon as the door shut behind me, I took off. I ran up the road past the workshop, then the galley, the air rushing past me. It felt like freedom. I couldn't wait to throw my things in my bags. I was leaving! I would be able to be a regular teenager! I threw open my dorm door with a thud, rushed to my mattress, and came to a stop. There wasn't much to do. Most of my stuff was in a bag already since there was no dresser in this empty room that I had been staying in. I laughed and lay down on my mattress. I let my imagination run wild with my future.

THE NEXT MORNING, someone knocked on the door. I opened it, and the cadet MAA thrust a paper into my hand.

"Thanks," I said sarcastically, but the cadet had already turned away. I shut the door and glanced down. It was a Knowledge Report on me from Mr. Hammond. My eyes caught on the list of people that this KR was being sent to.

Holy shit.

All the executives at PAC would be getting a play-by-play of what happened last night. I began to read the letter, the words flying past.

Well, there was no way I was convincing anyone that I was in-ethics now. I didn't care, though. I was leaving anyway. My eyes strayed to the top of the report.

Wait.

"Kathryn"?

My laugh echoed in the empty dorm. This was being

sent across PAC, and Mr. Hammond couldn't even spell my name correctly.

I thought of my parents, and my mood shifted. I was such a disappointment. I had tried and tried, and failed. But maybe they would be happier with me gone. They would stop receiving KRs about me. So yes, please, let them tell my parents that I didn't belong here. I threw the KR onto the ground and lay back down on my mattress.

New York, here I come.

41

AUDITING

I stared up at the ceiling, my foot jiggling off the edge of my mattress. I rolled onto my stomach and laid my head on my crossed arms. Two days had passed, and I was still here. I sat up and glanced at the clock on the wall. It was only 9 a.m. My plate sat by the door with an empty yogurt and spoon, waiting to be collected. I wondered who would come get it. Hopefully a friend so I could talk to them. I grabbed a comic book, but I couldn't get lost in the Marvel world. I sat up when I heard the door open, but the cadet who came grabbed my plate and turned and left without a word. I was alone again.

"Argh!" My voice echoed back to me. I collapsed back on the bed and turned my head to look at the clock.

9:10.

I leapt up and shoved my feet into my Converse. I stormed out of the dorm, the door slamming shut behind me as I marched down to the main office.

Without even taking a breath, I rushed inside.

"Mr. Hammond, when am I going to leave?" I demanded.

He looked up from his desk, startled, then leaned back in his office chair.

"What do you mean?"

"I thought I was supposed to be gone already. Why am I still here?"

"Well, Katherine, your mother is trying to arrange an auditor for you."

I stared at him.

"They want you to get help," Mr. Hammond said.

I didn't know what to say. I had never gotten auditing before. Auditing was what the Sea Org and Scientology was all about. People who got auditing became better people and succeeded in life. And now I would get a chance to get auditing myself? What if I got auditing and ended up being a good cadet?

"Okay. Can I at least be with the cadets while I get auditing?" I blurted out.

"If you're willing to be a part of the group and follow the rules, then that is fine with me. You will be assigned a post later today."

I nodded and rushed out of the office before he could change his mind. I moved my meager bag of belongings up to Dorm 10 and by lunchtime was catching up with my friends as if the last few days hadn't even happened.

THE NEXT DAY, my mom called and told me that I would be going down to PAC daily to get the auditing that my parents had paid for. I asked how she'd paid for it since they were always so broke. She said Lucas, my oldest brother, had helped.

"That's not fair," I protested. "Shouldn't the Sea Org provide the auditing? Why do you and Lucas have to pay for it?" I knew Lucas worked hard to save every cent of his Sea Org paycheck. Just $34 a week, and now he had to spend it on me.

My mom said the Sea Org was low on staff auditors, so they had to pay for a public auditor. It was the only way to get me help right away instead of waiting for months.

Now that I thought about it, my parents never seemed to receive any auditing services. My dad had been on OT III for at least ten years, even though the OT levels went all the way up to OT VIII. Didn't he want to keeping moving up the bridge?

"I don't know . . ." I said slowly.

"Don't worry about it," Mom said. "Lucas wants you to get auditing so you can do well. We all do."

My resolve wavered. My mom cared about me. Lucas cared about me. They wanted me to improve myself.

I decided I would give it a shot, on one condition. I made my mom promise she would pay my brother back.

"Of course, honey," she said. "Don't worry about that. You just focus on session."

As I said goodbye, I felt hopeful.

I WAS DRIVEN DOWN to PAC by an adult at the Ranch the next day. During the hour-long drive, I was told to report to ASHO, the Sea Org church that serviced the parishioners. The car pulled up in front. It was one of the blue buildings on L. Ron Hubbard Way, four stories high with a large brass lion in front, seeming to declare its importance. I trotted up the cement steps to the entrance. I opened the heavy double door and headed across the quiet reception, my feet making no noise on the gleaming tile. It felt so strange to be here as a public, getting service, instead of being here for a mission, like renovating a bathroom.

I took the elevator up to the third floor, where the auditing waiting room was located. It was inviting, with sofa chairs and lamps scattered in the corners emitting a soft, warm ambience. The carpet muffled my steps as I walked up to the counter that looked out over the lounge. A Sea Org member in a light blue uniform stood there, waiting to be of service. Behind him stood shelves containing the folders of the public and staff, which were filled with detailed manuscripts of their sessions. Soon my folder would be back there too. I let the Sea Org member know that I was here for auditing, and he said my auditor would come get me shortly and gestured for me to have a seat. I flipped through a Scientology magazine while I waited, but only a few minutes passed before I heard someone call my name.

"Katherine, are you ready?"

I looked up, surprised. It was Ross, a former cadet who had been on the TTC. He was a nice enough kid, but this was awkward. How the hell was I going to tell Ross anything private? There was no way.

"You're my auditor?" I asked just to be sure.

"Yes," he said. His face was a blank slate.

Damn.

I stood up and stared down at the neat part of his carefully combed hair. Ross had not grown much since leaving the Ranch. He only came up to my chin.

"If you'll follow me right this way?" he said. He pivoted and strode to the wood door that led to the auditing rooms. There was a sign that said "Silence Please. Auditing in Progress." I wanted to ask more questions, but I kept my mouth shut as we walked down a softly lit narrow hallway carpeted in beige, with framed posters on the walls of happy public climbing mountains and pumping their fist in the air. We passed rows and rows of doors that were shut, with signs on them saying, "In session." The silence was eerie, but I understood there was no noise so there would be no distractions. At the end of the hallway Ross gestured me inside an empty room. I crept in, sat down carefully in the chair facing the E-Meter, and looked around.

This was it. The famed auditing room.

It was small and nondescript. A photo of L. Ron Hubbard was mounted on the wall overlooking a shiny mahogany desk, with an E-Meter centered in the middle. Up in one corner was a camera pointed down toward where we would sit. Ross, the E-Meter, and me, perfectly centered in its sight. I looked away from it and focused on Ross.

"So . . ." I said as I adjusted my ponytail. "You're my auditor?" I repeated from earlier.

"I am," Ross said as he took a seat across the desk from me.

I wanted to mention how strange this all was, but he was maintaining his professional aura, and I didn't want him to feel like he was doing a bad job. I needed to take this seriously, I decided. Yeah, Ross was only fourteen, and I had known him since we were both babies, but that was just his body's age. He was a thetan that had lived thousands of lives, and now he was a Class V auditor trained on L. Ron Hubbard's tech. He knew what he was doing.

"Please pick up the cans," Ross said, breaking through my whirling mind.

I settled into my chair and picked up the two metal cylinders, which had wires connected to the E-Meter. I smiled expectantly, waiting for my mind to be blown.

"Squeeze the cans, please," he said. I squeezed them.

"Thank you. Please squeeze the cans," he repeated. I

squeezed them again, but this time more slowly, knowing he was looking for a certain pressure.

"Good." He looked up. "How do your hands feel?"

"I guess I can use some lotion," I said. I set the cans down and squirted my hands with some of the Lubriderm that was always present on auditors' desks. Dry hands affected how the meter worked.

"Thank you." Ross nodded and scribbled a note on the white sheet of legal-sized paper. This time, I passed the hand-squeeze test. Ross moved on.

"Have you had enough sleep?"

"Yes," I replied.

"Have you had enough to eat?"

"Uh huh." I nodded.

"Start of session," Ross said.

A shiver went through me. This was it. My first real auditing session, something I had been reading about since I was able to decipher words. I took a deep breath and smiled as Ross began.

"Have you had an ARC break?"

That took me by surprise. ARC break meant there was a loss or severance in affinity, reality, or communication with someone. This had to be cleared up before auditing started to ensure you weren't distracted. I thought back on my day so far.

"No," I responded.

"Great." Ross scribbled on the sheet of paper that was out of my view.

Ross explained he was running a process called PTS -1. PTS stood for Potential Trouble Source. I was always getting in trouble, so this sounded promising. Maybe we could fix the reason I was ethics bait.

"We will be going through a list of Scientology words,

and if you are unable to define the word correctly, we will look the word up in the Scientology Technical Dictionary," Ross said.

My heart sank.

This was what my parents had paid for? I had been hearing these Scientology words all my life, not to mention Chinese-schooling most of them. And now I had to look them all up if I didn't know the definition verbatim? This was horrible.

We spent the next hour going down the list of Scientology words, and any time the E-Meter needle reacted, I had to clear up the word in the tech dictionary. Although I tried to invest myself in it, I found my mind wandering and counting the minutes till the session ended. Tick tock, tick tock.

"Well," Ross said after what felt like hours had passed. "We've cleared up quite a few words. How are you feeling?"

"Great," I said brightly. Ross glanced down at the E-Meter. I knew he was looking for a floating needle, which is what would signal that I had a win, so I immediately began to think of Santa Monica Beach and how happy it made me.

"Your needle is floating," Ross said with a smile. "End of session."

"Thank you." I forced a grin.

WITH MY AUDITING SESSION COMPLETE, I was next instructed to head down to meet with the ASHO Day examiner. When I arrived, I saw my brother Lucas sitting in the examiner's chair. I plopped down in the chair across from him.

"Hi, Lucas!"

My brother's wide grin took over his face. I hadn't seen him in so long, but I still had an affection for him. He was

one of the kindest people I knew. And now I had to pretend
that I had had a win while I was in the session. I hated the
idea of lying to Lucas, especially since he was the one
paying for it. But on the bright side, I did like seeing my
brother looking so professional and happy in his uniform.
He was doing so well, and I was proud of him. It was easy to
make my needle float while looking at his face.

As soon as I left Lucas and headed back toward the front
entrance, I couldn't stop my mind's nattering. This was
auditing? It wasn't even interesting or exciting. I thought I
was going to do past life stuff! Ever since I was a little girl, I
had heard stories of Scientologists who remembered their
past lives. I had always been fascinated by them. When I
was around twelve years old, I had devoured the book *Have
You Lived Before This Life?* It had written accounts of
preclears' past lives that had been collated together. The
stories were so far out there, it was like reading a soap opera.
I couldn't wait to discover my own dramatic past lives. But
instead of doing that, here I was clearing words. What in the
actual fuck?

And this continued. Every day, I reported down to PAC
for session, and that was all we did. Clear words. Since
Lucas and my parents had paid for it, I didn't want to
complain. I just showed up and did the work. I knew they
wouldn't be allowed a refund. If you asked for a refund, you
were not allowed to be in the Church anymore. So, I had to
just get through it. At least it was only around an hour a day.

When I wasn't in session I was able to do whatever I
liked around PAC, until the evening, when I was driven back
to the Ranch. Most days I would visit my brother Judson,
who was posted at AOLA, down the street from ASHO.
Judson shared a post with Alexander. They were in the
Estates Division, which meant they fixed things around the

org. Every day, I would find them in their small office in the basement of AOLA with their legs up, goofing off and cracking up. Judson loved this post because he was left to his own devices with little supervision. He was sweet and friendly, and everyone loved him, but he did not seem to have the eye of the tiger like some. He was happy to sit around and hang out all day. Judson made me wonder if maybe I could join the Sea Org if I had a fun, easy post like his.

42

THE RECRUITMENT

It was funny how suddenly lineups didn't matter when a cadet was being recruited for the Sea Org. It was one of the few days that I was at the Ranch instead of in LA getting my auditing. Sea Org members had arrived that morning, trying to recruit cadets into the Sea Org. When they had spoken to me, I had been honest and said I had my courses to restudy. Yet here I was, called down to the main office, being blamed for the fact that no other cadets wanted to join the Sea Org right now.

"I'm not telling my friends not to join the Sea Org," I said. "Where did you hear that?"

"Well, the fact that you don't want to join the Sea Org makes your friends not want to join," Mr. Barlowe said.

"I am trying to finish the lineup that was assigned to me so I can be a better Sea Org member," I said.

"The fact that you aren't trying to join the Sea Org is affecting their choices. You are an opinion leader, so if you say you aren't ready, so will they."

"*Me*?" I scoffed. "No one listens to me."

"Oh, you would be surprised," Mr. Barlowe told me.

"C'mon, really? There's no way I am an OL." I laughed.

She shook her head. I could tell she didn't believe me.

I suppressed a grin. I liked being told I was a leader. Mr. Barlowe let me know I could go, and I was smiling as soon as I walked out the door.

I WASN'T AS happy the next day when I was put on full-time Scientology studies and forbidden from extracurricular activities. I couldn't go to the beach on the weekends, and I wouldn't be chosen for missions. The only relief I had was when I got to go to PAC for my auditing sessions. I hated the auditing, but since that only took an hour of the day the rest of my time down at PAC was spent hanging out with Judson or my old Ranch friends who were now in the Sea Org.

One day while I was at PAC, I was pulled aside by Casey, my old friend from the EPF. She led me to a small office and introduced me to the Sea Org recruitment officer, a girl a year older than me. Casey began the conversation by telling me how fun it was to be in the Sea Org. As I listened to her espouse how wonderful and fun the Sea Org was and the other member chiming in with other "cool" things about the Sea Org, the wheels in my head turned. Casey, the most deadpan, least fun person I knew, was telling *me* that the Sea Org was fun? I mean, wow. If even she was enjoying herself here, it must be true. Besides, a lot of my friends were in ASHO now, including Patrick. I would love to be in the same org as him. I missed our debates and arguments. There were no guys at the Ranch to challenge or flirt with me like him. And since I wasn't allowed to go on field trips, the Ranch was hardly any fun. On top of everything, I knew my parents would be thrilled if I joined the Sea Org.

"Okay, I'll do it," I said in a burst of spontaneity.

"Awesome." Casey gave me a high five. "Let's get you routed on by tomorrow. I can't wait for you to be in the Sea Org with me!"

"Me too!" I hugged her.

"I'll call the Ranch and let the Cadet Coordinator know you are ready to join," the Sea Org recruiter said.

"Okay, sounds good." I glanced at the clock. "Oh shoot—my ride back to the Ranch leaves soon. Gotta run, but I'll see you tomorrow!" I rushed to the horseshoe to catch my ride.

I ROUTED BACK onto the EPF the next day. It was back to its regular size of a few dozen. I didn't know anyone else this time, but that was a good thing. I had no one to go out-ethics with. The EPFers I met were all from Scientology families and followed the rules to the letter. Mr. V and I kept things courteous and formal, but when he saw how in-ethics I was being this time around, he lightened up and was more friendly to me. Within three weeks, I had completed all the courses. But I was caught by surprise when Mr. V told me he wanted me on the EPF for one more week, to make sure I was "really" in-ethics. This was infuriating. Was he just trying to torture me in return for the hard time I gave him before? Or . . . what if he wanted me to stay because we were back to our old ways of joking around? Maybe he even liked me? No . . . probably not. He was still married, and I was way too young for him.

A week passed, and a Sea Org member came to the EPF course room and told me the fitness board members wanted to meet with me regarding whether I was fit for the Sea Org or not. This was weird. Normally, the fitness board was done without the person present. They would review the person's ethics and student file and decide from there. Why did I have to be there? This didn't seem to bode well for me. I walked with the Sea Org member out of the course room, down the hallway, and out into the horseshoe. He led me toward the offices on Catalina Street. I thought they were all Golden Era Productions offices, the org that manufactured all of Scientology's promotional material. I was surprised when he stopped at one that was unmarked and knocked.

A voice echoed through the door.

"Come in."

The Sea Org member opened the door, and we walked in. The room was dark with no windows, and a lone fluorescent light shone down on four Sea Org members sitting at a long brown folding table facing toward the door. A single metal folding chair sat facing the Sea Org members. I recognized one of them. His name was Mr. Carnell. Mr. Carnell had overseen the cadets that had been put on the TTC until it was disbanded. I had heard he was pretty nice. I hoped he was, because he seemed to be the one running the meeting, since he sat front and center at the table with a thick manila folder bulging with papers underneath his folded hands. I had a feeling that folder was my ethics file, holding the many KRs I had accumulated over these past couple of years.

"Katherine, take a seat," Mr. Carnell said, pointing to the metal chair. I heard the door shut behind me as I edged over to it. I sat down, wiping my sweaty palms on my uniform shorts.

"Katherine, we are the fitness board, and we have a few questions before we can come to a decision regarding you joining the Sea Org," Mr. Carnell said.

"Okay . . ." I said slowly.

Mr. Carnell said I seemed to have a recurring situation of going out-ethics, but that Mr. V had said that I had shown ethics change and that I seemed to be ready to join the Sea Org. They were willing to give me this one chance.

"Is this what you want to do?" Mr. Carnell asked. "Is clearing the world your purpose?"

No, I'd rather go to regular high school and get a boyfriend.

I pushed the thought away.

"Yes sir. I am ready to join the Sea Org and take responsibility for this planet." I was pleased with my delivery. I sounded tone-40. Enthusiastic and confident.

"Good," Mr. Carnell said. "Now we do have some questions. We were going through your ethics file, and we came across this piece of paper. What is this?" He held up the note in question. It was full of scribbles and doodles in my handwriting.

"That's just a piece of paper I was doodling on while waiting for my auditing session," I said, confused by what that had to do with their decision.

"What's this mean here?" Mr. Carnell pointed to a scribble where I had written "life sucks" and "I hate this" all over the paper.

"Oh, I was bored." I shrugged. What was the big deal?

"Bored?" he said. "So, you aren't having any suicidal thoughts?"

"No!" I laughed. Jeez, why did they take everything so seriously? All teenagers wrote stuff like that. "I'm fine, I promise," I told them.

"Okay," Mr. Carnell responded. "We will get back to you on the results of your fitness board."

I got up from the chair slowly. "So, I can go now?"

"Yes."

"Okay, well, uh thanks," I said. I backed out of the room and shut the door quietly. I didn't know what would happen next. It was out of my control.

. . .

THE NEXT DAY, I learned that my fitness board had been approved. I was officially a Sea Org member.

I gripped the piece of paper in my hand that declared I was "fit." I looked up at Mr. V and flashed a smile.

"I almost can't believe it."

"Yeah, me neither," Mr. V said with a grin.

I laughed. "Now what?" I wondered aloud.

"Here is your routing form that has the list of actions you take." Mr. V handed me a checklist. "Good luck, Katherine. Don't disappoint me."

"I won't," I promised.

43

MY FIRST POST

I stood inside a cramped office lined with boxes of shoes, pants, and other miscellaneous uniform pieces and waited for the Uniform I/C to spare me a glance. She rummaged through items on her desk, her rotund body shaking as she vigorously sorted clothes. Her face was flushed as she muttered to herself. The Uniform I/C was my old dorm mate Tory's mom. I waited for her to recognize me.

"Here." She glanced at me and tossed a pair of slacks and two navy-blue blouses embroidered with the Sea Org logo onto the desk. "Go try these on in your dorm. This is what I have in your size." She reached down and grabbed a pair of ugly black shoes and thrust them toward me.

"Thanks," I muttered as I took them between my hands. "Um . . . how come there is only one pair of pants?"

"That's all we have right now," she said as she crossed her arms and glared at me. "We have a backlog."

"Oh, okay. Uh, thanks."

I picked up the uniform and hurried out of the room and headed to the elevator. Why was she so mean to me? Maybe she didn't like how often I borrowed stuff from Tory at the Ranch? I sighed. I stared at the pile of clothes in my hand as I waited for the elevator. I wondered how I would make this work with only one pair of pants. I guess I had to wear my pants every day and hope that they wouldn't start to smell. I could wash them on Saturdays. That was the day when those who were under eighteen studied for the California High School Equivalency Exam so we could pass it and no longer need to do school. At fourteen, I had no intention of passing. I already knew that Saturday would be the one day I didn't have to work on post or go on course. And of course, the one day I wouldn't have to wear this horrid uniform. I would milk my Saturday's for as long as possible, hopefully until I was eighteen.

I took the elevator up to my new dorm on the second floor. Once there, I pulled on my uniform and looked at myself in the full-length mirror hanging on the door. Ugh. A boxy navy blouse tucked into shapeless black pants, finished off with the ugly shoes. *It's okay,* I told myself. I would just have to spruce up my look. I pinned back my hair with some brightly colored butterfly clips. Next, I grabbed my small makeup bag. I smoothed on sparkly blue eyeshadow from True Colors, along with dark eyeliner and mascara. There. That livened up the uniform a bit. I put my shoulders back and headed out the door, ready for my first real day of Sea Org work.

"Take me off your damn list!" a former church parishioner screamed at me. I held the phone away from my ear and made a face at Marie, who sat at her desk across from me. I was working on my first post as a rudiments registrar. My job was to get public who had stopped coming to the church for services to come back on course or signed up for auditing. I had spent my first day calling a list of phone numbers and being yelled at, hung up on, or sent to voicemail over and over. I set the phone down with a flourish after I heard the dial tone once again.

"That woman was really happy to hear from us," I joked to Marie, who snickered. Marie was my age and a former cadet from the Ranch. "Is this what it's like every day?" I stared at my list of phone numbers.

"Yeah." She shrugged. "But some days we get to go to public's homes, so that's kind of fun."

"Oooh, we get to go off base?" I said excitedly.

"How's it going over here?" a rude voice interrupted our conversation. Our senior officer was Henry, another former cadet a year or two older than me. Henry had always been a goody-two-shoes, and now was no different. He looked over from his desk, his dark, gelled hair gleaming in the lights that beamed down on us from the tiled ceiling.

"I was just asking Marie if she had any tips for making these phone calls," I muttered.

"I have already gone over the patter with you," Henry said. "Please stick to the patter."

"Okaaaay, jeez." I picked up my phone and dialed the next number on the list. I glanced down at the sheet of paper in front of me, skimming over the script containing the lines to use in my calls. My eye was already watching the clock. I couldn't wait for dinnertime, when I could see all my friends.

"You have reached the voicemail . . ." a voice chimed. I sighed as I prepared myself to deliver the patter in a message. The minutes ticked by. My leg jiggled under the desk.

Finally, it was 5 p.m. I leapt from my desk.

"Ready for dinner?" I asked Marie.

She nodded, and we rushed out of the lobby, ignoring Henry as we pushed through the glass door leading out to the quad and up the stairs to the dining room. I asked Marie who she usually sat with.

"I guess I just sit wherever," she told me.

"Let's see who's inside. I really want to make sure we sit with our friends," I said as I walked in. I immediately spotted Patrick, my old crush/friend from the Ranch, standing by the buffet line. He looked over and grinned when he saw me.

"Katherine! All grown up and in the Sea Org," he hollered across the dining room. Other Sea Org members looked over, but he ignored them.

"Shut up!" I yelled back as I rushed across the vast dining room toward him. "You've only been in the Sea Org for like a month."

"Yeah, well, I'm a pro at it already," Patrick responded. "Hey, Marie." He nodded at Marie, who trailed behind me. "You guys wanna grab a table?"

"Yep." I grinned happily. We grabbed plates and loaded them up with chicken and potatoes. I ignored the pile of wilted broccoli that emitted a smell like rotten eggs. Patrick led the way to a table where a few other former cadets who I hadn't seen in ages sat. Immediately, we were the loudest group in the dining room, laughing and talking over one another.

44

THE REAL WORLD

It was a beautiful day and my mood matched it. I was going on my first car trip to get a disaffected Scientologist public back on church lines. It wasn't the thought of rehabilitating a Scientologist that thrilled me. It was knowing I was getting off PAC Base. I was entering "the real world." All the way to a place called Thousand Oaks. After several weeks of doing call-in every day at post time with no success, I was excited for an adventure.

Thousand Oaks was forty-five minutes away, so I brought my newest romance book by Sandra Brown. Marie and I slid into the back of the red Toyota sedan that belonged to ASHO. Henry had somehow gotten his license and would be driving. He must have CSW'd for time to practice driving or something. I was impressed that he made it happen since not many Sea Org members drove, including my parents. My sister still didn't drive and she was twenty.

It was a lovely drive. Listening to the radio, reading my book, and desultory chats with Marie whenever I pulled my nose away from it. Ahhh . . . Forty-five minutes with no phone calls to make? I reveled in it. But too soon, the car pulled up alongside a large house. Time to get into Sea Org mode.

"Ready?" Marie asked.

"Yep," I responded as I shoved my book back into my purse. I opened the door and slid out, then straightened my blouse and made sure it was tucked in as I took in my surroundings. The wind rustled the majestic trees towering above us. Large houses lined the street, looking straight out of a suburban movie. My mind immediately flashed to what it would be like to grow up on a street like this. In a normal home, going to regular school, maybe even having a boyf—

"Katherine!"

"Huh?" I looked over at Henry.

"Stop daydreaming and let's get a move on." He clutched his packet of Scientology materials importantly to his chest.

"Whatever. I wasn't daydreaming," I muttered, annoyed. I started up the pathway after Henry, whose long strides ate up the cement.

Ring. Ring. Ring.

I glanced at Marie.

Riiiiing.

Henry leaned on the doorbell.

"Did they not know we were coming?" I asked.

"No, it's best to surprise them," Henry whispered back to me. He looked around furtively, then stepped off the path and crept over to the window and peered inside, using his hand to block the glare of the sun. I glanced at Marie, and she made a face. We tiptoed after Henry as he circled the house, peering into each window we passed. I stifled a giggle. I felt like we were staking the place out to rob it.

"Damn." Henry frowned. "They're not here."

"Well, maybe next time!" I said gaily.

"Shhhh!" He glared at me. "Why do you always have to be so loud?"

"Sorry! I didn't realize we were supposed to be sneaky like a burglar," I whispered back. Marie snickered. I grabbed her elbow and leaned into her as I erupted into silent laughter. Henry stood there, glaring at us as we fell over each other in convulsions.

THE TRIP ENDED WITH HENRY, Marie, and me stopping at an Office Depot for supplies for the org. While we were browsing, a young guy who worked there offered to help us find what we needed. As he showed us around, he seemed to be flirting with me. I flirted back, pretending like I was in the real world. What if he asked me out on a date? I would have to say no, of course, but for now I enjoyed the fantasy. I laughed and giggled as he led us down each aisle, goofing off about where to find things. Marie wiggled her eyebrows at me behind my back, and I shrugged, smiling. Henry was oblivious as usual and followed pushing the cart.

When we were done getting the supplies, I said goodbye and thanked the guy for his help. It may have been my imagination, but it seemed like he was on the verge of asking me out. I opened the car door and slid inside. I stared out the window as Henry put the car in drive and pulled out and onto Hollywood Boulevard back toward PAC Base. I wished I could have stayed in Office Depot longer.

45

SEA ORG DAY

A week after my fifteenth birthday, it was Sea Org Day. This was the one day given to all the Sea Org members to celebrate working for the Church, and I had been making sure I stayed in-ethics enough that I could be a part of the celebrations. I had been looking forward to it for weeks. It had been the one thing that kept me going every boring day in the Sea Org.

When the day finally arrived, I put on the outfit that I had picked out: a bikini under cutoff jean shorts, a white Hanes tank top, and sneakers. Then I would change into a fitted black dress that a friend had lent me for the evening entertainment.

The day turned out to be the most fun I'd had in a long time. All ASHO Foundation staff were bused to Manhattan Beach, and we were able to do whatever we wanted. I played volleyball, went swimming in the ocean, body-surfed, laid out . . . Ahhh, this was summer! Then at the end of the day, there was a feast at a hotel. I sat with my friends and joked and laughed the whole night. After dinner, there was an open stage for Sea Org members to put on skits and plays that they had rehearsed during their lunch breaks or evenings.

The next day was the Sea Org Day ceremony. This was held at Celebrity Centre International. CC Int, as we called it, was a magnificent castle in the heart of Hollywood that the Sea Org had purchased many years ago. It operated as a service organization, delivering services to celebrities in Hollywood such as Tom Cruise, John Travolta, and Kirstie Alley.

That evening, we wore our formal Sea Org uniforms. My dad wore his epaulets to show his rank as an officer. My mom was only a petty officer second class. She had two more ranks to make it to full officer. I was the lowest rank listed, since I was new to the Sea Org. My rank was swamper. A swamper was the person out at sea who cleaned the decks of the ship—so, the lowest job you could have. Everyone who joined the Sea Org was a swamper, then worked their way up. If you wanted a promotion, you had to write a CSW listing all your accomplishments and why you should be promoted to the next rank. Then at the Sea Org Day event, they would announce them. No way would I have the nerve to write a CSW requesting a promotion.

That evening, I claimed a seat next to Ricky in the glass atrium where the ceremony was being held. He was getting promoted, and his leg jiggled with excitement.

"Calm yourself," I joked to him as I grabbed his knee to make it stop bouncing.

"Don't give me orders. I'll soon be a petty officer." Ricky snickered. "You'll be a little swamper having to follow all my orders."

"Ha!" I scoffed. I shoved him, and he nudged me back with his shoulder. A Sea Org member turned and gave me the fisheye stare I knew all too well.

"Stop!" Ricky whispered to me. "I have to set an example now." He straightened his uniform and his Sea Org cap.

I pulled myself together and tried to act more like a Sea Org member. As I looked around, I took in the other members dressed in their ceremonial uniforms. It was impressive. I was proud to be a part of this. Suddenly, the Commanding Officer PAC Base stepped out onto the stage. We all stood and cheered. She waved her hand and welcomed the Sea Org members. She listed the accomplishments that the service orgs had achieved this year, then announced each Sea Org member who was being promoted. I watched Ricky cross the stage and salute the CO. Then a few of my other friends from the Ranch walked across, including Allison and Lacy. I clapped and cheered for them. Look at them. Their strong salutes as they accepted their awards. Maybe one day that could be me?

46

I CAN DO THIS

After the Sea Org ceremony, I committed myself to working harder. But every time I picked up the phone to call a disaffected parishioner, I was filled with dread. Was I going to be yelled at again? Would I be hung up on? To make the list surmountable, I played a game where I would call ten parishioners, and once they hung up on me or I didn't reach anyone, I would allow myself five minutes to doodle or take a bathroom break.

Most days I would skip Scientology studies, but at least I would make it to the roll calls so that the supervisors thought I was there. Then I would sneak out and go to my parents' room to read. Every time I did that, I treated it like *Mission Impossible*. I would edge out of the staff course room as soon as roll call was done, then walk briskly to Lebanon Hall as if on an important task. Once there, I would sidle in against the wall, eyeing the elevator. Should I risk being seen by the security camera aimed straight at it and take the elevator to the seventh floor?

If I heard footsteps, I would book it up the stairs before anyone could catch me. Then I would dart across the hallway and up the stairs to the second floor, grabbing the doorknob to shut the door behind me. I'd made it to the RPF floor.

RPF stood for the Rehabilitation Project Force. It was where Sea Org members that had made huge mistakes on post were assigned to. They had a long study program, had to do hard labor and were on the RPF for years. They weren't allowed to talk to Sea Org members which meant they were separated from their spouse if they were married, and had half-pay. It was a very sad life. I always wondered how they stood being treated like garbage. Seeing them always made me uncomfortable so I'd swiftly move past their floor, avoiding eye contact with any RPFer in the area, and scurry up to the third floor.

I still had four floors to go to reach my parents' room, but the stairs stopped at the fourth floor. I had to quickly cross to the other end, passing door after door shut tight—all rooms for married couples in the Sea Org—the camera in the far corner burning a hole into my back. I would then rush up the remaining stairs to the seventh floor and darted down the hall to my parents' room.

Their room was nothing special, but to me it was sanctuary. It was the size of a small walk-in closet but had a nice cozy feel to it, with their familiar bed and dresser that had somehow stayed with them through all the years, traveling from room to room. They didn't have a bathroom, but this I was used to as well. They hadn't had a private bathroom in years. There was one down the hall that was dark with a leaky sink. But I wasn't there for the bathroom. I was there to read. I liked to pick out a book from the crammed bookshelf and lie on their queen-sized bed and get lost in it. My parents' books tended to be by authors like Ken Follett and WWII biographies, which wasn't my normal genre, but I didn't care. Books were books, and I wanted to be transported into another world.

HANGING out with my friends was the only thing I had to look forward to. So many Ranchers had joined the Sea Org and whenever we got together I had so much fun, whether it was goofing off at meal times, or even sneaking away to the ASHO library with Patrick and pretending to word clear each other but really just chatting. The silliness I had with the Ranchers was what kept me going through the monotony of Sea Org days.

One day Ricky and I were walking through the skyway that connected the Complex to ASHO. It was a long hallway, one-story up with windows on all sides. Anyone walking by on the sidewalk could see us. Despite the full view, Ricky and I started arguing over who was stronger and before I knew it, we were wrestling right there in the skyway. I pinned him, but suddenly he flipped me and pressed my arms back against the carpet.

"Whoa, you've gotten stronger!"

"Uh yeah, and don't you forget it," he said. He sat up to flex his muscles. At that moment I took him by surprise and knocked him over.

"Ah! Bitch!" he said laughing.

"What the hell are you guys doing?"

We stopped what we were doing and looked up. There was Mr. V with his arms crossed looking down at us. Mr. V had been promoted from the EPF I/C recently and was now a top executive running PAC Base.

"Oh shit," I said as I got up.

"Ricky, go return to post," Mr. V ordered. He then turned to look at me shaking his head. I thought he looked sexy in his CLO uniform. The black slacks with the black blazer, white buttoned down shirt and black tie was very manly.

"I can't believe you are still pulling this crap," Mr. V said. "You are in the Sea Org now. Stop acting like an oversexed teenager and get back on-purpose."

"I am!" I protested as I tried to tuck my uniform back into my slacks. "It's lunch time. We don't have to be perfect at lunch time."

"But you don't need to act out of valence either." Mr. V retorted. "Get back to your org. I don't want to see this shit anymore."

"Okay, jeez," I responded. But inwardly, I loved that I had gotten his attention.

A FEW WEEKS after Sea Org Day, I was daydreaming during ASHO muster in the quad courtyard. Suddenly I heard the word "interrogatory," and I started paying attention. I looked toward the front and saw the Hubbard Association Secretary standing in front of muster, holding bright golden-yellow legal-sized pieces of paper. Someone was getting an interrogatory sent out about them.

"Please fill this out and do not withhold anything," the HAS ordered. She handed a stack of papers to the front of each line.

I wondered who this was for. Whoever it was, was in serious trouble. An interrogatory would ask questions about the Sea Org member and every single staff member would report any out-ethics they had observed. These interrogatories were rare. I had done them a couple of times at the Ranch, but never in the Sea Org. This felt more intense. Interrogatories at the Ranch were put in your communications basket. They were not announced at muster and handed out in front of everyone. I pitied the poor Sea Org member who this was on. I glanced around, wondering who it could be. When the sheets of paper were passed down to me, I took one off the pile and passed the rest to Marie who was standing behind me. I glanced down quickly and felt like I had been slapped in the face.

It was *my* name. Right there in bold.

Katherine Spallino.

I closed my eyes, then opened them.

Was this real?

This interrogatory was on me?

Yes, I confirmed. "Interrogatory regarding Katherine Spallino" was the headline. This was followed by a series of questions.

HAVE you observed Katherine wandering around during post time and seeming unproductive?

HAVE you seen Katherine blow from course?

HAS Katherine said anything to you that is out-tech or off-purpose?

THERE WERE twelve questions in all. I read each question, my breath coming in short bursts. By the end I wanted to crawl into a nearby closet and cry. Right now, two hundred staff members were reading these questions about me, no doubt thinking I was the worst Sea Org member in the world. The air ruffled the trees above me as if it was a different world. Because where I was, it felt like I was in a deep, dark hole, with the eyes of the entire ASHO Org staring me down.

Just keep it together, Katherine, I thought.

I took a deep breath, then looked straight ahead. I kept the interrogatory clutched in my right hand while I waited for what felt like eternity for muster to be dismissed. All the Scientology Training Routine drills I had done at the Ranch, practicing to not let emotion show through, were coming into use. Finally, muster was dismissed. I moved quickly, squeezing through the staff members in front of me, avoiding looking at anyone's face. I didn't want to see the derision directed at me, or worse, pity. That would throw me over the edge, and I might end up crying in front of everyone like a baby.

"Where are you going?" I heard Bethany call as I stepped into the lobby. She was my department head and Henry's senior, as well as mine and Marie's.

"I have to go the bathroom," I said. I kept my stride down the short hallway. The bathroom door was almost within reach.

"Stop, Katherine," she demanded.

I gritted my teeth and turned around and glared. "Am I not allowed to go to the bathroom?"

"Knock off the attitude, Katherine!" Bethany retorted, flinging her perfectly curled hair behind her shoulders. "That's what got you into this situation in the first place."

"Whatever. I don't even know why I am being interrogated. I thought I was being in-ethics, but apparently not!" I turned on my heel and strode to the bathroom, letting the door slam shut behind me. I ran into one of the stalls and slammed the door again, flinging the metal lock shut. I closed the lid of the toilet, sat down, and put my head in my hands. My throat felt so tight, as if a hand was gripping it. I tried to swallow and breathe through it, squeezing my eyes shut. It felt like a dam was waiting to burst, but I didn't want to walk out with my eyes red.

Okay, fine, an interog is out, I thought to myself. *It's not the end of the world.* I took another deep breath. But then I replayed what had happened in my head, and my stomach tightened again. That had been so humiliating.

Fuck.

Calm down, calm down, calm down, I chanted in my head. *You can do this.* I wasn't going to hide in the bathroom, I decided. I was going to go out there with my head held high and stare down any asshole who looked my way. I swung the bathroom stall open, strode over to the mirror, and scanned my face.

My eyes looked a little bloodshot, but you would have had to look closely to notice. I set my black purse on the marble counter and leaned over to reapply some dark eyeliner. I added some lip gloss and rubbed my lips together. There. I was ready to face the music. I shoved my gloss in my purse as the Hubbard Association Secretary pushed the bathroom door open. Passing by me to get to a stall, she glanced at me.

"Shouldn't you be on post?"

"I'm allowed to go to the bathroom," I retorted. I pulled open the door and strode out without waiting for her response, then headed to my desk. I sat down as if everything was normal and began to rummage through my papers. I could see Bethany looking at me out of the corner of my eye. I pulled out the dreaded list of public to call and waved it at her.

"I'm getting to work now," I called. "Stop staring at me."

Bethany glared, so I swiveled in my chair facing away from her. I picked up the phone and listened to the dial tone. I began to doodle instead of calling the first number on the list. My mind was too wound up to call, anyway. I wondered what was going to happen after the interrogatory. Maybe they would say I was so out-ethics and then I could be allowed to leave. A part of me wanted that. I had been thinking about leaving over the years anyways. It hurt, though. I had been trying so hard, yet here I was in trouble. Yes, I didn't go on course, and I was still told I was "too loud," but why did the Sea Org care so much about the small things? At least I was on post. I was here trying my best.

A COUPLE OF HOURS LATER, I was called into the ethics office by Bertha, the ASHO Foundation Director of Inspections and Reports. Her job was to ensure staff and public kept their ethics in. If you got in trouble and a report was written on you, you had to see Bertha.

Bertha seemed like the epitome of a perfect Sea Org member. She was sixteen but seemed much older, with a subdued, serious air that emanated from her. She gestured for me to take a seat. I pulled back the wooden chair and plopped down. Bertha straightened the stack of interrogatory golden rods in front of her, the light above reflecting off the shiny desk.

"Katherine," she began. "In the interrogatories that we received from the staff at ASHO, there were numerous reports that you were seen goofing off, flirting with boys, that you set a bad example, and that you are frequently spotted in the bathroom doing your makeup during post time. This—"

"Seriously?" I interrupted. "I can't put on makeup? Don't I have to look professional?"

"Do that on your own time, not during post time," Bertha responded.

"Oh, you mean in the thirty minutes that I have to eat. Yeah, that's plenty of time to eat and get my make up done," I said sarcastically.

"Everyone else can do it." Bertha sneered. "And like I said, this is not the only issue here. We have many reports from the staff that you are not working and goofing off on post."

"Who were the people?" I crossed my arms. "Can I have some names?"

"It doesn't matter who it was, but let me just say, almost everyone had something to say about you."

"Well, that's harsh," I muttered.

I slouched down in my seat. I wondered if any of my friends had written about me too. They probably had. It was expected that you report any out-ethics, whether friend or foe, and friends reported on each other all the time. I crossed my arms and hugged my body tight.

"Okay, so what now?" I demanded.

"At this point, we are going to hold a Court of Ethics. This will convene in two weeks. In the meantime, you need to get your act together and behave like a Sea Org member."

"Fine." I stood up to go. "Is that all?"

"Yes, you can go on post now, but you better not be found slacking," she ordered.

I gave her a thumbs up and a smile like a Cheshire cat. All teeth and no warmth. "I'll be on my best behavior." I pivoted and strode out.

Fuck. Fuck. Fuck.

I trudged to my desk and plopped down. I wanted to lay

my head in my arms and go to sleep. I was suddenly so exhausted.

"Katherine, do you have your list of public to call?" Bethany stood over my desk.

Seriously, I thought to myself. *Couldn't she just give me a minute?*

I met her eyes. Bethany stared back.

I can't do this. I can't keep pretending.

"Well?" Bethany said.

I stood up.

"I'm going on the Decks," I said.

"What?" Bethany looked taken aback. "Are you serious?"

"Yes," I said. Marie was doodling at her desk. I could tell she was listening, but I didn't care if she heard. Smarmy Henry was nowhere to be found, thank god.

"I am obviously a failure at being a Sea Org member. I want to go on the Decks to get handled," I said.

"Fine." Bethany sneered. "Go join the DB's."

I glared at her. I resisted the urge to flip her off. Instead I turned and walked away, seething. Just because my friends were on the Decks didn't mean they were Degraded Beings. As I crossed the courtyard, I decided to look for Leslie and Casey, who I knew were on the Decks. The Decks were for those who had doubts about being in the Sea Org. Well, that was me, right? I had been doubting my place here for months, if not years.

I found Casey and Leslie in their dorm at the Complex, lounging around on their beds. My mood brightened. These two knew what it was like for me. How hard it was to follow the rules. Casey had been the one who had persuaded me to join the Sea Org but she hadn't been able to stay in-ethics just like me. Now I could be with them instead of fucking up on post.

"Guys, guess what?" I declared as I plopped on the floor next to their bed.

"What?" Leslie asked as she flipped through a magazine.

"I'm on the Decks now!" I grinned up at them in their bunk.

"Oh, cool!" Casey said. She propped herself up on one elbow. "Hey! You can help us wax the ASHO lobby tonight. Alexander has to do it for his estates manager post, and he asked us to help him."

"Yeah," Leslie added. "He said he will order pizza for us if we help."

"Okay." I smiled. I plopped down on the chair next to their bunk and grabbed a magazine. This was way better than being on post.

That night I spent hours waxing ASHO's lobby with Alexander, Leslie, and Casey. There was no one in the Org, since it was after 10 p.m. We blasted KROQ on the radio even though the security guard patrolling PAC that evening kept coming by and telling us to turn it down. As soon as he walked away, we would crank it back up. At midnight, we ordered pizza and lounged on the public couches in the reception area, laughing and joking around. Finally, we finished up the last of the waxing. We didn't get to bed until five in the morning. It was the most fun I'd had since Sea Org Day.

47

THE BEGINNING OF THE END

"Katherine?"

"Katherine?!"

"Katherine!!"

I jolted when I realized my name was being shouted across the room.

"What?" I said, confused. I had been standing at muster, lost in thought, but I was jerked back to the present. I was surrounded by ASHO Foundation Sea Org members inside the executive's office, where a muster was being held due to the pouring rain outside.

The Captain pointed at me from the front of the room. "This is the type of out-ethics that we shouldn't be allowing in the org. Katherine stands there, looking at her nails as if she has something better to do," he said, his brown mustache bristling up in a sneer. "We are trying to clear the planet. Is that something you might be interested in?"

I was at my first ASHO muster in two weeks. I had been enjoying the last couple of weeks sleeping in, slacking off in our dorm and, occasionally, doing a project with Casey and Leslie. I had moved out of my ASHO dorm and into theirs.

But today, I wasn't in my dorm reading, or listening to music. Unfortunately, Bertha had tracked me down in my dorm and informed me that I was required to be in uniform and go to muster even though I was on the Decks. I hated pretending to be a part of the group. I had been standing in the back of the muster, leaning on the wall while the Captain of ASHO Foundation lectured the organization about what gross income targets needed to be met. Since this had nothing to do with me, I had let my mind wander. But now I was fully present. And everyone was looking at me.

I stared at the Captain. Where did this hatred for me come from? My encounters with the Captain were few, but each time he had always been kind and courteous to me, even recently when I was in ethics trouble. But now, suddenly, he was coming at me? In front of the whole ASHO Foundation staff?

"Well?" He sneered at me. "Are you interested in clearing the planet or not?"

"Yesss," I said, drawing the word out.

"Yes what?" he demanded.

"Yes, sirrr . . ." I loaded my words with contempt. This was bullshit. Why was I being singled out? The Captain turned his attention away from me and continued his lecture while I simmered in anger. I knew he was under a lot of pressure to get the ASHO Saint Hill size because he was being shadowed by two personnel from the Religious Technology Center, the highest organization in the Sea Org. There was a list of goals we needed to accomplish, and we kept missing our targets. I had a feeling the Captain was taking out his frustration on me. When he dismissed the org, I pushed myself off the filing cabinet, ready to book it out the door and back to my dorm. But too late. The Captain was striding over to me.

"What the hell is your problem?" he screamed at me. He was tall and lanky with a graying mustache, not the toughest looking guy around. And now here he was, trying to intimidate me. Didn't he know I was from the Ranch, where we had Mr. Hammond, the scariest dude around, as our Cadet Coordinator?

"I don't know what you're talking about." I glared at him. His face turned red.

I leaned against the wall with a bored expression on my face as he started screaming, saying what a Degraded Being I was, how disgusting I was, that I needed to get back on purpose. His words landed like soft pebbles against the bubble I had built around myself. It was like I was in a movie watching this happen to someone else. As the Captain leaned in closer, spit sprayed out of his mouth and landed on my cheek.

I reached up and wiped it away with my hand, staring at it with disgust. "Say it, don't spray it! Jeez."

Bertha, who had been standing behind the Captain, shook her head at me. I couldn't believe I had said it myself, but I couldn't take it back.

The Captain pulled himself to his full height and turned to Bertha. "I want her Court of Ethics done today!"

"Yes sir!" Bertha glared at me.

"Good. We don't need this on our lines," the Captain said. "Get her handled." He turned on his heel and walked away.

"You are out of control," Bertha said as she grabbed my arm and pulled me toward HCO.

"I can walk," I muttered. I yanked my arm from her and followed her to the ethics area.

. . .

THAT EVENING WAS my Court of Ethics, but I couldn't work up the energy to care. I wandered into the Ethics Department conference room. Four Sea Org members stared at me as if I was a dirty piece of chewing gum stuck on the bottom of their shoe. I stared back as I pulled out the chair at the head of the table and sat down. I wanted to put my feet up on the table, but I thought that might be a bit much. A Court of Ethics was convened by an Ethics Officer or church executive who is senior to the church staff member being charged. The purpose of it was to decide on what sentence I had to serve for all the out-ethics I had been in. Bertha and the three other ASHO Foundation staff were chosen as part of the committee. The only staff member I knew besides Bertha was the chaplain for ASHO Foundation. She was an older woman from Mexico who had joined Division 6 when I had. She was new to the Sea Org, and we had gotten along well. But sitting here, you would never know that. She glared at me as if I had personally offended her. It took all I had not to snap at her and ask what her problem was.

The Court of Ethics began with Bertha listing my crimes. I was slacking on post, I was often late for muster, I seemed out of valence, and so on. Of course, they tacked on my altercation with the Captain this morning. I tried to remain indifferent, but it was hard to hear them list offense after offense. My confidence wavered as the list continued.

Keep your TRs in, Katherine, I whispered in my head. I lifted my chin, maintaining eye contact with Bertha as she droned on, my face immobile.

When she had finished, I still didn't move. I hoped to convey that I didn't care. That none of this was hurting me. Never mind the wreckage inside my body.

Suddenly, the chaplain leapt to her feet. "You are a

horrible Sea Org member. Don't you even care about saving the world?"

Before I could respond, she leaned closer and poked her finger at me, screeching, "What kind of thetan are you?"

I pressed away from her, but her long pointer finger scraped my cheek.

"You fucking scratched me!" I said, shocked. I put a hand to my cheek to feel if there was blood.

The chaplain sat back down and had the decency to look ashamed, but it didn't matter.

"I'm not staying for this crap," I muttered. I stood up and strode out of the room. I knew I would be in even more trouble, but I didn't care. I marched through ASHO, ignoring any faces that turned my way, through the long hallway, to the Complex, then raced up the stairs to my dorm. I flung myself on my bed and covered my eyes. How much more of this could I take?

THE NEXT DAY, I was called in for the final meeting for the Court of Ethics. I debated not going but decided to sit through it. I had spent the day yesterday thinking about leaving the Sea Org, and instead of being convinced to do it, I had scared myself back into wanting to try harder. My whole life I had been told horror stories about how awful the wog world is. People were not intelligent, made bad decisions, and didn't have Scientology technology to help them. What if I got sucked into that world and became a promiscuous slut who did drugs? With these thoughts running through my head, I decided to try to pull it together and be more on purpose. Besides, my contacts were really old and I had been trying to get a CSW approved to go to the eye doctor but it kept getting disapproved. Maybe it was because I was too out ethics. If I got my ethics in, maybe I could get new contacts and stop walking around with a ripped contact in one eye.

At the Court of Ethics, I explained that I was sorry and would try harder and they seemed to accept it and told me they would issue my findings that afternoon with what I had to do to get in good standing with the group.

Later that day I scanned the paper to see what my penalty was. I had to do lower conditions and write my overts and withholds. That wasn't too bad. I had been writing OW's since I was a young child, so this would be easy.

THAT AFTERNOON, I sat in the ethics area of HCO and wrote my OWs:

1. Overt: I blow from course often.

2. Time, Place, Form and Event: Almost every day after I go to roll call, I leave and go hang out somewhere instead of doing course. Sometimes I go to the ASHO library and just hang out there and pretend to study with a friend.

1. I snuck off PAC Base and went to the convenience store during post time.

2. During post time, on November 7, I didn't want to do event call-in, so instead of going to CLO to the call-in unit, I walked down Fountain Ave to the store and bought some chips. Then I walked back and sat in a stairwell for a while, reading my book and eating chips.

.   .   .

I SPENT the afternoon writing each transgression down. I put down my pen and felt a sense of calm come over me. I felt better, as if I had been cleansed.

THE FOLLOWING DAY, I wrote up my lower conditions, working my way up from Doubt to Liability. When working on the condition of Liability, it was expected that you make up the damage that you had done. Because of all the work I had done while on the Decks, I had plenty of work completed. I wrote about mopping and waxing the lobby all night, and about the hours of call-in I had done for the IAS event.

Next, I had to ask for acceptance back into the group by petitioning Sea Org members for their signatures. That afternoon, I walked around ASHO having Sea Org members read my condition of Liability and the work that I did. To indicate that I was accepted, they signed under the "yes" column. Once I had majority of the signatures from the ASHO staff, I submitted my CSW to the Captain. He approved it that evening, and bam, I was back in the good graces of the group.

48

SMOOTH SAILING

I spent the next month working hard on post as the rudiments registrar, though I was accomplishing nothing. It was all busywork. I was completing the tasks assigned but did not register one public back on course. It didn't matter as long as I kept my mouth shut and produced. Because I stayed in-ethics, I was able to participate in the Christmas party that the PAC Base had every year for the Sea Org staff. This would be my first party ever, and there would even be beer! The beer was only for Sea Org members that were twenty-one and over, and I was only fifteen. But I didn't care. I was determined to sneak in a sip. It was the only time of the year that alcohol was served at a Sea Org party, and I wanted to take advantage. Besides, my body was fifteen, but my spirit was billions of years old. The law didn't really apply.

The party was in the main mess at 10:30 p.m., after all the service organizations had shut their doors to the public.

Before the party, I applied my makeup carefully, and dressed in my best Dickies pants. They were sky blue and looked so cool. I paired the pants with a T-shirt and

Converse. Getting ready with me was Mirriam and Audrey, my old friends from the Ranch. Mirriam and I had connected again recently over our propensity for getting into trouble. She was a saucy one, with a sweet demeanor that could turn devilish in an instant. Audrey had always been quieter and more reserved than most Ranchers, but recently she seemed to have broken out of her shell. With her magenta lipstick and hot-pink shirt, she was ready to party. I had applied my own share of makeup, including my trademark icy blue eyeshadow, but I couldn't work up the confidence to wear deep-red lipstick like Audrey did. Mirriam was dressed similarly to me, with black Dickies, and a fitted T and Converse.

We sauntered down the hallway to the elevator, then to the dining hall, and strutted inside. I took in the scene around me with a wide smile on my face. The lights were dimmed, the tables and chairs were pushed to the side, and there was a large table bursting with snacks. Cookies, chips, licorice, cheese platters, grapes—anything you could want seemed to be on the buffet line. Next to it was the bar, with coolers filled with beers and sodas. There was even hip-hop blasting. This was a party!

Mirriam, Audrey, and I rushed to the food table, grabbed a paper plate and filled it with goodies, and sat on the chairs lined up by the wall. We whispered about how we could get a beer as we crunched through our Doritos, since Mr. V was standing right next to the drinks, as if he knew of our plans. Finally, we saw that he was distracted talking to someone and had his back turned. We walked casually back to the food table and grabbed some licorice, walked over to the drinks table and each grabbed a beer, and then wandered back to our spot and sat down. I scanned the room to see if anyone had noticed.

"I don't think anyone saw," I whispered.

We each took turns using our bodies as shields for each other as we poured the beer into the empty cans of Sprite we had chugged earlier. Then we discreetly put the three beer cans on the ground behind our chairs. When we were done, we looked at each other and grinned. We could walk around with our Sprites, and no one would know we had beer.

I took my first sip and almost spat it out.

"This tastes disgusting," I whispered.

"It's an acquired taste," Audrey said as she took a drink without a flinch.

I rolled my eyes. "Yeah, like you've had beer before."

"It is pretty gross." Mirriam laughed.

"I'm chugging mine." I tipped my can back and glugged it down.

Mirriam did the same. Audrey informed us she would be sipping hers.

By this time, a few Sea Org members had made it out onto the empty space in the dining room and had started dancing. Just then "Say My Name" by Destiny's Child blared over the speakers.

"I love this song!" Audrey said as she swiveled her hips, singing along. Her silky, white-blond hair brushed her shoulders as she moved them up and down.

"Me too!" I grabbed her hand and Mirriam's and tugged them toward the dance floor. "Let's dance!"

I let go of them and put my arms up and sashayed onto the dance floor, singing along to the music.

Mirriam and Audrey danced next to me. We put our hands in the air and moved our bodies. The next song came on. "Maria, Maria," by Santana. We grooved and swayed as more and more Sea Org members came out on the floor. As my body moved to the beat, I tipped my head back and closed my eyes. The music reverberated through my body. I opened my eyes and took it all in. It was so cool, seeing all these Sea Org members out on the dance floor, not just my friends, but the Sea Org members that were so uptight and robotic, now dancing and laughing right alongside me. There was Mr. Carnell, the man who ran my fitness board, dancing. Over there was Bertha. Okay, she wasn't dancing, but she was swaying to the music. Ricky rushed over to us, followed by Patrick. Our dance circle widened as more Ranchers joined us. At midnight, my head began to spin from the second beer I had snuck with Mirriam and Audrey. I made my way upstairs, talking and giggling to myself. I flopped onto my bed and fell asleep with a smile on my face.

49

BACK TO REALITY

I woke up on January 3, turned off my alarm, then shut my eyes. I didn't want to get up. I ignored the sounds of the other girls in my dorm rustling around, chatting as they dressed for the day, and pulled the covers over my head. The holidays had been fun and had given me the sense of purpose that I had been looking for, but now it was done. Over. I had eight long months stretching ahead of me until the next fun holiday, Sea Org Day. All there was was the daily drudgery of getting up, going on post, going on study, going back on post, and repeat. The only time that was my own was Sunday morning, but even that was monitored. We had to get a pass on our dorms for cleanliness before we could go anywhere. Then I would have two measly hours before post time. I felt a wave of despair wash over me. What was wrong with me? Why was I so unhappy holding a post and working in the Sea Org? The Sea Org was trying to make the world a better place, and I couldn't even work up the energy to get out of bed? I needed help. Maybe I could get auditing again? The last time I got auditing, it had not been what I'd hoped, but maybe I needed a different auditor who could help me get on purpose. The problem was that there were only two staff auditors, and there was at least a thousand Sea Org members at PAC Base. Maybe more. There was no way I would be slotted in to see an auditor when there were other Sea Org members who were more deserving of it.

A thought flashed through my head. *But what if I blew? Would they help me then?*

I pulled the blanket from my face, opened my eyes, and stared up at the metal links of the bunk above me as the wheels began to turn in my head. If I left PAC Base without permission and was gone all day, I would be considered a blow, which meant I would be sent to the Decks. From there, they might interview me to see why I left, and I could tell them I wasn't happy and needed help. Then maybe I would be set up with an auditor. I sat up and threw my covers back. I pulled on my uniform and plotted when I should blow as the other girls in the dorm dressed beside me.

I went to breakfast, morning muster and post as usual. After lunch, I went to CTO and answered at roll call. This was the time, I decided. As soon as the supervisor was busy talking to a Sea Org member, I slipped out the door at the other end of the course room.

I walked outside of CTO and up Catalina Street, then crossed the large parking lot past LA Org. I stepped onto the north end of L. Ron Hubbard Way, just twenty feet away from Sunset Boulevard. I could see one security guard on his bike at the other end of the block. Perfect.

I turned and walked up LRH Way to the corner of Sunset, then crossed the street walking straight ahead, ignoring the tickling sensation between my shoulder blades. I was worried a security guard was tailing me, but I resisted the urge to check. I was a block away, at the Metro station on Vermont Avenue and Sunset Boulevard, when I gave in and looked behind me. My stomach was in knots as I scanned the busy street. Cars sped past. Wogs were walking along minding their own business. But there was no one there. I exhaled a long whoosh of breath.

Now the next step. I planned to take the Metro to Universal City Walk. I didn't have any money; ASHO Foundation staff had not gotten paid this week due to not getting enough funds in from the public. I had gotten paid a few weeks ago, but it had been half-pay of only $17, and I had spent it on shampoo and conditioner and getting a meal at Fat Burger for a special treat during Sunday morning's personal time. I would just have to go on without the $2.00 ticket. I was sure it would be fine. There was never anyone checking tickets anyway.

I hurried onto the escalator heading underground. I had taken the Metro when I had an approved liberty day, so I knew which one would take me where I wanted to go. I sat stiffly on a marble bench and waited as the minutes trickled by. I crossed my arms and forced myself to take a deep breath. I craned my neck to look down the tunnel. Lights appeared around the curve. I leapt to my feet. The train came screeching to a stop. I quickly stepped on, and as the train pulled away, I melted into my seat. I had made it.

My relief was short-lived.

As the train arrived at the next stop, the doors slid open. A policeman entered.

Shit.

I hoped he wasn't checking tickets, but as soon as the train jolted ahead, he moved from passenger to passenger, making his way toward my seat at the back of the train. I shrank down and postulated that he would stop before he got to me. Two black-booted feet appeared in front of mine. My eyes traveled up the uniformed man and met his eyes.

"Do you have your ticket?"

I fumbled around pretending to look for it.

"I can't find it," I muttered. "Shoot! It was right here."

"Ma'am, please follow me off the train at the next stop."

My heart sank. Just my luck.

The train pulled into a station and I followed the policeman off and braced myself for the worst.

The cop told me he had to issue me a citation to appear at juvenile court on the date listed on the back of the paper. I couldn't believe I had pulled this in, but at least I wasn't going to be arrested.

"How do I get home?" I asked while staring at the yellow slip.

"This citation can count as a ticket for the day. Go ahead and get yourself back to where you need to be," he replied. The cop hopped on the next train that pulled up, no doubt to find other riffraff like me.

I sat down on the marble bench to think. I decided I would continue on my way to Universal City Walk. I had a "train ticket" now, so why not. I needed to make sure I was gone from PAC long enough to be noticed, and if I returned now, it would be for nothing.

I arrived at Universal City Walk and wandered around the shops. This quickly became boring since I didn't have any money to spend. I took the escalator up to the top level, climbed onto a roof ledge with my legs dangling over, and watched the crowds below as I thought about the day. I was surprised that I had not been caught by PAC Security. Normally they were so good at catching people who blew.

After a few hours had trickled by, I was not only bored but hungry as well. The sun had set, and the deep inkiness of the sky pressed down on me. I shivered from the cool wind and wrapped my arms around myself. Watching all the people walking by with their families, chatting happily, made me feel sad and alone. It was so rare that I was able to be with my family. Now that I was in the Sea Org, I just saw my parents in passing. The only time we had spent together was on Christmas Day, and my dad was only able to take a half day off. As I watched the families, it sank in how much we were not together. That was just the way of the Sea Org.

I hopped off my perch and meandered down Universal City Walk, a single solitary figure, lost in the crowd. I couldn't get past the feeling that I was so insignificant. I decided to head back. I waited for the Metro train on the marble bench, hunched over, with my fingers clasped. Would any one even notice I was gone?

Soon enough I was back at PAC. As I turned onto LRH Way I spied Bertha, standing by LA Org. I froze, wondering if I should walk to her or duck across to the other side of the street. I know I wanted to be caught, but I couldn't help being scared.

Before I could decide, her eyes caught mine.

"Katherine!" she called, waving me to her. I walked over slowly. This was it. I was about to be caught.

"Where did you just come from?" she asked.

"Oh, I just went for a walk," I responded.

"Don't pull that crap," she said. "You've been gone since dinner."

Are you kidding me? I left at 2:30 and they think I left at 5:30? Security is obviously not as tight as they think.

"Oh, it was just a long walk," I said, chickening out and thinking I might need to sneak away again in the future. If I told them how easy it was, they might monitor the sidewalks that I took to get off PAC Base. Bertha told me to follow her to HCO. We walked into ASHO.

Lana, an older girl from the Ranch, was posted at reception. We had become friends since I had joined ASHO Foundation, so I gave a quick wave to her. She rolled her eyes but smiled. She knew that I was back in trouble. I didn't care. I was feeling pretty happy. Now that I had been caught, I figured they would dig in to find out why I was having such a hard time and help me.

Instead, when we arrived downstairs, I was lectured about responsibility and told that I needed to get back on purpose and go back on post. I trudged off to my post downstairs.

That had all been for nothing.

A COUPLE OF DAYS LATER, a meeting was called with my seniors and Bertha, the Director of Inspections and Reports. At the meeting they said that I was showing bad indicators and not producing and slipping back into my old ways. I said that it was true and maybe I needed some auditing. I looked at them hopefully.

"What about going back on the EPF?" Bertha asked. "That way you can redo all of the courses and get back on purpose."

Huh. I hadn't thought of that. I was not happy in the Sea Org. But at least I had fun when I was on the EPF. It had also not escaped my attention that there were a few new attractive guys who had been recruited from Scientology families onto the EPF. Maybe one of them could be my future boyfriend once we graduated together.

"Sure," I told Bertha with a shrug. "I'll give it a try."

50

WHO IS LISA MCPHERSON?

S uppressive People were coming to PAC Base today, and I was determined to find out why. I didn't care that at muster earlier the EPF I/C had warned us to keep out of sight. I wanted to know what all the fuss was about.

I had been on the EPF a few weeks now, and I was enjoying it. This was not because I liked restudying the courses, but because there were hot guys to flirt with. I woke up each morning excited for the day. I was aware that my intentions were wrong, but I couldn't help myself. I should be focusing on becoming an ideal Sea Org member, but all I could think about was boys, boys, boys.

On top of that, there were not many girls on the EPF. It was as if I had arrived at the perfect time. The other girls in our dorm were younger than me, with the youngest being twelve. They had parents who were parishioners of the church and had gone to private schools called Renaissance Academy and Delphi Academy that used L. Ron Hubbard's study technology. They were shy, quiet, and obedient. Everything the Sea Org could ask for to be molded into top-performing Sea Org members. Being around them helped me be in-ethics. I followed the rules, I was less likely to be loud, and I was more "in valence," or at least in the valence of what the Sea Org expected of me. But now, I could feel myself reverting to the old me. I wanted to know what was going on with those SPs, and I didn't care if it was against the rules.

My chance came later that day as I was mopping the tiled hallway leading into the Complex elevator. A unit paused near me as they were passing through. Their unit I/C, Hannah, had stopped to chat with my unit I/C. I swished my mop back and forth, but my ears perked up when I heard words float to me. " . . . protesters . . . outside . . . not allowed . . ."

I spotted my friend Grant in the other unit. I wondered if he knew what was going on. I waved my arm at him to get his attention and he jogged over, his eyes shining with excitement.

"Are they here?" I asked.

"Yeah. They're in front of AOLA right now."

"What's on their signs?" I asked quietly. It was common knowledge that it was frowned upon to discuss what the protestors were there for. But my whole life I had never been given a clear answer for why these people hated Scientology so much. I was just told they were Suppressive People. I wanted to know what made them Suppressive. I knew I could trust Grant to not write me up. He was new to Scientology and had only joined the EPF a couple of weeks ago. He had already had the temerity to question LRH policy a few times.

Grant grabbed the mop bucket and pushed it so it looked like we were a team working together in case anyone looked over.

"I don't know," Grant said. "I tried to get Hannah to go closer when we were outside, but she said we needed to stay out of their sight."

Grant's unit was gesturing for him to join up with them, but he pretended like he didn't see.

"How often are protesters here?" he asked. I moved the mop back and forth as I thought about it.

"Well, since I was a kid there have always been random people trying to film us at the Ranch. That happened like once or twice a year. And then sometimes I've seen protesters here on L. Ron Hubbard Way, but it wasn't all the time." I frowned. "I feel like it's more often now."

As I said that I realized that it was true. This year there had already been several occurrences of protestors compared to the year before, when I only knew of two instances.

"I wonder why there's more?" I said.

"Grant," Hannah called. "Let's go!"

"Shit," Grant said, looking over at his unit. "I better go. Let me know if you find out anything." He turned and jogged over to his unit.

I continued mopping the floor as I thought about the protestors. Why were they here? Why were they coming more often? I knew that I shouldn't even be wondering, but I couldn't help it. I wanted to know what the SPs were so mad about. I finished mopping my area and joined up with the rest of the unit. My I/C, Shauna, was telling them that we could go report to the EPF office now for a ten-minute break before muster.

"I'll put away the mops," I volunteered.

Shauna thanked me, and the rest of them headed off. As I pushed the two mop buckets down the hallway, I decided that, instead of coming back through the ground floor hallway, I would cut through ASHO and walk back to the EPF office on L. Ron Hubbard Way so I could try to catch a glimpse of the signs. I put the mops away, then slunk out the front door of ASHO reception and headed out to the street.

It was a lovely sunny day. I felt the warmth beat down on me as I stood on the stairs leading down to L. Ron Hubbard Way. I looked over toward AOLA, using my hand to shield my eyes against the bright sunlight. I could see a small crowd of people standing in front of the building with signs. Most of them were in regular T-shirts and shorts. They didn't look at all as menacing as they were made out to be, but I guess Suppressive People didn't dress any differently than us. Some of the Sea Org security guards were on their bikes nearby watching them. I trotted down the stairs and started down L. Ron Hubbard Way, squinting my eyes to try to read the signs.

One of the security guards guarding the protesters peeled off and came biking over to me.

Crap.

I pretended like I didn't know he was coming and continued my stroll.

"Hey," he said as he pulled up next to me.

"Oh, hey," I said. "What's going on over there?" I asked.

"Just some SP's. But you need to go back inside. You don't need to see this bullshit."

"Okay, yeah, I'm going in. I was planning on going in through the canteen area because that's closest to the EPF office," I lied.

"No, go through the Lebanon Hall entrance," he said, pointing to the entrance nearby.

"Fine," I said nonchalantly, as if he hadn't just ruined my investigative plans. He biked off as I turned to head into Lebanon Hall.

Should I look?

I wanted to see the signs, but I was worried there would be OT information on them. OT meant you were an Operating Thetan and you were at the highest levels of spiritual enlightenment. Since I was a young girl, I had been told not to look at protestors' signs because they could have OT III data. It could ruin your chance to go up the Bridge and potentially cause physical harm and even death. I didn't understand how that could be possible, but it frightened me. Despite all this, I wanted to see what was written on them.

I turned my head and looked. Words jumped out at me. There didn't seem to be any OT information, so that was good, although how would I know, since the OT data was secret? But these signs just seemed to be talking about "Lisa McPherson."

I had no idea who that was. Maybe she was sending people to protest for her. Was Lisa McPherson another SP like David Mayo? David Mayo was a name I had heard since childhood. I knew he was the worst SP in the world, although I didn't know what for. No one ever talked about David Mayo anymore. It was like he was Voldemort, a.k.a. He Who Must Not Be Named.

"Hurry up!"

I startled and looked over. The security guard was still there waiting. He gestured for me to get inside.

I nodded and opened the door to the building. I made my way down the stairs to the ground floor and headed to the EPF office. I picked up my pace. I was excited to find Grant and tell him what I saw. Maybe since he had just been out in the wog world before coming here, he would know who this Lisa McPherson was.

. . .

EPFERS WERE SITTING at the tables chatting as they waited for muster to be called when I walked in. Grant looked up and gestured at me. I hurried over and sat next to him. Two other EPFers were sitting at his table too, but they were my friends, so I knew they would like to hear what I had to say. Hopefully they could be trusted not to write me up.

I sat down and whispered to Grant everything that I had seen.

"Who's Lisa McPherson?" he interrupted.

"I don't know." I shrugged. "I was hoping maybe you had heard of her.

"The sign said 'something' for Lisa McPherson. I couldn't see what the 'something' said—"

Grant made a face warning me to shut up when a hand grabbed my arm. I was wrenched up and out my chair.

"What the fu—" I said, turning to yell at whoever just grabbed me, thinking it was another EPFer getting overexcited about something. But before I could finish my sentence, I saw it was Mr. Johnson, the Commanding Officer for PAC Base. She gripped my arm and yanked me toward the EPF I/C's office, pushing me inside and slamming the door shut. Mr. Cromwell, the new EPF MAA, looked up from her desk, startled.

"Did you hear what this SP is doing?" Mr. Johnson shouted, standing over me as she pushed me away from her. I stumbled away to the far wall.

Mr. Cromwell stood up and came around her desk. "What hap—" Before she could get out her sentence, Mr. Johnson interrupted, her pretty face contorted, her lips pressed flat against her teeth. "You think it's okay to go around telling people what the signs say and get them enturbulated? Who the fuck do you think you are, you fucking SP?"

Her words hit me like bullets. I stood in shock as more came raining down.

"You need a non-enturbulation order! You are off-purpose. I see you in the hallway, flirting with boys, you fucking slut! Get your shit in order!"

My body felt hot as rage coursed through me. How dare she yell at me? She didn't even know me or my intentions. And to throw me into this office in front of everyone like I'm a piece of garbage? My hands curled into fists. I wouldn't let this bitch get me down.

"Fuck you!" I screamed.

Her face jerked back as if she had been slapped.

"You're the fucking bitch! All because I told the others what a sign said doesn't mean I'm a Suppressive Person! This is bullshit. I'm trying my best to be in-ethics and you think I'm garbage. Well, fuck this! You are just jealous—" I paused to take a breath. "You are just jealous," I continued, "because I have big boobs and you *don't!*"

I heard my words reverberate through the air and hang there like a comic book bubble. I knew how ridiculous I sounded, but my statement was possibly true. A friend of mine was Mr. Johnson's assistant. Tasha had told me that she was always commenting to her that I was the only one she knew in the Sea Org who could manage to get a uniform so tight on my chest. Tasha had told me she thought Mr. Johnson was jealous since Mr. Johnson had tiny boobs. The most ridiculous part of it was that I had no control of what uniform size I got, and Mr. Johnson knew that.

The room was silent.

"You are unbelievable," Mr. Johnson said, her face white. She turned to Mr. Cromwell.

"Mr. Cromwell, make sure she gets handled." She gave me a disgusted look and then walked out of the office.

Mr. Cromwell turned to look at me. She looked tired. "It's muster time, so I'm going to go run muster and then I'll come back to talk to you, okay?" she said.

I nodded. Mr. Cromwell shut the door, and as it clicked shut, I collapsed against the wall and slid down to the floor. My chest heaved as I tried to catch my breath. Tears flowed down my cheeks as sobs escaped me. I couldn't stop my tears no matter how tough I wanted to be. I was just a loser anyways. A loser, and SP and everyone hated me. I slumped down on the ground and let my tears soak into the carpet.

THE NEXT DAY I received a Knowledge Report from Mr. Johnson. She sent it to the top executives at PAC. As I read the report, I felt numb. She didn't mention any of the comments that she had made, and there was no mention of her losing her TRs and manhandling me.

This was so unfair.

I grabbed a pen and paper and began to write my own report. I scribbled down what happened and then reread it. I stared at it for a moment, then shook my head. I knew there was no way I could send it. No one would believe my version.

Over the next week, whenever I saw Mr. Johnson, we ignored each other. Then my unit was assigned to renovate a dorm. Mr. Johnson was in charge, and I was nervous about how she would treat me. She surprised me by being polite and respectful as if nothing had happened. There was no contempt in her voice. I wondered if I had scared her off by yelling back at her. Maybe she wasn't used to that. On top of that, there were no repercussions from the Knowledge Report. Then, two weeks later, I graduated the EPF and was back in the Sea Org.

51

CAUGHT

The police car pulled up in front of the horseshoe of the Complex at PAC Base. Mirriam and I slouched down in the back. The windows in front of us were prison plexiglass, the passenger doors locked tight.

"We are going to be in so much trouble," I whispered as the policeman exited the car and went around to open our locked doors. I couldn't believe this was happening.

I was a couple of months into being back in the Sea Org, and suddenly here I was again . . . in deep shit. I had been posted at CLO at first and then was reassigned back to ASHO Foundation as a filing clerk down in the basement. I had only agreed to it because I knew the post was easy and my two best friends, Mirriam and Audrey, were also posted at ASHO Foundation and we would be on the same schedule. It was a near-forgotten part of the building, and except for a handful of staff members assigned to work there, it was mostly avoided. Luckily for me, my mom also worked there. She was the letter registrar and wrote letters to public around the world, urging them to come to ASHO and do services. It was nice to be able to see my mom every day for the first time in my life.

Away from the view of the public, the basement was decidedly nondescript with its hospital-style linoleum hallway and simple furnishings. The tubed fluorescent lights beamed too brightly, as if in overcompensation for the absence of windows. There was a large room with sliding shelves, which contained thousands of folders. These files contained records of the public's correspondence with the church, along with their current addresses and phone numbers. Finding the time to goof off away from prying eyes, I soon slipped into a comfortable routine. I made sure that the folder requests were taken care of and that there were no backlogs, then I'd spend the rest of my time doodling or listening to music. Sometimes, Ricky would come down and we would play hide-and-seek among the shelves. On the days when I was bored and no one came down to hang out, I could just lay my head down and take a nice nap while I waited for the minutes to tick by.

Each night, when my hour of freedom arrived at ten o'clock, I would race from the basement out into the fresh air. My friends and I would sit on the fire exit stairways chatting or go for walks around the block. Tonight was no exception, yet somehow I had ended up in the back of a police car.

It all started when Mirriam and I had decided to take a walk to nearby Los Feliz. It was a perfect Los Angeles night for it, with the air so warm it caressed your skin. Los Feliz was a trendy neighborhood filled with restaurants, coffee shops, and boutiques. We had done this a couple of times before and had been able to leave and return inconspicuously. We loved to wander around and act like we were regular people, not Sea Org members dedicated to clearing the world.

Mirriam and I had changed into comfortable clothes: exercise sweats, fitted T-shirts and sneakers. Not the most attractive of outfits, but much better than our stiff uniforms. The two of us then strode up Catalina Street, where we were less likely to draw suspicion to ourselves and be prevented by a security guard from leaving. While there was no exact rule or policy saying we couldn't leave PAC to exercise, we had a feeling it probably would be frowned upon. With that in mind, we breathed a sigh of relief once we were on Sunset Boulevard and had crossed L. Ron Hubbard Way and were almost to Vermont Avenue. Away from the security cameras now, we relaxed and eased up our pace. It always felt so good to leave PAC Base and feel like a normal person.

I passed the time telling Mirriam about how Patrick and I had wrestled once in the cardboard dumpsters on Catalina Avenue when we were supposed to be flattening cardboard. After wrestling, we had laid on top of the flattened cardboard and talked while the sun set.

"That's so romantic!" Mirriam exclaimed.

"I know." I sighed. "It's too bad that he's a bad kisser."

Mirriam nodded her agreement.

Patrick had asked me out when I was posted at CLO, and it had only lasted a few weeks. When he kissed me, it felt like a snake attacking my mouth, and it had turned me off. I broke up with him a week later, saying we were better off as friends. Thankfully he had agreed. Maybe we were too much like brother and sister. It was a bummer because after years of flirting and crushing on him, it had turned out to be such a letdown.

A police car driving past suddenly screeched to a stop ten feet in front of us, the red brake lights of the vehicle lighting up. Mirriam and I stopped and glanced at each other.

"We're being paranoid, right?" I asked.

"Yeah, totally," Mirriam agreed.

We had each had our own separate run-ins with the LAPD. But this time we weren't doing anything wrong. Feeling confident they weren't stopping because of us, we started up again. As we walked, the police car reversed toward us until it was adjacent to us. We stopped and watched as the policeman in the passenger seat rolled the window down.

"What are you two doing at this late hour?" he asked as he leaned his arm out of the window.

"Uh, going for a walk," I answered.

"At this time of night?"

"It's only 10:15," Mirriam said with a shrug.

The policeman opened his door and swung his leg out, his black boot hitting the pavement. He unfolded his body out of his seat and stood. The driver also exited the vehicle and strode around to join him. Each of them stood with one hand resting on a taser, or maybe it was a gun, as if preparing for an attack. Instead of being scared, I fought the urge to laugh. Why did they even care that we were going for a walk?

"How old are you two?" the cop who had been driving asked.

"Fifteen," I said.

"Sixteen," Mirriam said.

"Do your parents know that you two are out here?"

"Uh . . ." I glanced over at Mirriam. This was a hard question to answer. We were considered adults since we were in the Sea Org. But that was hard to explain to a cop. We also knew it was important not to put the Sea Org or

Scientology in a bad light. We needed to keep our answers simple and not draw any concern or suspicion.

"Yeah, we're just going for a quick walk, but then we're heading back," I responded.

"Where do you both live?"

"Just a few blocks away," Mirriam said.

"We are going back now," I added.

"Well, did you guys know you are out past curfew?" the driver cop asked. "Curfew is at ten. You shouldn't be out on the street."

I looked at Mirriam, who looked as bewildered as I did. I had never heard of curfew before.

The cops told us they would drive us home. It wasn't safe out here this late, and we needed to be more aware, they lectured. They suggested that next time, if we wanted to take a walk, we should go earlier in the evening when it was still light out. We knew that this was impossible, we had to work until 10 p.m. every night but we agreed and politely declined their offer to drive us back. We could get home on our own just fine, we told them. Only it wasn't an offer, and they demanded we get in the vehicle.

"Are you going to handcuff us?" I asked, suddenly nervous.

The policeman looked at me like I was crazy.

"No, we're giving you a ride back. You're not under arrest," he said. He gestured for us to get into the car as he held the door open.

Mirriam and I slid in the back seat and silently waited as both cops got in the front.

"Uh oh . . ." I whispered to Mirriam.

She covered her mouth to stifle a giggle. Gone were our hopes of returning unnoticed. We both knew we were going to be in so much trouble.

"So where am I taking you?" the cop in the driver's seat asked, interrupting my thoughts.

"Um, do you know where the Scientology church is on L. Ron Hubbard Way?" I asked. I saw the cop glance at his partner.

"Yeah, I know of it. Is that where you guys live?" he asked.

"Uh huh," Mirriam said.

Again, I saw the cops exchange looks.

"Where are your parents?"

"Um . . . well, my parents are there . . ." I trailed off. I looked over at Mirriam as she nonchalantly told the cops that her parents didn't live there, but she had a legal guardian.

"Well, we would like to go in and speak with your parents and guardian when we arrive." He pulled away and drove down Vermont back toward PAC.

The police car turned onto L. Ron Hubbard Way, gliding across the brick-paved surface. The street was brightly lit, with Sea Org members in uniform purposefully walking to and from the buildings despite the late hour. Mirriam and I glanced at each other and sank down in the plastic vinyl seats so we weren't visible through the window. Mirriam's face glowed under the reflected streetlights. Her eyes were dancing, and she looked about ready to burst out in giggles. I put a hand over my mouth to stop myself from joining her. The police car took a right on Fountain Avenue and another right onto Catalina Street, finally pulling up next to the horseshoe.

Peering through the window, I could already see two security guards exit their office and walk over as the policemen let us out of the back seat. I slid out and Mirriam followed.

The security guards asked what was going on.

I could tell by their faces that they were trying to look pleasant and concerned, but underneath they were pissed. It was inconceivable that we would be so out PR. After the policemen explained where they'd found us, and that it wasn't safe for us to be walking around this neighborhood late at night, the policemen asked to see my parents and Mirriam's guardian.

One of the security guards spoke on their walkie talkie and asked another guard to get my mom and Mirriam's guardian. I knew my mom was going to be shocked and embarrassed, but I also thought this was kind of ridiculous. All we'd done was go for a walk.

I glanced at Mirriam. She suppressed a smile. I pursed my lips and tried not to laugh. The Senior HAS pushed open the double doors and strode over to the cops. Security must have called her in. She was in charge of ethics for the whole PAC Base. Mirriam and I stood off to the side, watching them confer.

My mom arrived, her glasses slipping down her nose, looking frazzled and annoyed. She spoke with the cops and let them know that yes, I worked for the church, and that I was now considered a responsible adult. But she would talk with me and make sure I knew not to go wandering the streets of LA at night anymore.

I had never experienced my mom being a disciplinarian to me, so it was interesting to see her in the role. I felt a little bad for her, because she was not used to it. I glanced over at Mirriam, standing near her guardian, a woman in her fifties with cropped gray hair wearing a CLO uniform. There didn't seem to be any familiarity between them, which confirmed my thoughts that this was merely a legal formality.

After a bit more discussion, the cops decided they were satisfied and got in their car and left. When their brakes lights were just small pin pricks in the distance, my mom began to lecture me about being out-PR. I listened to her saying that wogs don't understand how we work and that I was an adult now—I needed to make decisions based off of what was best for the group, not just what I want to do.

"It's not like we even knew about this curfew," I interrupted. "Don't you think we should have been told that fact in the first place?"

My mom sighed. "I see what you mean. But if you could please not get into any more trouble, I would appreciate it."

Poor mom. I felt a stab of sympathy for her. Always getting reports about her recalcitrant daughter. She looked so cute, standing there with her big glasses and curly hair. I leaned over and gave her a hug, and she reluctantly gave me one back.

"You stay in-ethics now," she said as she pulled away.

"Okay, Mom, I will," I said with a smile. She sighed but gave me a little smile in return, then turned to head back upstairs to her room.

"Bye, Mom," I called cheerfully and waved. She turned and frowned at me. I don't think she liked that I was still in such a good mood.

Whoops.

She shook her head and then continued on her way.

I turned to find Mirriam and spotted her being lectured by the Senior HAS. The HAS looked like a petite elf with her short blond pixie cut, tiny stature, and elfin face. It was hard to take her seriously.

And there.

I could see it.

Mirriam's lips began to curl up.

Uh oh.

Mirriam had a habit of smirking when people yelled at her. Her eyes would sparkle as she tilted her head to the side and one side of her mouth quirked up.

I wandered over to watch the proceedings.

"Do you think this is funny?" Mr. Hansley said.

"No," Mirriam responded immediately, but her face still had a smirk on it, as saucy as you please.

"You two are outrageous. You need to get your shit together, fast."

Oh shit.

The fact that she had called me out made *me* want to smile. I bit my lip to maintain my composure. I didn't want to make this worse!

"Yes sir," I said.

Mr. Hansley shook her head. "Get to bed. I don't want to hear about any more of this crap happening."

We nodded, then turned and walked sedately inside. As soon as we rounded the corner to the Complex elevator, I could feel my composure breaking. I glanced at Mirriam, and she looked about to burst as I jabbed the elevator button. The doors slid open and we rushed inside. As soon as they shut, we collapsed against each other laughing.

"Oh my god!" I gasped. "I can't believe we just got brought back here in a cop car!"

I thought we were in for it the next day, but nothing happened. Not even a Knowledge Report.

52

LET'S GET FRISKY

"I bet I could kiss anyone if I wanted to," I declared as I leaned against my bunk bed. Mirriam and our friend Ashley laughed. It was after post time, and we were lounging around in my dorm.

"I bet you $1 you can't kiss Logan," Ashley countered.

Logan was a nineteen-year-old that I had been flirting with since we were on the EPF together. He had this sarcastic, dry humor that I loved, not to mention his scruffy, mussed blond hair, piercing blue eyes, and full lips. Kiss Logan? Oh, yes please. I liked the sound of that!

"I bet you I can," I said. I leaned over and shook Ashley's hand, then Mirriam's.

"Wait," Ashley said. "Are you really going to just go and kiss him?"

"Yup. I'm going to go find him now." With that, I turned with an exaggerated flourish and opened the door.

"Go get 'em, girl," Mirriam called out.

"Oh, I will," I said gaily. "Wish me luck!"

"Good luck," they said in unison as the door shut behind me.

I laughed and skipped down the hallway, off on my mission. I glanced down at my outfit. Sky-blue shorts ending mid-thigh, a fitted white T-shirt, and sneakers. Pretty cute.

I decided to check the exit stairwell to see if Logan was there. As I walked down the hallway, I was brimming with confidence. I was pretty sure that he would kiss me. He flirted with me all the time. Besides, it was for a bet. He would probably think it was funny. But when I arrived at the exit stairwell and saw him leaning against the wall smoking a cigarette, talking with Alexander, my stomach flipped.

Great.

Of course Alexander had to be there. Spencer, another boy, was there as well. Seeing them made my confidence drop but I shook it off. I could do this.

Besides, Logan wasn't mean-spirited like Alexander. The worst that could happen was he would say he couldn't make out with me because it was out-ethics since we weren't boyfriend/girlfriend.

"Hey guys," I said as casually as I could. They nodded their heads at me and continued their conversation.

"Logan?" I interrupted. "Can I talk to you for a second?"

"Oooh," Alexander and Spencer said in unison.

"What are you going to go talk about?" Alexander asked.

I ignored his question and turned to Logan. My heart thudded in my chest as I waited for his reply.

"Yeah, sure," he said. He took one more drag of his cigarette and stubbed it out in the pot in the corner that was overflowing with butts. "Let's go."

I trotted up the stairs. Logan followed close behind, so close that I could feel the heat emanating from his body. I stepped into the hallway and walked over to the closet just down the hall. It was large and lined with metal shelves crammed with luggage. When you joined the Sea Org, you were only allowed to bring one bag of your personal belongings, and this is where they were kept until you graduated the EPF into the Sea Org. I stepped into the closet with Logan on my heels. I let him pass me, then closed the door and leaned against it.

"What's up?" he asked with a slight smile on his face.

I took a deep breath. I felt a little faint. It was as if my confidence had flown off, taking all of my energy with it.

"Okay, this is stupid. I made a . . ."

I stopped.

I didn't know if I could say it.

"What? Just tell me," Logan said.

I remained silent.

"C'mon," He said and smiled. The smile was what did it.

"Okay," I agreed. I took a deep breath and stared down at the carpet as I blurted out my plan. "This is silly, but I made a bet with Ashley that I could kiss you. It's only for a dollar but it's more for the principle of the thing. I want to prove that I can."

I raised my eyes to his, scared to see if he was disgusted. Instead, he seemed excited, his eyes sparkling, his lips quirked up in a sexy grin.

"I'll share it with you," I joked.

"Okay, let's do it."

"Oh, uh . . . okay."

Is this really happening?

Logan sat on a large black suitcase that was standing upright behind him and patted his lap invitingly.

I laughed, walking toward him.

I sat down on his lap and put my arms around his shoulders.

"Okaaaay, what's next?"

"I don't know, aren't you the one running the show?" he responded with a smile.

Suddenly, the door opened. Alexander, Spencer, and Jay, one of Logan's friends, peered in like three elves, one head above the other.

I jumped off Logan's lap.

"What are you guys doing?" Spencer asked.

"Nothing! Just talking," I said hurriedly.

I glanced at Logan, but he just lounged back, his hand across another piece of luggage as if he was in a living room and not hanging out in a closet.

"Riiight," Alexander drawled out. The three of them strolled in and leaned back on whatever suitcases were available.

"What are you guys *really* up to?" Jay asked with a smirk.

"Nothing!" My cheeks felt hot and I hoped I wasn't blushing.

"C'mon, you can tell us." Jay smiled and held his hands out entreatingly. Spencer looked on. Alexander just looked bored.

"No, it's nothing," I shook my head and glanced at the door. Maybe I should just forget this.

Logan cut in. "We're just having a talk. We'll be out in a minute."

"Oh, hmm . . . I wonder what it is that you guys have to talk about?" Jay said as he scratched his head like an idiot.

"Don't worry about it," Logan gestured his chin toward the door. "See you in a minute."

"So that's how it is." Jay chuckled. I exhaled as they left and turned to Logan.

"You know, we don't have to do this." I crossed my arms. "I just thought it would be funny. But now I feel stupid." I laughed.

"No, we have a bet to win, remember?" Logan grinned as he leaned back onto his sofa/suitcase. "Come over here."

My heart raced as I walked over and sat down gingerly.

"Now, where were we?" he said as he put his arms around my waist. He leaned in and lightly pressed his lips on mine. A jolt of heat went through my body. We kissed slowly and then with more intensity. My body felt like it was on fire. Logan pulled his arms tighter around me until my body was pressed close against him. We kissed for what felt like hours, until we heard a knock on the door.

"Are you guys still in there?" Spencer called out.

Logan and I looked at each other and smiled. I hopped off his lap and patted my hair down. I hoped it wasn't too obvious that we'd been making out.

"You can come in," I called.

Spencer walked in. "So . . . what's up?" he asked, grinning.

"Nothing." I tried to look innocent. "Well, I have to get going. It was nice chatting with you, Logan," I said with a saucy smile. I walked out and shut the door softly behind me. I was sure Logan would tell Spencer what had happened, but I didn't mind.

I headed off to my dorm. As soon as I opened the door, Mirriam and Ashley asked me what had happened. Of course, I had to fill them in on every little bit.

"Give me a dollar," I said to Ashley as my story came to its end. She laughed and passed it over.

"Yes!" I laughed.

That night as I lay in my bed, I replayed my kisses with Logan over and over in my head. I wanted to do it again.

The next day couldn't go by fast enough. As soon as post was over, I searched Logan out in the stairwell.

There he was. Standing with Jay and Spencer smoking a

cigarette. I took a deep breath to calm my nerves. As I walked down the stairs, they looked up at me. Logan grinned and gestured with his head for me to join them. I smiled when I reached them and leaned against the wall, listening to their jokes and banter. When there was a lull in their conversation, I leaned over and whispered to Logan.

"Here's your dollar," I said. I pressed the bill into his hand. "You can have all of it since you did so well."

Logan turned his head and locked eyes with me. "It was well worth it."

We stared at each other until Jay interrupted. "Get a room."

I glanced at Jay and rolled my eyes. "Whatever."

Okay. Yes, I want to get a room, but I'm not going to tell Logan that.

Then Logan said, "Maybe we should?"

I covered my mouth with my hand and smothered a laugh.

Logan was obviously joking. You can't just make out if you aren't even dating! Once, fine. But twice?

He tilted his head inquiringly. I stared at him and felt my heart rate go up again. He was serious.

"Okay." I grinned shyly.

Logan turned and led the way up the steps to the seventh floor. I followed behind him, avoiding the looks of Jay and Spencer. I tried to keep my cool, but when I heard a long whistle, I couldn't stop my laugh.

"Shut up, guys," I said. I made a face at them. Spencer and Jay's laughter followed me as I continued up the stairs. Logan held the door open for me as I passed by. He shut it and followed me as I took the final steps to the closet. I entered and turned back to Logan. He sauntered in and sat on the same suitcase that he had used the last time and gestured at me to join him. The confidence of this guy. I loved it. I laughed. I walked over and sat on his lap, wrapping my arms around his neck, pulling his lips to mine.

HAVING a boy to make out with at night made life in the Sea Org exciting. I knew we weren't boyfriend and girlfriend, so some girls might say I was being a slut, but I didn't care. Besides, we weren't going out 2D. Out 2D was when you touched each other below the belt or if he touched my breasts. We were just kissing. You couldn't do anything further unless you were married to the person. Sometimes he would press against me, and I could feel all of him, but we didn't go any further than that. But after a week of meeting each night, our fun came to a halt. One night we had sequestered ourselves in the closet again when Logan told me that we were going to have to stop meeting up.

"Oh." I swallowed. "Why?"

A thought flashed through my head. He was bored of me. I put my hand on the shelf and started to lift myself off his lap, but he wrapped his arm around my waist, tugging me back.

"No, no. It's not because I want to stop. Trust me, I don't. It's because I am getting a sec check and you are coming up in my sessions."

"Oh shit." I sighed. That was not good. But at least the reason wasn't me.

"I understand. I don't want to be the one preventing you from your program," I said.

Logan nodded but didn't seem too pleased.

Suddenly an incident flashed through my head. "Wait a minute . . ."

"What?" Logan asked.

"I was thinking that I was getting evil looks from some of the Sea Org members at Bridge yesterday in the hallway. They must be in HCO!"

"Oh," Logan said. He grimaced. "Yeah, sorry. The MAA and HAS pulled me in to the ethics office to talk about this. They told me that I have to stop."

"That sucks, but I get it." I gave a dramatic sigh. "I'll miss making out with you." I smiled down at him to show that I would be okay but inside I was bummed.

"Yeah, me too." Logan gazed at me.

We stared at each other until he broke the silence. "You know what? We've already made out tonight, so there's no point in stopping this evening. Right?"

He slowly moved his head toward mine. I closed my eyes, focusing on his warm lips and embrace. I wanted to remember every moment of this night that would probably never happen again.

At midnight I walked back to my dorm. I wondered what was going to happen next. It was obvious Logan was in some sort of ethics trouble and had been for a while now. He wasn't on post and was getting sec checked. Was he going to be leaving the Sea Org? I wanted to ask him, but I couldn't since it was against LRH policy. I hated not knowing. If he ended up leaving, I would miss him so much.

THE NEXT DAY I saw Leslie, and she pulled me aside.

"Logan's gone," she whispered to me in the corner of the canteen, next to the large coffee dispensers.

"I can't believe it! Just like that?" I said. "But he didn't even say goodbye."

Leslie had heard everything about our late-night meetings in the closet. She gave me a sympathetic smile. "C'mon

Katherine, you know how it is. He probably didn't even say goodbye to anyone. People who are leaving always just seem to disappear."

"Yeah." I nodded my head. "You're right, I guess."

"Shoot." She glanced at the clock on the wall. "It's almost muster time and I need to grab something from my dorm."

"Okay, I'll see you later." I turned toward the cash register. After paying for my items, I headed down through the ground floor to get to ASHO for muster. I saw Jay, Logan's friend, up ahead about to round the corner.

"Hey, Jay!" I called out. Maybe he would know why Logan left so suddenly.

Jay stopped and turned. His face changed from curious to disgusted.

I stopped walking and watched as he strode up to me with his eyes narrowed.

"What's wrong?" I said.

"Don't you have anything to say for yourself?" he asked.

"What do you mean?"

"All of your shit with Logan in the closet got him into more trouble, and now he's gone."

"Wait. What? It's not my fault! Logan was going to leave regardless of what we did."

Jay glared at me.

I reached out and touched his arm. "Jay. You know that's true."

Jay shook his head and turned and strode back in the direction he had been heading. I watched his departing figure. I couldn't believe he blamed me. I sighed. I had to get to ASHO for muster. I trudged down the hallway wondering how I would get through the days with nothing to look forward to. I was going to miss Logan so much.

53

I'M DONE

I wrote a letter to mail to Logan but then scrapped it. He was out of the Sea Org, so there was no point in sending it. There was no chance of pursuing any sort of relationship if he was gone. I spent the next week going through the motions, but I could see the future in front of me mapped out. Day after day of the same thing. Filing papers. Fetching folders. Every once in a while, getting a day off. But that was it. A never-ending monotony. At this point, I knew what had been building in me for the past year. I didn't want to be in the Sea Org. But how could I get Bertha to take me seriously and not try to offer me a solution like a different post, or worse, repeating the EPF? How could I make sure she knew I really meant it? There had been three instances now where I wanted to leave, and yet somehow I had been persuaded to stay. I didn't want to be persuaded anymore. I didn't want to do some "ethics program." I was done with the Sea Org.

Done.

I just needed to get it through to Bertha.

I'm going to have to blow again, I decided. The fact that it would be my second blow would be a big deal. I hoped it would be taken more seriously than my first one. The Sea Org did not like bad PR, and runaways were definitely bad PR. If I ran away again, they would want to kick me out.

THAT NIGHT I WAS READY. Post ended, and I slipped out the front door of ASHO and trotted down the stairs to L. Ron Hubbard Way, lit up by the bright streetlights. I didn't care if a security guard spotted me leaving. It would be better to be caught early than actually having to blow, since I had no idea where to go. If I was caught now, I could let the security guard know I wanted to leave the Sea Org and hopefully that would be that. I could be put on the Decks and on the path to routing out.

Unfortunately, no guard noticed me, and I was now on Sunset Boulevard. The streetlights cast long shadows on the sidewalk. Cars rushed by. The problem with waiting until it got so late was that I was now walking on Sunset Boulevard in the dark by myself. I felt a prickle on my back. I threw a glance behind me to make sure I wasn't being followed by anyone who looked suspicious. The sidewalk was dark, with shadows between each streetlamp, and there was no one that I could see. I turned back and continued walking. I shoved my hands in my uniform pants, which I had not bothered changing out of, and quickened my step toward the Metro.

I entered the Sunset/Vermont station, the sound of my shoes echoing on the tile and bouncing up to the high ceilings above. There was no one there. It was eerie with the wide-open spaces and not a soul in sight. I spied a sign with the hours and peered at it. Shit. Now I knew why it was empty. The Metro stopped running at 10 p.m.

I groaned.

I was screwed. I had been hoping to buy a ticket and had some half-baked idea that I'd wander around Universal City Walk like the last time I blew. But now I couldn't even get there. I sighed. I didn't know what to do now. I just knew I didn't want to go back to PAC. I slumped on a marble bench in an alcove of the Metro and looked around. Maybe I could sleep here. I lowered myself onto my back on the cold marble and put my arm over my eyes to block out the bright light. I figured security would find me here within an hour or two. The Metro was one of the first places they checked for blown Sea Org members. And if not, I could always spend the night here, and by morning it would be noticed that I had been gone all night.

I squirmed to get comfortable and eventually found myself drifting to sleep.

Thud, thud, thud.

I opened my eyes.

It sounded like a set of heavy footsteps walking down the hall from the escalators. I sat up and peered around the wall that shielded the view of the hall. I hoped it was security and not some weirdo.

Coming around the corner was a policeman, striding in his heavy boots, his hand on his holster. There was nothing that I could do but wait and watch him come closer. His eyes caught mine and pinned me to the bench as he strode over.

"What are you doing here?"

Shit.

"Uh, I didn't realize the Metro closed at 10 p.m., so I was just taking a rest," I said.

"Why are you out so late?" he said.

I didn't have any answers, so I shrugged. I couldn't say

anything bad about the church, so I guess all I could do was be quiet.

"Where do you live?" he asked.

I debated on what to say and decided to tell the truth. "The Church of Scientology."

His face seemed surprised and a little confused.

"Follow me." He led me back up the escalator to the sidewalk on Vermont. Another police car pulled up and a woman cop came out.

"She's going to do a quick pat down of you, okay?" he said.

"Why?" I asked confused.

"We have to make sure you don't have any drugs or weapons on you," he responded.

"Oh," I said. The woman came over and patted me down while the other cop stood there observing. When she was finished, he told me they would take me back to the address. Unfortunately, until they spoke with an adult, he would need to handcuff me until he got some more information. He had me turn around, and the woman cop handcuffed my hands behind my back. The cold metal clinked as they led me to the patrol car, opened the door, and guided me inside. I slouched down in the seat. The lights flashed as we pulled away from the Metro station. I postulated that we wouldn't go down L. Ron Hubbard Way and make a scene. I did not want to be spotted by anyone. Thankfully, they turned left onto Vermont and then onto Fountain Avenue. I directed them to pull up on Catalina Street by the horseshoe.

The police car pulled up and the cop put it in park. He got out and circled the car. He reached for the handle and opened my door. I slid out awkwardly with my hands still handcuffed behind my back. The policeman gestured for me to turn around, and he unlocked the cuffs just as a security guard came out of the double doors. I wanted to crawl into a hole while the cop explained to him where he had found me. The security guard spoke into his walkie-talkie, and my mom was summoned.

Ten minutes later, she walked through the double doors. She hurried over to the policemen, her ID extended. After she explained that I was her daughter, the cop seemed satisfied and left.

"What the hell do you think you are doing?" the security guard demanded as soon as the police car had pulled away. The question seemed rhetorical, as he continued talking without waiting for an answer. "You need to stop getting brought here by the police. Its fucking ridiculous. Act like a Sea Org member instead of a teenager, do you understand me?"

I stared at the sidewalk and nodded.

"At this point, you can't be trusted. We are putting you on twenty-four-hour watch."

I glanced at my mom to see her reaction. She frowned as she peered at me through her thick glasses. I wrapped my arms around my waist, feeling small. I knew I had disappointed her. Again.

The security guard gestured for me to follow him. I turned away and left her standing there under the streetlight.

54

DECKS AGAIN

That night I slept alone in a room security seemed to have reserved for people like me who blew. A security guard was stationed outside my door, but I didn't care. I wasn't going anywhere, and with the door shut, I didn't notice they were even there. The day's events had exhausted me, and it wasn't long before I fell asleep.

I woke up in the morning and wondered what time it was. There was no window, and I didn't have a watch. I swung my legs out of bed, wandered over to the door, and peeked out. Noah, a former Rancher, was sitting on the ground outside reading a book.

"Hey!" I said. "What are you doing here?"

Noah looked up. "You're finally awake. I've been assigned to watch you."

"That's funny. A Rancher watching me." I laughed.

I looked over him, noting his white uniform. "Are you training to be a security guard?"

"Yeah," Noah said. "Who would have thought?"

"No kidding!" I stepped out of my room and plopped

down next to him. He looked startled. "When did you graduate the EPF anyways?" I asked. Noah was my age, but I
didn't remember ever seeing him around.

"I was on when you were on. When you were running
around with Jamie and Leslie."

"Oh yeah." I nodded like I remembered.

"So, who do you hang out with now that you're in the
Sea Org?" I said.

"Oh, you know, my regular friends—Craig, Joel, and
Steven," Noah answered.

"Cool. So what music are you into?" I pointed to the
Discman on his lap.

"Right now I'm listening to Blink 182."

"I love Blink 182!" I reached my hand over. "Can I listen?"

"Uh, sure," he said. He handed me one earpiece and I
popped it over my ear. He did the same and pressed play.

I nodded my head to the music, smiling. I noticed Noah
staring at me. I stared back, noting how cute he had become.

The song ended.

"Thanks." I handed him the earpiece back.

"No problem."

"Did you know you have really nice lips?" I said with a
tilt of my head.

Pink spread over his cheeks. "I do?" Noah asked.

"Yeah." I paused. "Very kissable."

Noah stared at me, then looked away. He busied himself
with his Discman while I began to daydream about what
kissing him would be like.

The rest of the morning passed in a happy blur, with the
two of us chatting away. But at lunchtime, another Sea Org
security guard came to replace Noah. With Noah gone, I no
longer had a distraction. I lay on my bed and mulled over

the events that had happened yesterday. Would I finally be able to leave the Sea Org? Had I created enough problems that they would let me go? How could I convince Bertha to let me leave?

THAT AFTERNOON, I was escorted by the security guard to the ethics area. My head was clear. I knew exactly what I wanted to say. I walked straight into Bertha's office, pulled out a chair, and sat down.

"I don't want to be in the Sea Org anymore," I said in a rush of words. She didn't flinch a muscle.

Damn. I was impressed. She had good TRs.

"I don't think I am an asset to the Sea Org. I am always getting into trouble and creating Dev-T for you. I just think it's best that I leave. Also . . ." I paused and took a breath. This next part was my clincher, to make sure Bertha didn't try to persuade me to stay. "I know that one day I want to have kids. If I want to have kids, I need to have a life outside of the Sea Org, since I know that rule about no children allowed will not be changing."

There. I had done it. Put it out in the open.

"Okay, Katherine." Bertha tapped her pen on the table. She paused. "You have been getting into ethics trouble since you joined the Sea Org. You are not a good fit. I will work on getting an auditor set up for your sec check."

I knew she was saying I was a horrible Sea Org member, but I didn't care.

"Okay, thanks." I wiped a hand over my face to cover my grin. "Should I move into the Decks dorm?"

"Sure." She gathered her papers and stood. From the look in her eyes, I could tell she was done talking to me.

"Okay." I stood as well. "I guess I'll go find where the other people on the Decks are." At her nod, I turned to go. No Sea Org member followed me as I left ASHO. I guess now that I was officially leaving, they didn't care to watch me anymore. With each step I took, the weight on my shoulders felt lighter.

THAT EVENING I searched out my parents at their dinnertime in the main mess. I needed to let them know that I was leaving the Sea Org so my mom could try to figure out where I could live. I scanned the crowd of members until I spotted her curly head next to my dad's balding one at their dining room table. I wound my way through the crowd, a bounce in every step.

I plopped down next to my mom in the empty seat.

"Hi, Mom! Hi, Dad!"

"Hi, honey." My mom gave me a sad smile. I guess she was still upset about the police bringing me back to PAC again. Whoops.

"So," I began, looking at each of them. My dad continued to eat slowly and methodically while my mom set her fork down and pushed her salad away. All around us, Sea Org members sat eating their meals and conversing, their voice like white noise. The large windows on the east side streamed in light from the midday sun, matching my bright mood.

"What is it?" she asked.

"I am going to leave the Sea Org," I said in a low voice as I glanced at the man across the large round table. You were not allowed to say that in public, but he seemed busy reading the newspaper, so I plowed on. "I don't do well on post here. I feel like I am creating Dev-T instead of helping.

Also, I really want to have a family one day. It's not like I can leave at twenty-five and just go have a baby. I need to start my life first! And then get a husband and one day have children." I smiled at this. "Don't you guys want grandkids one day?"

My mom peered at me, then shrugged. "I would prefer you stay in the Sea Org."

"Really, Mom?" I stared at her. "If I had kids, you wouldn't care?"

Her face softened. "No, no, of course I would. I just don't want grandkids to be one of the reasons you left."

Ah. I understood. The Sea Org guilt. She didn't want to be the "why" for the reason I was leaving.

"Oh no, I'm doing this for me," I said as I leaned over and put my arm around her and squeezed her shoulders. After a moment, she lifted her hand and squeezed mine. "The kids are just a nice side-benefit for you," I added.

My mom gave me a weak smile, but it was a smile nonetheless.

"Just do me one favor," my dad said as he wiped his face with a napkin.

"What?"

"Don't embarrass the Spallino name."

I burst out laughing. I couldn't help it.

Don't embarrass the Spallino name? What did that even mean? I honestly hadn't even thought he cared about the Spallino name. I had never felt like we were a close family. More like we were six people connected by blood, who chatted with each other when we saw each other in the hallways or the main mess and occasionally spent Christmas together. But hearing him say "Spallino name" did warm my heart. At least he cared that I didn't tarnish it.

"I'll make you proud, Dad," I said.

He shook his head at that. Maybe he didn't believe me because I was laughing when I said it.

THE NEXT FEW days were spent lounging in my dorm hanging out with Casey and Leslie. At night we sometimes would do estate projects that were assigned to us, but other than that, we were left to our devices. Casey was eventually persuaded to go back on post.

Poor girl, I thought sympathetically. Back to working long days on post forever.

Mirriam joined the Decks the next day, and I invited her to take Casey's empty bunk. That afternoon we walked across the street to the convenience store to get some super pops. As we walked back, sucking our pops, I regaled Mirriam and Leslie with my ideas of what it would be like when we left the Sea Org.

"I hope I get to go to a fun high school," I said as I walked beside them. It felt so good to be able to speak about what I wanted to do out loud. Especially since I knew Leslie and Mirriam wouldn't report me because they were doing the same thing. We all wanted to leave.

A FEW DAYS LATER, a PAC Base Sea Org member told us that we had to vacate our dorm for reasons unknown. We were told that we had to move into a dorm called the Pigs Berthing on the second floor, which was renowned for being disgusting and dirty. Pictures of it were posted on the bulletin board in the main mess to shame the Sea Org members that lived there.

Leslie, Mirriam, and I headed to the dorm to investigate our new living situation. We opened the door and saw bunk beds crammed into the sprawling room. Susan, a former Rancher, was plopped on the floor reading. *Of course* Susan lived in this dorm. She'd had a reputation at the Ranch for being slovenly, and it had continued in the Sea Org.

"Hi guys!" Susan said.

"Hi," I said. "Do you live here?"

"Yeah, why?"

"We are supposed to move in," I said. I wrinkled my nose at the idea.

"What are the empty bunks?" Leslie demanded.

"Oh, they just set up that one," Susan said, pointing to a bunk with no sheets.

"What's in here?" Leslie asked, poking her head in a door off to the side.

"That's the closet," Susan said.

"Guys, check it out," Leslie said. She waved us over. I poked my head in.

"It's large enough for our bunk bed!" Leslie declared. "Let's move all of their stuff out and move in here."

"Yes!" Mirriam agreed.

I nodded. This would be perfect. They thought they could punish us, but we would make the best of this!

When we were done, our three-tier metal bunk bed took up most of the room, with just enough space to squeeze in two battered dressers by the entrance. Luckily the closet had a window at the far end which let in a lot of light. Within a day, Mirriam had painted a beautiful picture of a woman on the wall with watercolors, I had put up posters by my bunk of Ben Affleck, and Leslie had posters up of the Clash and The Smiths. We had made our sanctuary.

. . .

THAT EVENING we were told by a security guard to help Alexander do Sophie. Afterward, we headed to the main mess area to eat some snacks that we had grabbed from the canteen and ran into a few other teenagers who were on the Decks, including. Sophie was my age, and gorgeous, with hair so blond it was almost white. All of the Rancher boys had crushes on her, but she didn't care. She was ready to leave the Sea Org after only being here a few weeks. I was impressed that she knew straightaway she didn't belong.

I sat next to her and asked what her plans were.

"I'm already getting my sec check," Sophie said. "So I hope to be done by Friday and home by the weekend."

When Sophie said "home," jealousy flared inside me, but I tried to tamp it down. She knew exactly where she was going to go—back home to her mom and back to school. Her life was waiting for her on a platter, whereas for us Ranchers, the future was a hazy void. I was excited for it, but I didn't know what it would be. I wondered if I would end up staying with some relatives in New York that I had visited once when I was eight years old, but I wasn't sure. My mom said she was still working it out.

I asked Sophie about the school she'd gone to and soaked in all the details, trying my best to be happy for her. Maybe when I left, I would have a life like hers.

THE DAYS WENT BY QUICKLY. I slept in, read books, and listened to music and chatted with Mirriam and Leslie. Not having a lot of work to do was strange. I felt a little guilty. But, I reasoned, it wasn't my fault that Bertha seemed to have forgotten about me. If I was able to sleep in in the morning and read, then I wasn't complaining.

All this waiting around was because we needed an

auditor for our sec check. A sec check was required before leaving the Sea Org. You were to be interrogated so the auditor could find out every overt you had committed in the Sea Org. This was per policy by L. Ron Hubbard. No one was to leave the base until the interrogation was complete, otherwise you would be considered a blow. On top of that, you would be in bad standing with the church. I wanted to leave through the proper channels and make sure that even though I would be considered a freeloader for leaving— someone who owes money for the courses they took—they wouldn't declare me a Suppressive Person. If I was declared a Suppressive Person, my parents would no longer be able to talk to me, and I didn't want that.

The problem was that our respective orgs oversaw setting up auditors for the sec check, but there never seemed to be one available for the former cadets. The other kids who had parents outside of the Sea Org received auditors quickly, like Sophie. They would be gone within a week, whereas it had already been three weeks for Mirriam, Leslie, and me with no auditor in sight. I think because our parents were in the Sea Org, it just didn't matter as much to get us routed out. But the teenagers with parents who were Scientologists living in the regular world had to get back to their old lives.

What really made me angry was that whenever I went to ASHO to check on the status of getting an auditor, I felt like I would get dirty looks because I was on the Decks. While their stares stung me on the inside, on the outside I smirked at any Sea Org members who gave me the side-eye. *Fuck you all,* I thought. At least I wasn't stuck doing boring Sea Org work. They were. Besides, I knew they thought I would turn out to be some degenerate out on the streets of LA, but I would prove them all wrong once I left.

Oh yes. I had plans. I would be successful and come back to the org as a public Scientologist with money pouring out of me. I would donate to the church and be on course, and they would have to be oh-so-polite to me. How I would become successful, I didn't know, but I was determined to do it.

55

SECURITY CHECK

"Start of sec check."

After a few months on the Decks, I was finally getting my sec check so I could leave the Sea Org. My auditor was Rebecca, a young woman with a permanent scowl on her face. She was always smoking a cigarette with her thin blond hair covering her face. Whenever I had talked to her, her eyes seemed to gaze right pass me, as if I was a fly on the wall. I suspected that she thought I was annoying. But when you are an auditor, you have to be nice to your preclear, so she was halfway friendly to me today.

After we had greeted each other, she led me into the security office, to one of two small rooms. It was just large enough to fit a desk and two chairs. Rebecca indicated for me to sit in the chair facing the door. She took a seat across the table from me with her back to it. The E-Meter and cans were set up between us on the table. Part of the E-Meter included a shield so I couldn't see what notes she made. In the far upper right corner of the wall behind her was a camera that would record our session.

I sat in the chair and grabbed the cans. My knee jiggled

in anticipation. Maybe I would get a win from this sec check. I knew sec checks were set up so that you could reveal all of your worst secrets, but you still had to end the session on a win. Rebecca began by asking me if I was hungry or tired, to which I quickly replied that I was fine. She started the sec check by telling me what a sec check was and read from a policy by L. Ron Hubbard.

"We are about to begin a security check. We are not moralists. We are able to change people. We are not here to condemn them. While we cannot guarantee you that matters revealed in this check will be held forever secret, we can promise you faithfully that no part of it nor any answer you make here will be given to the police or state. No Scientologist will ever bear witness against you in court by reason of answers to this security check. This security check is exclusively for Scientology purposes. The only ways you can fail this security check are to refuse to take the test, to fail to answer its questions truthfully, or if you are here knowingly to injure Scientology. The only penalty attached to failure of this check is processing or our refusal to employ you or issue you a certificate, and this will happen only if we find that you are trying knowingly to injure Scientology. You can pass this test by 1) agreeing to take it, 2) answering each question truthfully, and 3) not being a member of a subversive group seeking to injure Scientology."

A lot of this didn't surprise me, having heard this my whole life. I nodded that I understood when Rebecca prompted me.

Next, she asked me a series of questions:

"Is this Earth?"

"Yes."

"Have you ever drunk water?"

"Yes."

"Are you holding up a tree?"

"No." I laughed.

"Am I an elephant?"

I knew where this was going. This must be some sort of test to have a baseline so she could see if I was telling the truth or not.

"No," I responded.

"Are you a table?"

Seriously. These questions.

"No."

After a few more, she switched gears.

"Is this a security check?"

"Yes," I responded.

Then the questions became more interesting.

"Have you ever lived or worked under an assumed name?"

"Oooh, like a spy? Nope!" I grinned. Rebecca's eyes flicked at me before she continued, her voice smooth as stone.

Almost none of the questions applied to me. They were so outlandish that I laughed at a few. She even asked if I had ever practiced cannibalism. She didn't react at all while asking me these questions, so I stopped laughing and just answered "no" over and over while holding the cans.

Then came the next question.

"Have you ever masturbated?"

My heart skipped a beat. I wasn't sure about that one. I didn't fully understand what masturbating was for a girl, but I wasn't about to ask her. Besides, this had nothing to do with me leaving the Sea Org. And even though everything in session was marked confidential, I didn't believe the Sea Org did a good job of keeping PC folders confidential. I flashed back to when the Bridge Sea Org members had known all about Logan and me making out. They must have read his file. Who would be reading mine after this?

"No." I looked her straight in the eye.

Rebecca moved on to the next question.

"Are you guilty of something?"

"I feel guilty leaving the Sea Org, but I think it's better for me to go, because I want to have kids."

Rebecca didn't bat an eye at this, which made me feel better.

After a few more questions, she ended the session.

I stood up from my seat with a big grin. I was done. I could finally leave the Sea Org.

56

AWAY I GO

I slid onto the seat next to my mom's desk.

"So," I said as she set her pen down, "I am done with my sec check."

"I heard," she said. "Well, I have figured out a place for you to go."

I sat up straight, my back taut with excitement. "Where?"

"You are going to stay with my sister Millie and her husband in Florida."

"I have an aunt in Florida?"

"Yes, you do." She nodded. "She's my youngest sister. She has three daughters . . . I can't remember their names. But one of them is about your age. You two will be sharing a bedroom."

"Oh, okay." I was slightly disappointed. I had been hoping for my own room. But I pushed the thought away. I had a place to go, and my cousin was my age! Maybe we would be become super close.

"I have to get back to work now, but I hear that security is booking your flight soon," my mom said.

I said my goodbyes and rushed to my dorm.

. . .

THAT NIGHT IN THE DORM, I gushed to Leslie and Mirriam about Florida. I told them about my hopes for high school. Maybe I would join a cheerleading squad. What if I got a boyfriend? I lay on my bunk bed, rhapsodizing about my plans.

As for Mirriam, she had decided that she was going to be transferring to the Sea Org in Saint Hill, all the way in England. I couldn't believe that she had decided to stay in the Sea Org. She was telling me how she was looking forward to a fresh start in a new country and that she hoped there was a good-looking Scottish boy there who she could fall in love with. She was so excited about it, but I was just confused. Why would she choose to stay when she hated the Sea Org so much? What would be different? I didn't want to bring her down tone and dampen her excitement, so I didn't ask. If she wanted to get back on purpose that was a good thing, right? Instead, I asked how this had all happened. Why England of all places? Mirriam told me her dad had pulled some strings to get her posted at the Gold Rep Office there.

"Wow. You are going to work for Gold. You'll be an exec!" I said, surprised.

"I know!" Mirriam laughed. "Isn't that ironic?"

"Ha, yeah, it is." I smiled, but internally I was disappointed with her choice. She had been sucked back in, and there was nothing I could do or say to change her mind. Even if I did say something, it could come up in her Sec Check and I could get in huge trouble. Instead, I told her I was happy for her.

As for Leslie, she was still in limbo. All of her extended family was in France, so she didn't have anywhere to go.

There was talk of her staying with a friend of Garrett's, the security guard in charge of us. The friend lived out in Nashville, and Leslie wasn't too enthusiastic about it. But she supposed as long as she could leave the Sea Org, she would take what she could get. This I understood. It was worth the risk, just to be free.

A FEW WEEKS LATER, Mirriam told us she had her passport renewed and was flying out. We couldn't believe it was happening so fast! Leslie and I got together with the other Decky girls and decided to throw a party for her. We would do it during the day in the dorm attached to our room. We would invite all the boys who were on the Decks too. Since it was during post time, no one would notice them being in there, and if they did, who cared? We were leaving the Sea Org, so it's not like we could get into more trouble.

The next day was the party. We had picked up a few liters of soda and chips to munch on from the convenience store. We blasted some music and danced around. We all hugged Mirriam and wished her well. Early the next morning, in the dim blue light, she grabbed her packed bags and prepared to head out to her new life in the Sea Org in England. She whispered goodbye to me, and I sleepily waved and went back to sleep. When I woke up, I looked at her empty bunk. It felt so surreal.

A FEW DAYS LATER, I met with Garrett to sign my leaving papers. He led me into the small office in security that I was now familiar with and showed me the forms I had to sign. One paper said I agreed that I owed the Sea Org over $5000 for the courses I had taken on the EPF, and for the plane ticket to Florida. This was per the policy by L. Ron Hubbard regarding "freeloaders." Anyone leaving the Sea Org had to pay for the courses or auditing they had received. Luckily, since I hardly ever went on course and never received auditing, my freeloader debt was small. Some of my friends who were on the TTC would have a freeloader debt of up to $50,000 if they ever left, because they were trained auditors now. It looked like being out-ethics and blowing from course had worked to my advantage. I smiled to myself as I signed the papers with a flourish. After years of daydreaming about leaving the Sea Org and spending months on the Decks, I had achieved what had seemed impossible. I was officially routed out.

That afternoon, security drove my mom and me to the airport. We checked in, got my ticket, and checked my one suitcase, then walked to the escalator leading toward the boarding gates. I put my arm around her as we walked, grateful that she had taken time off post to be with me. We stopped at the bottom of the escalator, and I leaned over and gave her a hug. My mom teared up as I pulled away.

"Stay in-ethics," she said sternly. "And don't go out of valence!"

I laughed. "Okay, Mom. I won't be sucked into weird wog valences."

"Don't worry about me," I called down to her as the escalator moved away. "I'm gonna be just fine!"

She smiled through her tears as she waved at me. I waved back, then turned toward the boarding gates. I felt like I was on top of the world, riding the escalator to my new life. I hoped that I would be successful and have an amazing career one day. I would pay off my freeloader debt, do lower conditions, and donate thousands of dollars to the IAS. I would be the epitome of an ideal Scientologist.

ABOUT THE AUTHOR

Katherine is no longer a Scientologist and is a stay at home mom happily raising three rambunctious boys (two of whom are twins) in Minneapolis with her husband.

Katherine is working on her second novel, *The Bad Scientologist,* which follows her journey as she enters the "real" world. Follow her on Instagram @thebadcadet and twitter @badcadet to receive updates and news.

ACKNOWLEDGMENTS

Thank you to my dear friend, Mirriam, for being my biggest cheerleader during the entire process of writing this book. You have been an amazing friend to me since the ATA days. Even though you live in Australia, we have remained so close and talk about anything and everything. I love our conversations that can go for hours. From the moment I told you about my idea of writing this book, to the many, MANY drafts of it, you have championed me every step of the way. Your edits and suggestions are what helped shape this book. I couldn't have done this without you. I'll always be grateful.

To my friend Lucy, who had no idea about the world of Scientology. Thank you for being my first beta reader. Your feedback was just what I needed to figure out how to tell my story. And then you read it again for me after those edits! To give me so much of your time and thoughtful insight was priceless.

To Jessie and Plume, who I met on the EPF. Thank you for wanting to read my book. I value your opinions and thoughts since you experienced a lot of what I went through right along side me. It means so much that you support this book and related so much to it.

Megan, Anne, and Gayle, my final beta readers, who did not know much about Scientology. Thank you for your encouraging feedback. You made me feel more confident about publishing this book.

To the Ranch friends that I grew up with that are still in

my life. We've lost our parents, siblings and close friends through Scientology's disconnection policy, but we still have each other. Every time we get together, it's like no time has passed. When we're together, it's a whirlwind of laughing and talking over one another, with silly jabs and inside jokes. I love you all so much. Thank you for listening to me talk about this book for years, for filling in the memory gaps for me when I had them, and for encouraging me. I can't wait for our next girls' trip.

Thank you to my brother Jason for still being my brother. So glad to still have you in my life.

And a huge thank you to my husband—you met me when I was still a Scientologist, and you exposed me to a world that I knew existed, that I had been searching for since I was a child. I love the family we have created with our three sweet boys, and the many adventures we have together. I am living a wonderful life and I get to do it with you. On top of being an amazing husband and father, you also happen to be a terrific writer. Thank you for reading and editing many drafts and supporting me every step of the way. Thank you for everything. I love you, babe.

Printed in Great Britain
by Amazon

25366498R00199

To my dear friends,
Tony Conway & Colin Trier,
who share their Elders' Way with me;
and to the memory of
W. Bro. John Gunton,
stalwart of the
Old Bromsgrovian Lodge

Introduction.

When an operative mason became a master of his art, we have a fairly good idea of what that might have meant. He would be an expert carver, able not only to make perfectly square blocks from rough stone, but he would also be able to sculpt figures and to create intricate, flowing designs. No part of the building work was beyond him. And in addition to his practical skills, he would also understand the physical laws governing proportion and scale. He could lay out the work, plan the building, instruct less experienced craftsmen, oversee costs and wages. In short, he embodied all the knowledge required to build even the most intricate, the most beautiful, the loftiest of structures.

But what of speculative masons? When we become Masters, what is it that we are masters of? What skills do we acquire on our path to becoming?

The answers to these questions, I believe, hold the key to the future of Freemasonry and to the possibility that it continues to be a real force for good in the world. Without a deep, meaningful inner life, Freemasonry faces the danger that it declines into being no more than a quirky social club, famed for its charitable giving but, ultimately an institution without depth and without a spiritual or religious dimension; somewhere we can enjoy good fellowship but not a place where we dig deep into the realities of the world, the hidden mysteries, the truth of what we are and what we can be. The choice is ours. Do we want this ancient and honourable Order to become something that ignores the ineffable nature of our relationship with each other and with that almighty Creator in whom we profess belief or do we want to spend our time and energy exploring our true selves and achieving our true destiny.

Our rituals are full of hints and suggestions as to what it might mean to be truly a Master Mason and our legend tells us of an ideal Master who gave up his life rather than debase our art. If we are willing to take the time to dig below the outer form of our rituals, we can follow this Master and find clues about the kind of people we can become on our path to perfection.

What if we took these clues, these suggestions seriously? What if we conscientiously followed the injunctions found in our rituals and determined to live by them as far as we are able? Would that make us masters of something real: something deep and precious and worthwhile?

This book imagines a Master Mason, crafted by the ritual he follows and visualizes him perfected and complete, a shining example to others: an embodiment of the 'true godliness' of which our ritual speaks. It contemplates the rituals and lectures of each degree through his eyes and sees him integrate into himself the teachings–even the smallest hints and suggestions–that shed further light on the end of the journey he undertakes–the journey we all undertake–on the Masonic path.

Let us imagine, then, this ideal Master Mason. Let us walk with him, at least for a while, and see where his way may lead.

JAM
October 2021

The Meditations:

...let us invoke the assistance of the Great Architect of the Universe in all our undertakings;

The first thing that a Mason does before any major work is to invoke divine aid for that which is to come. Not only do we believe that God will give us the help we ask for, but the very act of prayer, our willingness to acknowledge a higher power and the stilling of the mind that results from the act of 'tuning in' to that power, give us a calm focus and a moment of being centred.

It is an act of communion with our higher selves, a setting of intention, a drawing in of energy before we open ourselves out to act in the world. It is a reminder that we are something more than a physical automaton that acts without thought, tossed about by currents over which it has no control.

A fully realised Master Mason stands on the threshold between humankind and God. By his strict obedience to Masonic line and rule, he aims to be perfect in all his parts and to become an ever clearer and more effective channel for God to work in the world. His every act is a prayer; his every wish is an intercession on behalf of his fellows; his every word seeks to uncover the love which is the true light of the world.

...of his own free will and accord, properly prepared, humbly soliciting...

The aspirant who sets out on a spiritual path must always act from his own conviction and not be swayed by the opinions or desires of others.

A Freemason, even before initiation, has proved himself to be a person who is brave and who has the courage of his convictions. He is someone who has studied and researched and who has undertaken at least a measure of inner preparedness. Most importantly, he is someone not ashamed to be humble and to accept that he still has much to learn.

A Master Mason, further along the same path, consciously maintains this inner balance and is able and willing to guide and be guided; to both lead and follow as the situation demands.

A Master Mason is aware of the strengths inherent in such a position as well as the difficulties that will be encountered and overcome as he strives to maintain it in his own life. He aims to develop the inner poise necessary to be humble yet strong; firm in his faith, yet always willing to learn. Above all, he cultivates the inner strength to hold fast to his convictions and to do, always, what he feels is right.

I will thank you to kneel while the blessing of Heaven is invoked...

The first thing a candidate is required to do upon his entrance to the Lodge, is to kneel to receive the benefit of Masonic prayer. Before each subsequent ceremony, this procedure is repeated, as we consider that no Masonic business can take place until 'the blessing of Heaven is invoked.'

A Mason is not afraid to humble himself before his Creator, nor is he ashamed to be seen to be thus in front of his brethren within the Lodge. The first step to wisdom is to acknowledge our own powerlessness, and our dependence on God.

With bended knee and lowered gaze, we ask for God's blessings on the next step along our path, and so we begin to understand that there is a higher power to whom we must answer and on whom we must rely.

A Master Mason's fully aware presence is vital in any ceremony. He can never be a disinterested observer. His duty is to add the weight of his prayers and the focus of his intentions to the words of the Worshipful Master and the movements within the ritual. The self-realised Master is a powerful force, and he acknowledges that he has a responsibility and a part to play in setting the new initiate securely upon his path, and to guide his newly made brother into the future.

...he may the better be enabled to unfold the beauties of true godliness,

If a Master Mason is to truly embody the 'beauty of true godliness' he can only do so through a proper understanding of the wisdom and knowledge available to him. The more he integrates what he learns into the way he lives, the more he is able to assist in the creation of himself in God's image. Knowledge and wisdom are the keys to manifesting our highest and truest selves and they can both be found within the teachings of Freemasonry. If we wish to become true Masters, we must be willing to find the hidden gems of knowledge that are 'veiled in allegory and illustrated by symbols' to be found within Masonic lore.

Hearing these words spoken to a new Initiate, the Master Mason should take a moment to reflect on his own progress along the path and to assess how much his actions reveal the nature of God. It is a moment when we can rededicate ourselves to the highest ideals of Freemasonry and understand that we are the lights by which our new-made brother will be guided through the darkness. It is an opportunity to feel anew the thrill of expectation as the path unfolds before us, and to strive for the things that will lead us to perfection, so that we may be fitting vessels for God's light and love on earth.

In all cases of difficulty and danger, in whom do you put your trust?

A Master Mason, hearing this question asked in Lodge, feels the answer not as a rote-learned affirmative, but as a deeply heart-felt statement of total faith. He knows he is not exempt from the trials and tribulations of life; nor is he so arrogant as to think that he is able to rise above them, as if the everyday concerns that trouble others need not touch him in his elevated state. No; the Master Mason is someone who is fully immersed in material life but without being swept away by its seductions. He responds to all mankind as a true and faithful brother because he knows the pain and the difficulties that all must bear. He is able to offer help and succour to those who are in need because he holds in his heart - in that quiet centre of his being - the firm, unshakeable faith that God is with us and that, though our trials are hard and we are stretched and tested to the limits of our endurance, our sense of being held in His hands gives us the strength to pass through all dangers and difficulties.

The Master Mason is always ready, able and willing to reach out his hands to help his brothers and sisters in their hour of need.

...unbiased by the improper solicitation of friends against your own inclination...

In becoming a Freemason, we take our leave of the mass of humanity and set out upon a lonelier and more difficult path. By the time we are initiated, this quality, this strength of purpose and will, is present within us and it develops further as we progress. Although we tread the Masonic path in the company of sworn Brothers, the individualism and focus that led us to knock at the door of Freemasonry in the first place continues to serve us well as we take on the mantle of Master Mason. It is in this role that we accept responsibility for our own lives and our own relationship with our Maker.

As Master Masons, we also take on the task of teaching others and of helping our less-experienced Brethren to appreciate and honour the path they now tread.

The Master Mason walks lightly but firmly, sure of himself and trusting his choices. He is true to himself above all else.

...uninfluenced by mercenary or other unworthy motive...

A Master Mason is a person for whom the selfish desires of the ego have melted away. He is the perfect ashlar, smoothed and squared by a lifetime's striving for self-knowledge. He seeks nothing for himself beyond what is due to any member of civilised society and, while he works to secure the physical, emotional and spiritual well-being of himself and his connections, he never loses sight of wider society and his place within it.

Keeping a due medium between avarice and profusion, he is prudent yet generous. He gives of himself because he understands profoundly the truth of our interconnection, and he always has the well-being of all as his wider hope and aim. He conducts his business honestly; he is kind and patient. He understands that it is through putting aside the petty, selfish ego that he will find happiness and communicate joy.

...a general desire of knowledge

In this world of instant access to information, it is possible for us to discover almost anything we wish to know. But it is not possible for any individual to know everything, and so one of the most important things we can learn is discrimination: the ability to identify what is worth knowing and what is not. A new Initiate has already made great strides in his ability to recognise a worthy endeavour but, as Master Masons who are further along the same path the Initiate treads, we understand that Initiation is just the first of many steps, and that the search for knowledge is not ended but has only just begun.

Masonry will bring us to knowledge, but it is only though our own efforts that we attain wisdom. A Master Mason is truly a seeker of knowledge but the truths that he seeks are not those of the outer world. The rituals of Freemasonry guide us to that which will make us better, stronger men: balanced, centred, patient and kind; trusting in the benevolence of our Creator and, at the end of it all, fearless in the face of death.

A Master Mason seeks the knowledge that will make him a 'master' of himself because he understands that until we know ourselves, we cannot fully know our Maker.

...a sincere wish to render yourself more extensively serviceable to your fellow-creatures?

The great wisdom of a Master Mason is that he understands the interconnection of all living things. The concept of the Brotherhood of Man under the Fatherhood of God is more than just an abstract idea to him. He feels it deeply in that quiet centre of himself and, in time, he learns that when he acts fully from that centre, the benefits will ripple out from him to affect his family, his friends, his brethren, his workmates and eventually the entire world.

A Master Mason will happily engage in charitable work both as an individual and through the initiatives of his Lodge, but he also understands that his efforts to make himself a better man, to be more attuned with his highest purpose and to serve God, is also a form of work that benefits all of humanity and, indeed, the entire world.

Thus, every genuine act of self-betterment is an act of service and a Master Mason's inner landscape is one that connects him with all his fellow-creatures.

…I will always hele, conceal, and never reveal…

Discretion is a key part of a Master Mason's armoury. He holds his tongue and watches closely the flow and currents of human interaction. He is generous with his time and his care; he can focus his attention to listen and respond with true brotherly love to the distress and needs of others. He makes no secret of the factors which motivate him, and he will talk freely and passionately of his understanding of the relationship between Creator and creature.

But on some matters, he remains silent - not because any actual physical harm could result in speaking of our Masonic secrets, but because he is alert to the psychological damage he can do to himself if he does not live a life that is faithful and true.

A Master Mason does not make promises lightly but those he makes, he keeps. It is this that gives him moral strength and it is this level of integrity that makes him a trusted friend to all.

…what…is the predominant wish of your heart?

The light of this world is not true light but, as Initiates, we are still encouraged to seek for it and to understand it as a symbol and a shadow of knowledge and goodness. Later, after undergoing the trials and ordeals of a Master Mason, we come to realise that worldly light, the absence of darkness, is not the true object of our search. We learn to let go of the idea of light as a symbol, and we come to experience its reality: a growing sense of certainty, a sense of being grounded; a sense of being centred, of being held and, above all, a real sense of knowing and of being in communion with that Supreme Being to whose power we all willingly subject ourselves.

Having once felt this communion, a Master Mason cannot help but turn his steps onto the path that will lead him to a greater knowing, a deeper connection and a limitless peace. He knows that there is nothing better and so, having fulfilled his allotted tasks in the outer world, he joyfully allows himself to seek his heart's desire: that oneness with the Divine that is our sure beginning and our hoped-for end.

...to stand perfectly erect...your body being thus considered an emblem of your mind...

A Master Mason seeks to control all aspects his being. He learns to surrender his ego to a higher power and he seeks to feed his mind with knowledge that brings him ever closer to that perfection which is his true self and his natural state. But before that, he must learn to control his body so that it might become a fitting vehicle for the spirit it carries through this material world. He understands that the body reflects the mind, but he also knows that the reverse is true: the more we train our body, the more easily our mind can be free to follow its proper course.

A Master Mason treats his body well and with respect. Ever mindful of Masonic line and rule, he holds himself erect so that his actions will be true and square; he walks tall and proud, a living plumb line in the world, to demonstrate the benefits of uprightness. He is a beacon for the world to follow and his light shines out in the darkness for all the world to see.

...the badge of innocence and the bond of friendship.

A Master Mason must learn to tread a fine line between the open-hearted innocence that allows him to experience this world in all its fulness, and a naivety that is, in fact, marked by an absence of wisdom and understanding.

True innocence is a captivating and charming quality. Used correctly, it allows us to be fully in tune and at one with the natural currents of the world. We laugh at that which is funny; we cry at that which is sad; we are empathic and sensitive to others because our hearts our open and receptive.

But innocence is not foolishness and so, as we walk the Masonic path, our innocence is upheld and strengthened by wisdom, knowledge and understanding. We aim to remain open-hearted always, but we must also learn discrimination: to understand that some experiences and behaviours will strengthen us, our brotherhood and our intimate relationships, and we learn to guard against those influences that weaken our resolve and undermine our determination to live our best lives.

It is on the foundation of this innocence, tempered by deep understanding, that our sense of self stands firm and our bonds of Brotherhood remain unshaken.

...and work with that love and harmony which should at all times characterise Freemasons.

One of the duties expected of a Master Mason is that he guides and teaches those who tread the path behind him. In doing so, he should not just impart the knowledge and understanding that he has gained; nor should he focus solely on the importance of learning ritual. One of his greatest tasks is to be an example to his 'younger' brethren. This means that he must relate to them with a sense of care and sensitivity that is the mark of a Mason who has fully integrated knowledge of God and self and is thus able to act from a calm centre with a loving heart.

A Master Mason embodies the virtue of brotherly love, and he does so by keeping himself ever mindful of his true relationship with his Creator and his fellow creatures. He knows that he is a child of God, and he sees all living things as his kin. He avoids judgement and cultivates love as his daily practice, seeing in every person a brother or sister of the dust. He may have come far along the road to salvation, but he never forgets to look back and to help those who may still be struggling to attain the heights that he has won. He is kind and solicitous, sensitive, caring and calm.

...may you raise a superstructure perfect in its parts and honourable to the builder.

The work begun at our initiation is not completed just because we pass to a higher degree. The superstructure that we aim to build is our life's work and it will take us all our lives to complete it. What we must remember, though, is that we do not know the number of our days and so we cannot think to ourselves, "I will dedicate myself to being a fitting temple for the in-dwelling of God next year, or in thirty years, when I am old."

The span of our lives is a mystery to us and so, as Master Masons who have already been given the insight that it is our clear duty and in our best interests to contemplate the truth of our mortality, we must not put off the opportunity we have been given to make of ourselves perfect ashlars, able to be of use in the building of that Great Temple beyond this world.

As we listen to these words, spoken to our new-made Brother, let us consider how well our building is progressing and rededicate ourselves to work alongside him to create lives of true value and worth.

...that virtue which may justly be denominated the distinguishing characteristic of a Freemason's heart; I mean Charity.

Charity, in its Biblical sense, may be understood as the highest expression of love, signifying that reciprocal relationship between God and humankind, and it is manifested through an unselfish outpouring of good-will and fellow feeling between ourselves and others.

A Master Mason who has attained the summit of Jacob's Ladder and who is in possession of this highest virtue is more than kind and generous: he understands deeply and with utter certainty that we are all one, that we are all creatures of the dust and at the same time the beloved children of our Almighty Creator. As such, he cannot help but manifest that love, care and attention that is the birthright of all of us who choose to place our lives in God's hands.

The Master Mason knows that any apparent separation from God is illusory and temporary and that, when the veils of this life are lifted from our eyes, we will see that we and He are one and that by loving each other we love ourselves and our Maker.

...part to be spent in prayer to Almighty God, part in labour and refreshment, and part in serving a friend or Brother in time of need...

Freemasonry is not a path of renunciation. Vows of poverty and chastity are not required of us, nor are we expected to withdraw from the world in order to turn our thoughts to affairs of the spirit.

A Master Mason understands, though, that his path is, in some ways, more difficult. It is easier to resist the temptations and attractions of the material world if you remove yourself from them, but a Master Mason walks in this world. He accepts its burdens and its duties; its responsibilities and its distractions, and he aims to remain focussed and centred, aware always of the spiritual, even in the midst of the physical.

We tread a middle path: we avoid fear and rashness; avarice and profusion; we hold our centre – that still point from which we know we cannot err – and we live immersed in the world, open and alive to all its joys and all its disappointments, but we carry within us the knowledge that those disappointments are temporary, passing clouds, and that a greater, more lasting beauty is to be found if we take the time to look within. Freemasonry teaches us how we might divide our time so that all aspects of our lives and our true selves may be nourished and nurtured: our body, our mind, and our soul.

...the force of conscience, which should keep down all vain and unbecoming thoughts...

Conscience is defined as a person's moral sense of right and wrong, which acts as a guide to their behaviour. The common gavel, such a basic tool but so important as the 'powerhouse' behind the primary work of an operative mason, is a clear signal that a well-developed conscience is the first tool required by a Speculative Freemason as he sets out along his path.

A Master Mason later learns to work with other tools, but he never loses touch with those fundamental principles which are his anchor and his pole star. His sense of right and wrong is the pillar that supports all his other work, and it forms the circumference of the circle within which he builds his life.

A Master Mason renews and recharges that sense every day, through the regular use of all the tools at his disposal. Knowledge, wisdom and understanding; virtue, honour and mercy; brotherly love, relief and truth: all of these things keep him in due bounds with himself and others and, through a daily contemplation of the significance and import of all these building blocks in the Temple we aim to build with our lives, the Master Mason keeps himself focussed, undistracted by those thoughts and behaviours that undermine character and weaken the soul.

…the advantages of education…

In becoming Freemasons, we step on to a path that directs our learning in particular ways.

At our Initiation we are encouraged to study the liberal arts and sciences; in the Fellow Craft degree we look more deeply into the hidden mysteries of nature and science and those areas of knowledge are enumerated for us. We understand from the Charges of the two degrees that this knowledge, fully studied and integrated into our characters will manifest as wisdom and in a life of usefulness, service and true happiness.

It is not until we become Master Masons, though, that the most important aim of education is revealed to us: the knowledge of how to die. The Master Mason gains and uses knowledge to be a better person and to live a better life, but he begins to understand, as he walks the Masonic path, that his true goal is knowledge of himself and his relationship with that Supreme Being who encapsulates all knowledge, all learning, and all wisdom.

The Master Mason learns to seek the hidden truths behind the outer appearance. He knows that his stay in this world is transitory and brief, but that he is part of a greater, infinite life that exists beyond the realms of all human learning. Education leads to the door of knowledge; the Master Mason opens that door and steps beyond.

...the practice of every moral and social virtue.

Living true to our principles, with the generosity and spontaneity of spirit that is the mark of a Master Mason, whilst maintaining a sense of self-care, is not easy.

A Mason is obligated, from his earliest moments in the Order, to live the best life he can in terms of his behaviour within the context of his family and connections, and his contributions to society at large. He is called upon to develop a practice of conscious living that exemplifies the best to which humanity can aspire.

The Master Mason, more established in this daily practice, understands that he does not need to trumpet his virtue to the world, and he realises that, often, more can be accomplished by working in the background, quietly and steadily.

Therefore, the Master Mason develops an inner resolve and strength with which he develops clear boundaries between himself and those aspects of modern life which he knows serve neither his own good nor the good of society in general. From his strong centre he demonstrates the benefits of living true to his principles, and he is thus able to walk the roads of this life in peace and contentment. In cleaving always to the highest good for all, the Master Mason transcends all political and religious divides, and is able to hold out the hand of Brotherhood to all.

...and to regulate your actions by the divine precepts it contains.

Our sense of right and wrong is not arbitrary. We do not take it upon ourselves to cast certain behaviours as either good or bad and we aim to focus on our own actions rather than judge the actions of others. We do, however, look to a higher authority when it comes to our own interactions with the world, and we try to regulate our lives and actions by the moral principles and divine tenets of our chosen volume of Sacred Law.

We also learn to trust our own intuitions and, as we become more established on our mystic path and centred in ourselves, we weigh up the principles laid down, sometimes thousands of years ago, and contemplate them in the light of our modern world. In this way we are able to remain true to those original principles whilst living comfortably and compassionately in the society within which we find ourselves.

Ever mindful of the fact that divine principles may be expressed differently in different sacred books, a Master Mason is not afraid to look for the common ground that unites us in Brotherhood, rather than the differences that could divide us. Where doubts arise or potential conflicts appear, he is guided always by that golden rule, to love God with all your heart and your neighbour as yourself.

To God, by never mentioning His name but with that awe and reverence which are due from the creature to his Creator...

A Master Mason makes it his practice to cultivate a sense of Brotherhood. First with his fellow Masons and then with all of humanity and, eventually, with all living things. Understanding that we are all creatures of the one Creator, we learn that we do not stand above or apart from the natural world, but that we are an integral part of it, connected to all other parts in an indissoluble web of interdependence. Through living in the light of this understanding, we come to realise that all life is an expression of the Divine and that the bright spark of life shines out in the darkness of this material world in the heart of all living things.

The Master Mason comes to understand this oneness and so treats all life with reverence and awe, including his own. Through contemplation of the teachings imparted to us on our Masonic journey, we come to understand that we, too, are sparks of the Divine and that, if we are, so is every other living thing.

Therefore, a Master Mason cultivates a sense of the sanctity of all life. He protects and preserves it where he can and, where he cannot, he takes it reverentially, with gratitude and compassion.

...by imploring His aid in all your lawful undertakings,

If a Master Mason is to live true to himself and close to his God, he must first ensure that his thoughts, motivations, and actions are pure and clear. We cannot use our position as a cover for anything that we would not be proud to declare before our brethren, our families, or the world in general. This is why our undertakings must be 'lawful' before we presume to invoke God's presence and aid.

A Master Mason acknowledges that human beings are not perfect, and he understands that God does not require perfection of us before we approach Him. But we must at least try to be the best we can, and so a Master Mason is one who will always be willing and ready to test himself against "...the square of God's word and the compasses of his own self-convincing conscience." To be able to do this, he must maintain a level of awareness that can only be achieved by constant practice and self-examination.

Therefore, a Master Mason is introspective and meditative; contemplative; compassionate with others whilst being unswervingly honest with himself. How otherwise will he be qualified to stand in God's presence and implore His aid?

...by looking up to Him in every emergency...

It is easy to be swept away by the tides of this world, to be caught up in the pitfalls and vicissitudes of material life; it is easy to lose our centre and to find ourselves, heart racing, catching our breath as another apparent misfortune surprises us. However focussed we are, however established in our practice, very few of us are immune to the feelings that such setbacks engender within us.

A Master Mason, though, is equipped with certain tools that help him cope. Firstly, he lives in constant awareness of that still centre within himself that is his base and the strong rock upon which he builds his life. But, more than that, he has faith, and through his faith, he trains himself to rely on God to sustain him in times of difficulty. Freeing himself from desired outcomes, he understands that all things happen for a reason and that every calamity comes bearing commensurate gifts.

Thus, a Master Mason is not so easily swayed; not so easily pushed from his path; not so easily distracted and un-centred by the ways of this world. His sights are set on another, more distant horizon and he knows that it is from there, the true East, that light will come to him.

...by acting with him on the square...

A Master Mason lives without guile. He is upright and clear in his dealings with his brethren and, more than that: clarity, honesty, uprightness of purpose and all the other excellences of character that make a person trustworthy and dependable are fundamental parts of his character. Using the building blocks with which Freemasonry equips him, he aims to build a structure that is both beautiful and strong.

Whilst maintaining a high level of self-care and the strong personal boundaries that are the mark of a well-balanced personality, the Master Mason makes himself available to help others in need, to guide those who are faltering on their way and to support those who are making their first steps on the path that leads to knowledge, wisdom and understanding. As far as possible, he avoids judgements and is open-hearted and generous in his giving. He gives time, care, and material aid to those who come to him, and he is a rock – steady and unshakeable – for those who are fortunate enough to come within the circle of his family and connections.

In an ideal world, everyone, brother Craftsman or not, should be able to rely on the integrity of a Master Mason. Let us all determine to enhance each other's reputations by making it so.

...by rendering him every kind office which justice or mercy may require...

To find a balance between the strict imperatives of justice and the 'gentle rain' of mercy requires a delicacy of spirit and a deep understanding of human nature. It asks us to mitigate the punitive aspects of justice with the possibility of repentance, forgiveness and redemption that mercy can offer, and it forces us to reflect on the possibility that everyone, ourselves included, can fall from grace, and so forget themselves as to act in such a way as to cause hurt or distress to others.

As Master Masons, we try to look with humble eyes, to understand that we are all human and that we are all, therefore, fallible. If we are in a position to administer justice, we will aim to temper it with mercy and even when we do something as minor as correct the mistakes of a younger Brother, we will do so with kindness and understanding, always aware that we, too, were once rough ashlars, living in the darkness of ignorance.

A Master Mason becomes a vehicle for God's light to shine in the world by always striving for this balance between what is right and fair, and what is kind. By acting thus, a Master Mason manifests true Godliness as, through him:

"...earthly power doth then show likest God's
When mercy seasons justice."

...by relieving his necessities and soothing his afflictions...

A Master Mason learns to cultivate a high degree of inner strength and resolve. The fully realised Master is master of himself: his thoughts, actions and emotions. This perfect self-control can lead to a lonely place and so it is important that we do not lose sight of the gentleness that real strength allows.

A Master Mason can afford to be soft in his dealings with others, and because his mind is ever fixed on the interconnection of all life, his heart is genuinely moved by the suffering he sees in the world. He is not disturbed by unnecessary drama, but he acts swiftly to give practical support wherever he finds a real need.

It is not an easy balance to achieve, but a Master Mason strives to maintain his centre whilst keeping his heart open to the needs of others. He understands that it is through fully sympathising with their suffering that he will learn to find his own humanity and reveal his own needs. He also knows that from this position of vulnerability he will learn to find and appreciate his own strength.

A Master Mason responds from his heart to the suffering of others and thus manifests that virtue considered to be the summit of Freemasonry: Charity, which is nothing less than love-in-action.

...as in similar cases you, would wish he would do to you.

The 'golden rule', to treat others as you would have them treat you is found across many cultures and reaches far back in time. Arising in the East, surfacing again in Greece and then to the Middle East where it became a central tenet of Christian philosophy.

It seems obvious that a Master Mason would observe this rule because he understands that he and his neighbour are not different and are expressions of the same divine life. It appears that this stricture exhorts us always to consider the needs of others before we consider our own, but it could also be as much about self-care and self-interest as it is about altruism. In modelling how we wish others to act towards us, we are ensuring that all of us, ourselves as well as our fellows, are treated as well as can be in any given circumstances.

In a way, this is only a starting point for the Master Mason because, as he deepens in self-knowledge and as he approaches ever closer to the Godhead, mutuality is subsumed into something greater, and the fully awake Master does not think in terms of self and other but his entire being is suffused with the reality of oneness and his actions, to himself and to others, are motivated increasingly and exclusively by love.

We do not live in isolation and although sometimes our Lodge meetings and the coming together of our brethren can feel like an oasis of happiness in troubled times, we must still do what we can to function at our best in the outside world.

It is not enough for a Freemason to obey the law: it is a given that a Mason will be a peaceable subject and a law-abiding citizen. But we also have a duty, as Freemasons, to raise up our fellows by any means we can, and when we see the injustices of inequality and greed, we do what we can to ameliorate their effects, and even agitate for them to be lawfully addresses.

A Master Mason is not a blind follower of authority. As he progresses along the Masonic path, he takes on an authority of his own, one based on higher laws and on more meaningful imperatives. He recognises and acknowledges the laws of the country wherein he resides, and he respects them without reservation. But he is not silent when those laws are misused, misapplied, and abused or when they result in exclusion, suffering and division. It is in those circumstances that the Master Mason can truly exercise his authority as he is well-placed to lay a path that stays within the due bounds of the law, but which leads to a better, kinder place.

...the practice of every domestic as well as public virtue:

It is not just out in the world that the Master Mason strives to achieve peace and harmony. The centre of his life is his home, and it is there that the principles he espouses are most needed and most regularly put to the test.

It is not difficult to present a calm and dignified demeanour to colleagues and strangers. Even at Lodge meetings, it is not hard to project the self that one aspires to be, but it is at home, in the routine of daily life, of domestic chores and of constant exposure to others to whom we are answerable, that we can know whether we are really the person we wish to be.

If a Master Mason is kind, thoughtful, caring, selfless, mindful of others, generous, etc., etc., then he must also be all these things at home, with the people who are nearest and dearest to him.

It is in this way that a Master Mason demonstrates and maintain his centredness. If he can be all the things he wishes to be at home, he will have a strong foundation on which to build the life that he longs for, the life that he will eventually dedicate to the service of his fellow creatures and to his God.

...let Prudence direct you,

The virtue of prudence is the Pole Star of the Master Mason. It is by prudence that he navigates his way amongst the thorny roads of this life, ever mindful of the obligations he has taken to be a good man and true. Prudence bids him consider carefully before he speaks and even more carefully before he acts. Prudence is the beginning of wisdom because it is the enabler of reason. A Master Mason uses his intellectual faculties to make wise judgements and discover his own happiness as well as enhance the happiness of those around him.

Thus, the Master Mason is forever mindful, using his knowledge and wisdom to tread a careful path of right thoughts, right speech, and right actions. He is an example to others who look up to him, inspired and reassured by his calm composure.

Other virtues are strong in him too, but it is his prudence that directs the others; it is prudence that allows him to understand the importance of temperance, to clothe himself effectively in the armour of fortitude and wield, always for good, the sword of justice.

It is prudence which places the Master Mason among the best of men.

...Temperance chasten you,

Temperance is not about abstinence; it is about control. In this sense, temperance is a natural consequence of prudence. The Master Mason understands that if he is to live well, at peace with himself and in harmony with the world around him, then he must learn to control the vagaries of his mind and his passions. He is constantly alert to the demands of his body for gratification and pleasure, but he will allow it to be satisfied only when he can do so honourably. He is not a slave to his body, he controls it with his will, and although he is kind, he is also firm and strong.

As he progresses along the path to wisdom, the Master Mason also learns to observe and recognise the working of his thoughts. Again, the mindfulness of prudence supports him, and he gradually comes to understand that his mind is yet another facet of his being that can be tamed and trained to seek his highest good.

Avoiding vice which tarnishes the spirit, the Master Mason seeks to walk a path which leads to purity and peace.

Fortitude is the inner strength that enables us to maintain our centre and hold fast to our ideals. Whenever we are knocked back by the vicissitudes of life, it is our fortitude that picks us up and sets our feet back on the path. When our minds are troubled and our inner calm is lost, fortitude gives us the patience and understanding needed to regain it; to refocus and reaffirm our intention to progress and grow.

A Master Mason uses his strength to uphold the right, whether it be in his own life or in his dealings with others. Physical strength is not the issue here: the flesh is subject to all manner of affliction and to the degradations of age, but our will, our inner compass and guide, and our sense of ourselves as co-creators of a perfect world, can all, with correct effort, deepen and expand with the passing years.

Thus, a Master Mason grows in strength with age. He comes to understand that the signifiers of worldly strength and material gain lead, inevitably, to the cold and lonely grave, but that things of the spirit, those things which cultivate our sense of ourselves as spiritual beings inhabiting a physical body, allow us to increase our understanding of our true and eternal relationship with our Creator, and so to establish an inner strength that is unshakeable, even in the face of death.

...Justice be the guide of all your actions.

Justice is the dividing line between right and wrong. It is the 'no man's land' that transcends race, creed, gender, politics – everything that has the potential to divide and separate us. Justice is blind to all our differences, and desires only for every person who seeks her aid to be treated equitably, with fairness and without distinction.

It is the virtue to which all Master Masons should aspire. Even if all other virtues fail and fall away from him, let justice be left to ensure that this Master of the Craft has learned its most important lesson: that all are brothers and sisters, children of one God; that an indissoluble bond unites us all. In the light of this understanding, the Master Mason treats his fellow creatures as they deserve, and advocates for fair laws and equal rights for all with no taint of prejudice or discrimination.

By acting justly in the world, the Master Mason does his bit to ensure that civil society remains truly civil and that all members of society can achieve security and happiness.

If justice is the highest of virtues, so the Master Mason should strive to act by its principles and aim to become not just a good Mason, but the best of men.

Be especially careful to maintain in their fullest splendour... Benevolence and Charity.

Benevolence is not so much a way of doing things but is more a way of being. It is a positive mindset, a default position of goodwill to all and, at its most developed, it is a sincere wish for all beings to attain freedom and peace.

Charity is about doing; about acting effectively in the world to improve the lot of those afflicted by the miseries of poverty, illness, war, civil unrest and all the other troubles that can beset us.

But the two are mentioned together here and a Freemason would do well to take time to contemplate the link between them. It is not difficult to fathom: by cultivating benevolence, our hearts are moved to charity, and so we begin to act in a way befitting Free-masons who are sworn to uphold the Brotherhood of Man.

A Master Mason, well established in his practice of cultivating benevolence, becomes a centre of loving actions and charitable service to his family, friends, connections, and beyond, into the wider communities of which he finds himself a part. He is the one in whom those troubled and afflicted will find both a sympathetic ear and an open heart. And provided it causes no impediment to himself or his family, he will offer, as far as he is able, practical support and succour.

Secrecy,

For Freemasons, secrecy is synonymous with silence but it could be more accurately defined as the skill of judicial reticence: knowing when to speak and when not; knowing what to say and what to hold back.

Ironically, a good Freemason is always willing to talk about the Order and its many benefits because he is always on the look-out for other men who might be brought to consider the possibility of knocking on that welcoming door.

But a Master Mason, well-versed in his art, develops discrimination. He understands how the keeping of his obligations maintains his inner strength and gives him a sense of being truly anchored to the values he has sworn to uphold. He will not put himself in a position where he may inadvertently reveal that which he has promised to conceal. and if he is pressured to do so, he will speak instead of the wider principles of Freemasonry which he knows are more important and more valuable to explain to the uninitiated.

The Master Mason understands that his secrecy or silence is one source of his moral strength and that, being so personal and so integral to his individual being, his secrets cannot be known except by those who come by them honourably.

Fidelity.

Fidelity is not just simple faith. We can believe in God and still stray from the path we know to be the right one. Fidelity is more than faith, it is a fierce adherence, an unwavering determination to maintain integrity in all things. It is not about believing in God so much as being true to ourselves and our beliefs. We take vows of fidelity; we pledge our fidelity, and we aspire to emulate the fidelity shown by our Master who chose death rather than to live a life dishonoured by an abandonment of his vows.

Fidelity is one of the key traits of a Master Mason who has studied and searched and meditated upon the truth. He has found his centre, and he walks through the world unshaken by its vicissitudes. He understands that there will be sorrow and pain as well as happiness and joy, and he learns to approach all vagaries of this material existence with equanimity. He holds true to his core beliefs and renews his commitment to them every day by living out the philosophy of brotherhood in all his interactions with his fellow creatures.

It is this rectitude of understanding and of action; this firmness and commitment to live true to our beliefs that is what we mean when we talk of fidelity. It is one of the signs by which a true Master Mason may be known.

Obedience.

Obedience may be taken to be a strict adherence to the precepts and principles of Freemasonry. We are expected to be obedient to the Master and officers so as to play our part in the wise ruling and good order of the Lodge. We are expected without question to obey the rules of our Order with regard to keeping our secrets inviolable and our rituals private in order that we may preserve their value and power.

But, for us, obedience is never blind. We act from a position of understanding and acceptance, and we are therefore actively involved in the practice of obedience as an extension of that inner discipline which leads us to a true mastering of ourselves and our passions.

Therefore, a Master Mason is not a passive follower, nor is he blindly obedient to dictates delivered to him from above. Instead, he is actively committed to developing self-discipline and inner strength and he understands that to do so, he must remain true and hold fast to the principles of Brotherly Love, Relief and Truth.

Thus obedience, for a Master Mason, is not an externally imposed set of rules to follow, but is a strict and conscious adherence to those principles he willingly embraces and openly espouses. It is obedience to his true, higher self.

…to study more especially… the liberal Arts and Sciences…

The study of the seven Liberal Arts and Sciences is enjoined upon us to "… ever render us susceptible to the benignity of a Supreme Being." In other words, the more that we understand those subjects, the more we will come to understand that they are an expression of the human understanding of Divine laws and that within their constructs of shape and form, of proportion and symmetry, of harmony and order, are to be found the traces of Divinity for which our hearts long and which we, as Master Masons, aim to manifest and embody in our lives.

Intellectual understanding is not an end in itself, and knowledge unadorned by understanding and wisdom serves no real purpose. But knowledge, understanding and wisdom together are the keys to the door that gives entry to the Holy of Holies, where we will encounter the divine presence we know, in our hearts, is there.

A Master Mason is thus enjoined to study these Liberal Arts and Sciences to increase in knowledge and understanding, but his learning is always tempered by the wisdom to grasp the fact that human learning is but a reflection of universal truths and laws, and that all knowledge of any worth will lead us eventually to our true selves and to God.

...to endeavour to make a daily advancement in Masonic knowledge.

To reach the summit of Freemasonry, that "...ethereal mansion, veiled from mortal eyes, eternal in the heavens..." is a lifetime's work and we understand that continual practice and constant study are vital aids to us in our journey.

But to make a "...daily advancement in Masonic knowledge..." does not just imply that we must learn something new, or even that we must deepen our understanding every day. It might also mean that we must make the effort to act from the base of our understanding of the teachings of Freemasonry.

In other words, we move forward, not just by our own learning, but also by acting in such a way that our actions and interactions with others are fully informed by our integration of the fundamental Masonic teachings of unity and Brotherhood.

And so, advancing in Masonic knowledge is not just an intellectual exercise in academic or ritual understanding, but for the true Master Mason, it is moving through the world in such a way as to share and communicate the light of wisdom, knowledge and understanding, the summit and peak and culmination of which is love.

...indelibly imprint on your heart the sacred dictates of Truth, of Honour, and of Virtue.

For a Master Mason, truth is never partial and is never divisive. Through study and contemplation, he comes to understand the Truth that underlies all truths, that great yet simple comprehension of oneness.

Nor do Honour and Virtue imply anything other than acting in the light of that Truth.

But a Master Mason must do more than act. He must become the embodiment of the truths and virtues he seeks to comprehend. It is not a question of remembering to act in a certain way although, of course, that must be our practice as we embark on our path. But practice makes perfect, and the true Master Mason does not need to 'remember' to act honourably; he is honourable, deep into the core and centre of his being and so it is impossible for him to act in any other way.

To imprint a way of being on our hearts is no simple matter. It is a lifetime's work, a slow and steady treading of a noble path. It is the narrow way of self-discipline and conscious intention; of presence, of kindness and, always, of love.

As Masons we should so act on the Square, as to enable us to part on the Level with all mankind,

Even if we consider the fact that we are Freemasons to be one of our key self-identifiers, we must remember that to be a Mason is not to be separate from the rest of humanity, but, on the contrary, it is to fully and deeply acknowledge that we are fundamentally and irrevocably connected to our fellow creatures; to understand that we are one. But if, as Masons, we are to be of any use to the world, we also need to adhere to those precepts of Freemasonry that are peculiarly ours.

In the same way that yeast is not flour but becomes an integral part of the dough, so a Master Mason learns that he is both intimately bound up with humanity and, at the same time, apart from it. His nature is all human but, through the knowledge he gains and the wisdom he acquires, his gaze is no longer fixed on the minutiae of human affairs but on loftier, more distant horizons.

Thus, the Master Mason acts in the world, able to love and empathise with his fellows but aware always of a higher calling and a greater Light. Like yeast: inseparable in the mix but vital for the process that will cause the dough to rise and fulfil its destiny, to become a perfect loaf!

To learn to rule and subdue my passions, and make a further progress in Masonry.

The path to becoming a Master of any craft is not an easy one. An operative Master Mason would have served at least seven years as an apprentice and journeyman, and yet we, speculative Masons, can become Masters in a far shorter time. In some parts of the world, it is even possible to receive all three degrees in a day! If this is true, we must wonder what our Mastership is for and what it can mean.

A Master Mason is not made so by ceremony alone but by a lifetime of study, contemplation, and self-improvement. A true Master Mason is not just a master of Masonic ritual or of Masonic history and lore. A true Master Mason is master of himself. He has faced the darkness within himself, he has overcome the traumas and learned the lessons of childhood; he has acknowledged and learned to subdue his passions.

Self-knowledge is the aim of all our rituals and all Masonic teachings. A Master Mason knows, or at least, he is clearly told, that within his mortal frame there resides a Divine spark and it is this Divine spark that is the object of our research. When we make our 'further progress in Masonry' it is not in mastering ritual, it is in mastering ourselves. A true Master Mason understands this and knows it to be his life's work.

...and to be brought from darkness.

We enter Freemasonry in a state of darkness, and through various symbols and rituals, we are gradually led towards Light. We know that darkness represents ignorance, our 'infant state' of being unformed and unpolished and, as we grow in understanding and self-knowledge, we become perfected, smoothed and squared, fit to become a part of that great temple of humanity, yearning and striving for the Divine. Our blindfolds are removed, our compasses are fully revealed, and we are able to work with the full range of our abilities to delve deeper into the hidden mysteries.

And so it is that a Master Mason, in his fullness, is a co-creator of all that is worthy in life. He has the tools at his disposal that will allow him to see the Universal Truth within every partial, partisan truth and he will be able to speak and act with the authority of real knowledge and deep understanding. Having trodden the hard road himself, and having climbed Jacob's ladder, he is full of compassion for those still on the way. He has not only emerged from darkness himself, but he is also an instrument by which others may do the same. A fully realised Master Mason is, truly, a Light to the world.

...a Freemason's, tongue, which should speak well of a Brother absent or present,

Our tongues are the most potent weapon in our bodies. With them we can inflict terrible wounds or apply the most healing of balms. We can destroy reputations or build them up; we can encourage and teach, or we can undermine and create confusion and ignorance. We can use them to open up a path to Truth or we can conceal and obfuscate. The choice is ours.

Our obligations remind us, time and again, to use our tongues wisely. To keep silence where necessary and to speak well of others, particularly our brethren. We can even use them to gently correct and admonish when appropriate, but the point is that we should always use them kindly and mindfully.

There is another teaching, though, that we would do well to remember, because we also need to understand the damage we can do to ourselves if we speak negatively, slanderously, or unkindly:

"Not that which goeth into the mouth defileth a man; but that which cometh out of the mouth, this defileth a man."

And so, one of the greatest challenges a Master Mason faces is that of mastering his speech, to understand its power and to use it only to promote the common good.

That my heart might conceive before my eyes should discover.

A Master Mason must learn to be in touch with the inner workings of his own heart and mind. Whilst Freemasonry encourages us to use our intellect to study and learn, it also recognises that the ultimate lesson of Freemasonry – the calm acknowledgement and facing of our mortality – can only be accomplished by contemplation, and not by intellectual effort.

And so, while we aim to cultivate our minds through learning, we must also develop a practice that will allow us to come into what Krishna Das calls 'the heart space,' that part of ourselves that is at once the centre and circumference of our being.

As Freemasons, we symbolise it as the point within the circle from which we can only act from the truth of our being and, at the same time, we understand it to be the circle which sets the due bounds of our earthly existence.

This is the great mystery: that everything we seek can be found within us, in this great cathedral, this glorious Temple of our hearts.

A Master Mason is not made by book learning alone because he must learn to bring the consciousness and peace of this 'heart space' into his everyday life. It is by this peace, this 'centredness,' this loving heart, that he may be known.

Having sought in my mind, I asked of my friend, he knocked, and the door of Freemasonry became open unto me.

A Master Mason can be completely self-sufficient as he has all that he needs to live well and happily. He has an inner calm, a sense of peace, a clear understanding of right and wrong and he holds fast to the great virtues of Faith and Hope.

At the same time, he knows that his life has not achieved its zenith if he is unable to practise that crowning Masonic virtue of Charity – and to do that, he needs other people around him.

The path of a Master Mason is not that of a monk or ascetic, cut off from the world, seeking his own salvation. A Master Mason must learn to walk through this world and yet remain as calm, as centred and as full of love as any self-realised monk. This is not easy. It requires a daily practice of contemplation and inner focus and, above all, it requires support.

We find our centre within; we find our purpose within, but to work effectively in world, we need a friend or brother to open the door for us and, without doubt, we must be there to open the door for others to come into the light and begin the long ascent to the Godhead.

As Baba Ram Dass said, "We are all just walking each other home."

...to cause me never to shut my ears unkindly to the cries of the distressed, particularly a Brother Mason,

The summit of Freemasonry is Charity and, indeed, Freemasonry is known for its charitable work across much of the world. But Charity is also love in action and the Master Mason who truly aims to achieve the highest peaks of the Masonic path must be willing to do more than simply put his hand in his pocket.

To be charitable in the worldly sense – to be moved to give to those in need – is the first manifestation of this virtue but we can climb higher still. Beyond an intellectual understanding of the need and desirability of helping others, is an opening and flowering of the heart that leads us to a wonderland of compassion and connection. At this deeper level we come to understand that the highest teachings of Freemasonry are not about generosity, but are about unity.

When the apprehension of Charity leads us to that outpouring of love, and when that love leads us to a spontaneous and unstoppable urge to lift all of humanity out of their ignorance and suffering, and to help show them the way to the heights, it is then we may consider ourselves to have taken the first step on the final few rungs of Jacob's ladder.

Wisdom to conduct us in all our undertakings,

Mastership in not conferred in an instant and, although it is theoretically possible to become a Master Mason in the length of time it takes to perform the three ceremonies, true Mastership takes longer to develop and is more difficult to attain. Just as a rough ashlar cannot be smoothed and squared by a single blow, so a Mason's mind and heart must be perfected over time.

With sometimes rough blows, we are shaped by time and effort, and eventually, we may arrive at a point where we are fit and ready to become a part of that great eternal Temple where all divisions and strivings cease.

The virtue of wisdom, like Mastership is the achieved by time and effort. As Master Masons, we tread the earth with firm and humble step. Our hearts and minds are open to the possibility of communion and through study, contemplation, and disciplined daily practice, we gradually acquire knowledge and understanding. If we also learn compassion and tolerance; if we accept in both our hearts and minds, the reality of our Brotherhood with all, then it is possible that, in time, we will also come to wisdom.

Strength to support us under all our difficulties,

It is not just by our own strength that we stand upright. Wisdom, Strength and Beauty are the three great pillars that support every Freemasons Lodge and while it is true that our individual strengths add to the strength of our Lodge, it is equally true that our Lodges, founded as they are on these Divine attributes, lend us their strength, their wisdom, and their beauty.

A Master Mason who manifests these attributes in his life is aware that he is inspired and nourished by the institution of Freemasonry as a whole: its teachings, its philosophy, its blueprint for living a good life. But it also means that he is inspired by his own Lodge or Lodges in particular: their peculiar atmosphere and ambience; the way they foster brotherhood amongst their members. And, of course, it means by the individual members of his Lodge: those brother Masons with whom he has particular and personal friendships and with whom he is able to practise the wider principles of Universal brotherhood on a daily basis.

An individual Freemason can see that he does not need purely physical strength to make progress, but a Master Mason understands something deeper: that he relies on all facets of Freemasonry to arm him with a strength that transcends his physical limitations.

Beauty to adorn the inward man.

The third great pillar supporting our Lodges is Beauty. If we are to cultivate an inner beauty, we must look to the world to gain an idea of what it is we are trying to achieve.

As Masons, we recognise in the world of forms a symmetry and order that point undeviatingly to the Divine Will that created it. Even on a molecular and atomic level we can observe forces of balance and attraction that hint at the ultimate beauty of universal love.

Within our own lives, Master Masons strive to emulate that sense of symmetry and order. We, too, move through the world balancing and attracting those forces that keep our feet on a righteous path and our eyes on the highest peaks of human attainment.

This idea that we must cultivate an inner beauty is one of the keys that enables us to open the door to ourselves as Masters of our Craft.

A man who is inwardly beautiful is one who is at peace with himself and the world. His relationships are marked by openness, kindness, and a generosity of spirit. Upheld by the wisdom of knowledge and understanding, and the strength that comes of true faith, he manifests a love for all in his dealings with others. He is a man perfected by his longing for, and his clinging to, the Divine.

The bedrock of a Master Mason's ability to be in the world and yet remain untroubled and at peace, is his Faith in a Supreme Being.

We are not called upon to try to define the nature of that Being, nor to adopt any particular set of beliefs in that regard. Nevertheless, the Masonic conception of God – or rather, the concept of God shared by many Masons – is hinted at throughout our ritual: the great virtues of brotherly Love, Relief and Truth; the references to Wisdom, Strength and Beauty; the use of the terms 'Great Architect,' 'Grand Geometrician,' 'Most High' and others; all of these things point towards a Spiritual Nature ineffable in essence and yet, we are assured, able to be experienced directly by contemplation and the communion of true prayer.

A Master Mason has read the signs and has performed the labour necessary to have taken the first step on Jacob's ladder, which is Faith. The second is Hope, and again, a Master Mason who has devoted his life to exploring and deepening his Faith can well afford to hope for salvation. But there is a third rung, and the Master Mason who has taken that step in its fullness has moved beyond Faith and Hope into the knowledge that all life is one. This knowing has its own particular vibration or flavour: that which we call Love.

Hope in Salvation;

To hope for salvation, for enlightenment; to be free from the tribulations of this material life; to rest always in the presence of the Divine: this is the position we hold when we step up onto the second rung of Jacob's ladder. Our Faith is well founded, and we have begun to feel that numinous presence in our lives as we dedicate ourselves more and more to become vehicles for the Divine Light so long hidden behind the veils we have placed in the temples of our hearts.

Every step we take lifts one of those veils and the Light shines ever more brightly. Our Faith has led us to realise the great Truth of our eternal communion with God; we realise that we are included in the promises that such realisation holds out to us. Suddenly, our own future is assured: we have found our way to the summit of Freemasonry.

But then we see there is a further step.

A Master Mason, if he is to be worthy of that name, cannot step into the Light and leave his brothers in darkness. The final step is Charity, or Love, and on this rung the Master Mason confronts what is known in Buddhist traditions as the Bodhisattva vows: to forgo the reunion with God that is our deepest longing until he can make a path for all. This is Charity. This is Love. The is Master Mason's Way.

...to be in Charity with all men.

To be in charity with all men is the natural consequence of a life of faith and hope. A Master Mason
who is rooted in his faith and who has recognised that
he is worthy to partake of the blessed promises of reunion with our divine source, also understands without doubt that his life and the lives of all other creatures are but different expressions of the One life, that
Supreme Being whom we are taught to adore.

A Master Mason's love for others is not based on
personality or on any sense of individual worth. It
is based on his understanding that, in part, he is his
brother and his brother is him. By learning to recognise the Divine in himself, the Master Mason learns
self-love, and because he understands that the same
Divine spark resides in every living thing, he comes,
eventually, to have a heart open wide enough to comprehend the beauty and sanctity of all life.

The third step on Jacob's ladder is achieved by manifesting this universal, disinterested Love. A Master
Mason may be understood to have attained perfection only in so far as he is willing to hold out his hand
and assist his Brethren to ascend this final step and to
stand on the summit alongside him.

...not to boast of anything but to give heed to our ways, to walk uprightly and with humility before God,

A Master Mason is not impressed by worldly measures of success. He understands that the signifiers of worldly achievement are no more than tools to help him achieve and manifest his spiritual fullness. What is wealth if it is not used for the betterment of others? What is fame if it is not used to draw attention to the plight of those who suffer and are in need?

A Master Mason's success is measured in hearts and lives touched; in the manifestation of Masonic virtues in daily life, and in the measure of happiness and satisfaction found within his own heart.

The Master Mason does not boast of his successes, but he uses them wisely and kindly, understanding that with one small turn of Fortune's wheel, he could be in very different circumstances.

Understanding the connection of all life and seeing in every person a '...brother of the dust,' a Master Mason remains true to his principles and treads the paths of his life with wisdom and humility, knowing that there will come a time when his 'success' will be weighed in a very different set of scales.

...practice charity, maintain harmony, and endeavour to live in unity and brotherly love.

Charity is a natural by-product of a Master Mason's life. It arises spontaneously out of his understanding that all life is an expression of the Divine, and that the Divine spark which animates him is the same as that which animates all living things. When this understanding is underpinned by the knowledge that comes from study and research into the hidden mysteries of nature and science, and when it is constantly and faithfully applied, then we have the beginnings of perfection: a life lived wholly in the Light.

But such knowledge and such understanding do not come easily. This is why a Mason is enjoined to 'practice' Charity – it must become a daily, an hourly, a moment-by-moment habit in our lives if we are to achieve it in its purest sense.

Our regular efforts to study and learn and improve ourselves result in increased knowledge and understanding, and it is from this knowledge and understanding of the truth of our relationships with God and each other that Charity spontaneously arises. The process is no mystery: a certain course of action will lead to a predictable set of results. This is why a Master Mason lives as he does: because he seeks the outcome that such a life will undoubtedly yield.

Thus the Square teaches morality,

Morality is the very core and heart of Freemasonry, and it is symbolised for us by the Square.

It is important to note that, while geometrical principles underpin a Masonic understanding of the Universe, the square is not commonly a naturally occurring shape. The ashlar is not lifted from the quarry ready squared and when we look at natural forms, we are more likely to encounter spirals and curves than 90-degree angles.

For the Master Mason, the lesson here is both fundamental and infinitely profound: he understands that our task on Earth is to act as co-creators of perfection. But if our symbol of moral perfection is the Square, what does it teach us?

The Master Mason understands that it is through his own labour that he will come to attain this symbolic perfection. He understands that the purity within his heart must be found and uncovered, just as the perfect ashlar exists within the rough stone and must be modelled and wrought into due form.

A Master Mason sees in the Square the blueprint for a greater life and a higher calling: the completion and perfection of himself and all of Creation.

...the Level equality,

If Morality is to be our core and our heart, then it must be based on a foundation that is true and strong. The Level speaks to us of many things, the first of which, of course, is equality.

To a Master Mason this does just mean equality under the law: this would imply that it is an earthly quality, limited in its scope to our worldly lives and relationships. But equality to a Master Mason goes deeper than this: it is a quality of the soul, and it brings us directly to the most fundamental and important teaching of Freemasonry: the truth of Oneness. As a drop of sea water is qualitatively one with the mighty ocean; as the tiny spark is one with the great inferno, so are we - each individual, divine spark - one with that great Divine life from which we all spring. Thus, a Master Mason lives his life with an over-riding sense of sympathy and compassion for his fellows, for he knows that in their weaknesses, he too is weak and that in their failings he, too, fails.

But the Level is also a strong and stable tool, made to sit atop and firmly across two perfect ashlars. A Master Mason, through study and practice, also becomes a strong and stable force in the world because he knows that, in his strength, others may become strong and through his stability, others may find their own stable centre.

...the Plumb Rule justness and uprightness of life and actions.

Through his uprightness – his adherence to the moral law – the Master Mason connects Heaven and Earth. In his fullness he represents the two great pillars which stood at the entrance to the Temple; he represents the triple virtues of Wisdom, Strength and Beauty, and also the pillars of fire and cloud that were of such aid to the Israelites as they fled their captivity.

As such, a Master Mason is a beacon of light, learning and inspiration for all the world. He is wholly centred in the core of himself, in that Divine spark which is the point within the circle from which he cannot err.

But such a position is attained through great effort; through a lifetime of striving for the best that is within us and through years of study and inner work. A Master Mason must come to learn that identification with the ego must be left behind as he climbs Jacob's ladder, and that, as he goes higher, he must also go deeper to find that place where distinctions cease, and the fact of our inter-connection becomes his only truth.

Thus, rooted in the certainty of oneness and in constant communion with the Divine spark within, the Master Mason is enabled to hold himself upright in every sense of the word and be an exemplar of a just and noble life.

To be happy ourselves, and to communicate happiness to others.

Like everyone, Freemasons wish for happiness. To this end, we pursue, where possible, a life that will bring a measure of material prosperity and we hope to enjoy loving relationships that lead to a fulfilling home and social life. But we also understand that worldly happiness is fleeting and insubstantial, here one minute and gone the next.

Therefore, the Master Mason must go deeper and seek a more lasting happiness, founded on eternal principles. He learns to subdue his passions and to see beyond his identification solely with the material body and its senses. He searches for a lasting identity that aligns his true self with the Divine spark within his breast. In time he comes to live, to speak, to breathe, to be wholly centred in that point within a circle from which he cannot err.

And from this point, he sees clearly. He is no longer ruled by emotion and base passions. He is secure in a spiritual, eternal sense of himself that allows him to be truly happy in life and which allows happiness to emanate from him.

It is from this position that a Master Mason communicates his true secrets: that life is joyful and that lasting, reliable, well-founded happiness is one of the fruits of the Masonic path.

...to regard the whole human species as one family,

The Master Mason experiences the symbolic annihilation of the Self in a clear and graphic manner during the ceremony of Raising. That which is laid in the grave is different from that which is raised from it: in the experience of figurative death lies the secret to a fuller life: a life of the Spirit.

After this figurative death, we are raised into the arms of our brethren and, through the five points of fellowship we are shown that, from now on, our lives are to be lived for others as much as for ourselves.

It is through this ceremony that a Master Mason is given the tools to begin to understand his connection with all creatures. From there, through study and contemplation of the lessons given, he comes to realise with all his being, the fact that all living things take their rise from that one Divine life from which all goodness emanates.

Thus, the Master Mason comes to appreciate and to manifest in his dealings with others, the true teaching that, under the Fatherhood of God, all of us are brothers and sisters – sharers of one great life and one great destiny.

Good Fellowship.

The concept of universal brotherhood is founded on and anchored in our understanding of ourselves as children of the One Supreme Being whom we all acknowledge. It is an understanding reached through study and meditation, through contemplation and observation and a keen adherence to Masonic teachings and lore.

But to be a Master Mason is more than dry learning and solitary study. A Master Mason lives his knowledge out in the world and so he does not hold himself back from the joys that are to be found in worldly relationships.

A Master Mason's interactions with his brethren are not cold, lofty affairs. On the contrary, they may be rooted in the highest philosophical principles, but they are completely down-to-earth too. They are warm and genial and, often, full of good humour and laughter.

A Master Mason is not someone who engages in emotional games or dramas. He is centred and calm; he is in control of his passions and has learned to ride the waves of emotion that beset all human beings without being swept away by them. It is this that makes him dependable and trustworthy, and which allows him to act from that most natural and most attractive of human states: that of happiness. A true Master Mason is a great friend and is always convivial company.

Freedom...

Freedom is the first of three qualities with which an Entered Apprentice should serve his Master. At first, this may seem something of a paradox – service and freedom do not obviously go together. But a clue to the meaning is given in another part of the lecture where we are reminded that freedom means a perfect freedom of inclination.

Therefore, we can appreciate that a Master Mason understands – because he learned it as an Apprentice – that service must be joyfully and freely rendered if it is to be of value.

A Master Mason is master of himself, master of his passions and his emotions. He is self-sufficient; contained and complete within himself. And yet, he chooses to engage with the outer world through service, knowing full well that it is only through subduing the ego and living life for others that he can truly come to know and understand himself.

On an intellectual level, the Master Mason understands that he exists in an eternal relationship of loving service to the Divine, but it is not until he learns to live his life as an offering to the Divine in all life that he is able to fully realise the truth of that relationship with all his heart.

Thus he serves. Willingly, joyfully; freely.

Fervency...

The second quality expected of an Entered Apprentice in his service to his Master is fervency. This quality is symbolised by charcoal which is described thus: "Nothing more fervent than Charcoal; for when properly lighted no metal can resist its force."

The Entered Apprentice is expected to serve with a fierce, red-hot concentration; an all-consuming passion. The operative mason was learning his earthly livelihood and knew how important it was to mark his lessons well; the speculative mason is learning to embrace eternity and must do so with equal focus.

Therefore, the Master Mason learns to bring his attention to bear on those things that touch on the core of his self: that divine spark that resides within his mortal frame. The point within the circle of his life and connections is like the rays of the sun focussed though a magnifying glass: able to burn away the impurities of materiality and leave the pure brilliance of the untarnished soul.

A Master Mason learns to bring the burning flame of fervency to bear on all his thoughts and actions and with that mental focus he is able to see and to reveal the truth in all situations. He is a purifier; a light bringer; a beacon and a flame.

Zeal.

The third quality of the Entered Apprentice is Zeal, and this is represented by clay: "Nothing more zealous than Clay, our mother Earth; she is continually labouring for our support. Thence we came, and there we must all return."

If Fervency is the focused white heat of burning charcoal, then Zeal is the slow and patient perseverance of the earth. It is the quality of patience and determination over time. It is the walking of the long path home, the joy of chance meetings along the way, the happiness in the support of brotherly love that collaborates instead of competes.

The Master Mason recognises the immediacy of his fervency and uses those bright bursts of flame to attain the heights himself and to inspire others onwards, with lofty words and righteous actions. But he also knows that the strength and endurance required to see the journey through to its end, come from a steadier, more reliable energy.

He acknowledges the support that comes from others and the many gifts given by Mother Earth. He knows his body to be of that earth and so he treads humbly but resolutely towards the darkness of the grave, which is but the doorway to Light.

Free to good fellowship, and ought to be free from vice.

A Freemason is described as "Free to" and "Free from."

"Free to good fellowship" is the Mason whose heart has been released from all sense of externally imposed obligation. "Free to good fellowship" is the Mason who chooses his path – with all its responsibilities and obligations – freely and joyfully. "Free to good fellowship" is the Mason whose only Masters are God Almighty and the dictates of his own self-convincing conscience.

To achieve this level of freedom is a lifetime's work. It requires the sloughing off of all our conditioning, releasing ourselves from childhood trauma and neuroses; the willingness to look deep into the dark side of ourselves; to acknowledge and take responsibility for all that we have done.

A Master Mason's main work is on himself, and he needs to be scrupulously honest with himself if he is to make progress. If he wishes to build a perfect Temple, fit for the indwelling of the Divine, he must clear himself of all impurities of thought, word and deed and he must dedicate himself to live to the highest of ideals in every moment of every day of his life.

This is the path a Master Mason must tread and this is why, to be a true Master, he must be "free from vice."

Virtue,

The only way to Honour is through the cultivation of Virtue, and a Master Mason who wishes to live an honourable life must first learn to be virtuous in the fullest sense of the word.

The Master Mason comes to knowledge through study and contemplation. In time, through daily practice, knowledge becomes understanding, and from understanding wisdom may arise. But it is not until all of these things are exercised through the filter of virtue that they may be said to have come into their fullness.

True knowledge and understanding of the world are powerful and dangerous tools. In the wrong hands they have the potential to cause harm, to manipulate and twist desire into self-serving authoritarianism. But guided by virtue, they are powerful tools for the betterment of all humanity.

Thus, a Master Mason, seeks not just worldly knowledge and worldly power, but he strives always to season his knowledge with virtue so that when he acts, he acts for the highest good. He knows in his heart that a life lived without love, compassion and empathy is a life that has missed its purpose and is, ultimately, a life without joy and direction.

And what are love, compassion, and empathy but the crown and summit of all virtues?

Honour,

In a beautiful passage, the Emulation Lectures suggest that both religion and honour, although they have different origins, will lead a man to God. They both have Virtue as their foundation, but the religious man is virtuous because his beliefs enjoin him to be so. The man of honour is virtuous because it is the right and beautiful thing to do.

The religious man fears to do wrong, but the honourable man scorns wrongdoing; the religious man avoids acting in a way that he believes will be offensive to God; the honourable man sees vice as something contemptible and unworthy of his time or attention.

Thus, the honourable man goes beyond the strictures laid down by religion and acts honourably because he knows it is the right thing to do. He sets his sights higher than mere compliance with the Divine law and becomes a conscious agent of that law, as incapable of disobedience to it as he is incapable of denying his own nature and the dictates of his own heart.

A Master Mason, whilst often being religious, must also strive to live life as a man of honour, motivated by the highest principles and driven, not by a desire to obey, but a by an irresistible, undeniable compunction to be the best he can be.

Mercy.

Mercy is the crowning glory of all virtue. It is the sweetest and most generous of all human attributes because it is the reflection and the embodiment of the Divine.

A Master Mason seeks to judge and act with mercy in all the various facets of his life. He looks kindly on the faults of others even as he looks to guide his Brethren away from error and towards the right. And whilst he holds himself to the highest of standards, he is also kind on himself and is forgiving of his own faults.

Whilst honour may call upon us to always strive for that which is right, mercy understands that we may all sometimes fall short and must be allowed to get up when we fall, and try again.

A Master Mason understands that he must be merciful in his approach to others because he will rely on God's mercy when the time comes for him to stand before the Throne of Glory, naked and defenceless, to account for his actions in this life.

Mercy is the key to unlock Grace and it is through Grace that we will all eventually come home. A Master Mason expects to receive this greatest of Divine gifts and so, without hesitation, he understands that he must give it to others.

...see that the Lodge is properly tyled

Tyling is about turning inwards; about shutting out the world and allowing the work of the Lodge to proceed. It is the act by which the distractions and demands of our daily lives are temporarily set aside and we are able to focus on something higher, which will enrich us and satisfy us on the deepest levels.

A Master Mason understands that there is a personal and symbolic level to this too. He knows that he must ensure that his inner life is also properly tyled, that he has the inner strength to withstand the seductions and temptations of the material world that can lead his feet to stray from his chosen path. To do this, the Master Mason develops a daily practice of contemplation, charity, and study. A daily advancement in Masonic knowledge is not just about learning ritual, it is about finding and holding fast to that firm centre, to that point within the circle of our lives from which we cannot err.

This is the key to developing a sense of inner beauty: to be consciously and inseparably connected at all times to that inner Divine spark that resides within our mortal frame. It is thus that the Master Mason learns to hold steady and to steer his boat calmly on the turbulent seas of human passion.

In my heart

There are many ways in which to be a good Mason, and there are many ways in which a Master Mason may manifest his understanding and realisations of the truths he has learned to live by.

There is one thing, though, that all Masons must possess if they are to be able to call themselves Masons, and one thing that all Master Masons must live by if they are to be worthy of the name, and that one thing is Love.

From our earliest moments in Freemasonry, we are reminded that we came knocking at the door because of a preconceived regard for the Order, and we learn very soon that the highest step on Jacob's ladder – the summit and pinnacle of Freemasonry – is Charity: Love in action.

A Master Mason is, by definition, one who has attained the summit of Freemasonry and so it must be that his life is distinguished by the love he manifests in all areas of his life.

Based on our understanding that we are all children of God and that all living things are but different expressions of the one life that animates us all, we come to Freemasonry with hearts already predisposed to learn a greater, impersonal love: a love that transcends all superficial differences and sees only that one life, glorious, eternal, Divine.

Do you pledge your honour as a man, and your fidelity as a Mason...

A Master Mason's word is something that carries weight in the world. It is not given lightly and it is not negotiable. Because of this, a Master Mason learns to consider carefully before he gives it. He weighs up carefully and learns to see to the heart of any given situation. He is cool, although his heart is warm; unemotional even though motivated always by love.

And once given, a Master Mason's word is binding. It is dependable and trustworthy because it carries with it the weight of the entire superstructure of the Order. A Master Mason holds in his hands the reputation and good standing of Freemasonry as a whole, for it is by the actions of its individual members that Freemasonry is judged by the outside world.

Therefore, a Master Mason is exemplary in his deeds and in his intentions. He is steadfast and reliable, and if he says he will do a certain thing, it is as good as done. He is the most honourable of men and his fidelity to Freemasonry is unshakeable.

...to act as a true and faithful Craftsman,

A true and faithful craftsman not only possesses the skill he needs to execute his work, but he also has the mental focus and determination to see it through. He does not take his work lightly but brings to it all of himself, giving it the care, attention, and respect that it deserves.

A Master Mason, understanding that his work is to perfect himself and then help humanity at large towards perfection, brings the same dedication, the same singularity of purpose, the same love, devotion, and respect to his chosen Craft.

To develop the skills necessary for this inner work, the Master Mason is willing to devote time and energy to do what is necessary to make a daily advancement towards his goal, and to develop a regular practice of study, contemplation and positive actions that will move him forward.

To cultivate the necessary faithfulness, he learns to hold himself still and quiet; to act always from the centre of his being: that divine spark from which he cannot err. He lives happily in the world but patiently, step by step, he moves himself and his connections towards that Light which is both our source and our ultimate destination.

A true Master is one who is constantly aware of himself, his surroundings and of others around him. This is not a nervous state – there is no stress involved – it is more one of loving alertness: a desire and a readiness to respond to need and suffering as long as self and family are not compromised.

All manifestations of need are signs for a Master Mason to answer, be they from his nearest and dearest or from total strangers. There are specifically Masonic signs that a Master will recognise and respond to, but his response is not quicker or more caring towards a brother: the very foundation of his understanding is that he responds equally to all, knowing that all are brothers.

A Master Mason is awake; he is conscious; he is loving awareness, and he is ready and able to help. He looks after his body as far as is practicable and he cultivates a steadiness and strength of mind which allows him to serve his community at all times.

The true Master Mason strives always to be the best of himself for he understands that he may be called upon at any moment to manifest all those virtues which our Craft professes to offer the world at large. It is a huge responsibility but the Master Mason will always rise to the challenge.

A Master Mason understands that his inner strength derives, in part, from the collective strength of his Lodge and from the institution of Freemasonry as a whole. A Mason who stops attending Lodge cuts himself off from a web of mutual support and encouragement that has the potential to nourish his spirit and provide practical help in times of trouble.

Also, the Master Mason who does not involve himself in the communal life of his Lodge, denies his brethren the opportunity to share his understandings and to benefit from all that his presence may have to offer. His absence means one fewer person to share the work, to encourage younger Brethren or to represent the Fraternity to the world at large.

In contrast to this, the Master Mason who is fully present in the life of his Lodge is able to bring all his experience, all his wisdom, knowledge and understanding to bear on the communal life and, through this, he fulfils all his obligations to be a 'true and faithful craftsman.'

The summons to attend Lodge is more than a casual invitation; it is a reminder that we are obligated to support each other in all ways, and it is for that reason that a Master Mason, when he can do so without detriment to himself and his connections, will always obey that summons.

...without evasion, equivocation or mental reservation of any kind.

There can be no holding back in the life of the spirit. If we wish to bare our hearts to God and fully become co-creators in a life of true communion, we must be willing to look honestly and fearlessly into the depths of ourselves to acknowledge and exorcise the darkness that we find there.

Freemasonry is full of symbolism that hints at this descent into darkness, and it is always in the descent that light and knowledge are found. In seeking that light, we must be prepared to shed the layers of dust and dirt that have been laid down over the years of our lives and we must be willing to do the work that is necessary for us to be able to shine in our fullness and reflect that glory from which we spring.

A Master Mason cannot truly call himself Master until he has done this inner work. He must understand that the conferring of the title 'Master Mason' is the beginning and not the end of the path. This is why he learns to remain open, honest, and true. He acknowledges and strengthens his weaknesses whilst dealing kindly with the weaknesses of his fellows. But he does not hide from the light, seeing that it illuminates his shortcomings whilst also making visible the path that will lead, in the end, to his perfection.

...to shield the repository of your secrets from the attacks of the insidious.

Whilst the Master Mason is open-hearted and generous, giving of his time and his energy to those with whom he comes into contact, and always seeking another's good, he must also learn to protect himself from that which will weaken his resolve and undermine his inner balance.

We are taught clearly in Freemasonry that there are boundaries we must not cross: we are not to overstretch ourselves in ways that are detrimental to ourselves and our connections. In other words, if we give to others so much that we have little left for ourselves or our loved ones, then our helping of others is inappropriate and misguided.

The repository of our secrets is our heart. and attacks upon it come in many forms: there will be those who seek to denigrate Freemasonry itself; those who pressure us to reveal our secret signs, words and tokens, thus violating our obligations; those who will try to cause a rift between us and our sworn brethren; those who will try to tempt us away from the morality with which we have chosen to cloak ourselves. Some of these things are clearly seen and easily repulsed. Others are not. Therefore, a Master Mason remains awake and alert, always conscious of his true self and always centred upon that Divine spark within.

The caution exercised by a Master Mason is not in any way driven by fear. In fact, the opposite is true: a Master Mason's caution is the natural and inescapable outcome of his being fully present and alive in the moment.

His caution is a constant and careful weighing up of possibility, a surveying of outcomes before action; above all, it is being always mindful of the myriad possibilities that unfold from the present into the future.

The caution of a Master Mason is not driven by fear because he has learned to overcome the ultimate fear, the fear of annihilation. It is this fearlessness in the face of death that allows a Master Mason to be fully present in the here-and-now, and which enables him to weigh up the right course of action in every situation.

Of course, in our ritual we refer to being cautious in the context of not revealing our 'secrets' but for a Master Mason, caution as mindfulness is a state of being that he seeks every day, in every moment. With caution as his watchword, he treads a path of conscious awareness within the bounds set by his Square and Compasses, at the centre of which rests that still point from which he cannot err.

...you are expected to make the liberal Arts and Sciences your future study,

The intersection where the human mind and the liberal Arts and Sciences meet is the ground upon which the Master Mason treads in peace and certainty.

These liberal Arts and Sciences are a portal between the human and the Divine worlds, where the laws of Nature are able to interact, to mix and mingle with human creativity to begin to allow us to discover and express the great truths of our existence.

This is a liminal space, between worlds, where the intellect and the Spirit meet, and where the opportunities for us to fulfil our potential as co-creators of that great Temple we Freemasons strive to build and inhabit, are at their most accessible.

A Master Mason is a familiar of both worlds; he walks comfortably through this material existence, but he is aware, always, that beyond this world of forms, a mere heartbeat away, there lies another: more vibrant, more real, more full of Divine Light. It is his great work to reveal that other world to the denizens of this one and it is through a full and deep understanding and application of the seven liberal Arts and Sciences that he is able to accomplish this task.

...and estimate the wonderful works of the Almighty.

What we see in the world depends as much on our state of mind as on what is actually there. Every moment of our lives presents us with a choice and an opportunity to decide how we interpret what we see, and the significance we give to it.

A Master Mason brings all of his training to bear on this matter of the everyday because, through his practice, through his effort to put Masonic teachings to the test and through the exercise of his trained will, he sees the world around him as the work of God and he sees God's hand in everything.

Thus, the Master Mason cultivates the highest level of God-consciousness and manifests it in his daily life.

The true mark of a Master is not knowledge or power; it is happiness – an unshakeable ability to see God working in every aspect of our lives and to rest calmly in the knowledge that all is well, and all will be well. The trials and tribulations of the world may rock his boat, but the Master Mason sails, unperturbed, across its stormy seas.

...you are now permitted to extend your researches into the hidden mysteries of Nature and Science.

As we grow in knowledge and understanding, so we begin to understand the unity that lies behind all outer forms. We come to understand that all life is one, that God is one – that we are one.

The highways of science and the paths of Nature may seem to follow different routes, but if one travels either of them very far, one will find that they, too, converge and become one.

A Master Mason is encouraged to travel both of those roads and, even if he is more drawn to one than the other, he is led, by a winding way and by mystical steps to that point of convergence. Both roads have the potential to lead us to the truth and the Master Mason, through studying their outer forms, is guided towards their inner truth.

Thus, the Master Mason's mind is led gradually away from the world of form, illusion, and appearance and into that secret and hidden world where the barriers between us dissolve into unity.

Through study, contemplation and a rigorous testing of Masonic principles, the Master Mason eventually becomes the very light that he set out to find.

The life of a Master Mason is not just one of study and contemplation; it is not a selfish pursuit for inner peace, for spiritual superiority or power. It is a life of service, lived out in the 'real' world where spiritual insight must be translated into right action if it is to have any value at all, either to the Master Mason in question or to his connections.

Freemasonry gives us many tools by which to regulate and measure our conduct. We are enjoined to add to human happiness, to make the world a better place for our having passed through it and to improve the individual lives of those with whom we come in contact.

A Master Mason understands that study and contemplation and all the inner work that those things imply, are vital to make of our lives that great and glorious Temple fit for the in-dwelling of Divinity. But he also understands that they are not the entirety of the building: the inner work is the foundation; the true beauty of the superstructure can only be seen out in the world in a life well lived.

Like a stained-glass window that only reveals its beauty when the light shines through it, so a Master Mason's inner work does not fulfil its true purpose until illuminated by the light of loving, noble conduct in the world.

...level steps,

Above all things, a Master Mason learns to find balance; to walk through the world, coping equally with its extremes of emotion, its times of great joy and happiness and its times of disappointment and grief. He understands that the great wheel of fortune is forever turning and that the only way to remain completely at peace through all its revolutions is to find the still, calm centre of being that is the point within the circle of his life.

The level steps of a Master Mason are not just about equality – that is a lesson learned early on the path – but also about equanimity: the ability to cultivate calmness in all circumstances; to be able to stand firm and true, no matter what the problem or provocation to give in to fear or superstition.

A Master Mason walks calmly through the world because his feet are set on a path that is difficult but well-trodden. Ahead of him are those who have gone before and who show him the way; behind him are those who will follow in his footsteps. and it is partly for them that he walks on fearlessly, sure of this mystic way that leads him to his home.

The intention of a Master Mason is not a vague sense of obligation, nor is it an ill-thought-out plan with an undefined outcome. Nor does it carry any sense of regret for what might have been achieved. When a Master Mason sets his intention, it is a statement of fact: the first step in an act of will that cannot but result in the achievement of the desired aim.

There are some factors that will always contribute to such a positive outcome. The first is that that the intention is, in every sense, 'upright.' In other words, that which the Master Mason wishes to accomplish is something that brings about or encourages goodness and virtue. If Freemasonry truly '...inculcate[s] the practice of virtue among all its genuine professors...' so the actions of a Master Mason must, necessarily, do the same.

A Master Mason always exercises control over both his thoughts and his actions. Thus, his mind is clear and focussed, and when he acts, he acts with the force and clarity of a stone dropped into a pond: he moves towards his intention in a straight and undeviating line, leaving no more than tiny ripples to bear witness to his passing.

...to whom we must all submit and whom we ought humbly to adore.

As a Master Mason grows in knowledge and understanding, he also develops and deepens in power and authority. In learning to overcome the baser elements of his physical being and focussing his mind with true and positive intention, he becomes a creative force for good in the world.

The idea that power corrupts is a well-established one and so, for a weak-willed or morally corrupt person to arrogate power to themselves for selfish gain is a real danger. It is for this reason that Masonry stresses the importance of moral uprightness on every step of the way, because power without discipline, without morality, without devotion and service is a destructive and empty exercise.

The Master Mason, however powerful, whether in worldly, mental, or spiritual terms, always recognises a power higher than himself and is thus saved from the perils of arrogance, greed, and selfishness. He knows that, however 'great' he is, God is above him, and by practising an attitude of selfless service and loving devotion, he is keeps himself within due bounds with all of humanity, with his brethren in Freemasonry, with himself and with his creator. And thus held, he cannot help but use his knowledge, power and wisdom for the common good.

...remember that wherever we are, and whatever we do, He is with us,

All good habits require time, dedication, and practice to develop. Whether we wish to integrate healthy eating or physical exercise or a positive mental attitude, we have to work at them, practise them every day until we see them gradually become integrated into our lives, and those habits become a natural part of what we do and who we are.

It is no different when we aim to develop a consciousness of God in our lives. Like all habits, it must be encouraged and cultivated, and like all habits, it will become a part of us in time.

A Master Mason makes the effort to cultivate this God-consciousness. He chooses, in every moment, to see the Divine working in the mundanity of the everyday and he practises the disciplines of appreciation, gratitude and joy at all times.

The mark of the God-conscious Master is not necessarily silence and seriousness; sometimes it is found in a ready smile, in spontaneous laughter, in the unbidden upwelling of love and connection between brothers.

A Master Mason worthy of the name must first remember that, before anything else, he is a humble servant, ever mindful of his Master's wishes for him to be a light to the world.

…a point from which a Master Mason cannot err.

To find and act from the centre of our being is the first task of a Master Mason. All our learning of ritual, all our study and contemplation and all our charitable acts point us towards this one truth: that there is a divine spark within all living creatures that unites us and that is our true and eternal self. The path of Freemasonry leads, first, to this understanding and once it is achieved – and it can take a lifetime to achieve it – a Master Mason is able to be in the world but not be of it. He is able to feel deeply the full range of human emotion without being overturned by it; he is able to demonstrate equanimity in all that he does, so that all aspects of his private and public lives are harmonised and beautiful.

From his calm centre, the Master Mason radiates peace; he is the one to whom the troubled and sore at heart will come for solace. He is patient and kind; firm and strong in righteousness but understanding and forgiving of the faults of others.

Within the due bounds of the square and compasses, the Master Mason rests content, understanding that his place in the world is to help build that great Temple which will allow us to properly manifest God on Earth.

...with what grand ideas must such knowledge fill our minds!

To study geometrical laws and structures and then to contemplate their deeper significance cannot but lead us to a place of awe and wonder.

A Master Mason looks at the world through eyes that see beyond mere outer forms. He sees the order and beauty in all things, from the microscopic strands of DNA to the mighty sequoia. From the humblest bird's nest to the greatest temple, he sees the Great Architect's hand, upholding the material universe, pointing at possibilities for a life beyond.

And from earthly structures, the Master Mason lifts his eyes to the Heavens and there he sees the wonders of the Universe spread before him. He contemplates infinity and knows, from the centre of his being, that he is part of all that is; that his life is the intersection where physical and spiritual meet; where God descends to earth and where humankind has the chance to realise the essence of divinity within.

If we believe in a Supreme Being and if we believe that "...all his law is concord..." then it necessarily follows that a full understanding of any of His laws will lead us to Him and that, as we study those laws, our minds will be filled with Him. It is this connection that a Master Mason seeks to cultivate.

In this one creature was amassed whatever is excellent in the whole creation;

A Master Mason recognises that he is not separate from the rest of the natural world but that he is an integral part of it. Rather, he accepts his responsibility as the crowning glory of Creation: all the gifts of the plant and animal kingdoms; all the instincts, intuition and knowledge with which those kingdoms are imbued; all of their beauty; all their grace; all their natural 'rightness' of being are his.

But a Master Mason also knows that the Great Architect of the Universe has implanted within him something else: something wonderful and fearful; something joyful and terrifying; a gift that sometimes feels like a curse.

He remembers, always, that humankind is made in the image of God, only a little lower than the Angels, and that, unlike any other creature, he has choice, free-will and the ability to influence and decide his own path. Therefore, a Master Mason is always mindful of his thoughts and actions because he knows that, within the depths of his soul, the natural communion of the animal and plant kingdoms with their Creator has been superseded by the great gift of freedom. Appreciating the true nature of the gift, the Master Mason strives always to seek the path of return.

...integrity, and uprightness, should ever influence him to adore his Benign Creator,

One of God's great gifts to humanity is the ability to craft our own reality; to be able to control, not necessarily what happens to us, but our attitudes towards it. And thus, we come to appreciate the true meaning of free will and understand our place in the hierarchy of Creation.

It is also true that we attract into our lives those things that resonate with our own hearts and minds and so it must be true that the more we learn to live in tune with divine attributes, the more we will resonate with and attract the Divine into our lives.

A Master Mason understands these links between thoughts, behaviour and being, and so he is not surprised to find that living a life of integrity and uprightness should bring him closer to the source of those virtues.

As he learns to cultivate and appreciate the Masonic virtues in himself and in his brethren, so he learns to feel and appreciate them in his growing understanding of God.

Becoming a vehicle for Masonic virtues is the aim of a Master Mason, because he understands that, through their cultivation, his ego is overcome and he becomes an increasingly pure channel through which true brotherhood and true Godliness may flow.

...and endued him with that noble instinct called reason.

Masonic teachings mark out a path between knowing and feeling; between logic and sentimentality; between reason and an ineffable love. It is such a hard path to define because, from the outside, it seems to make little sense, but once on it and walking with level steps, we see it clearly and are able to follow it fearlessly.

With our minds we reason and understand. We hear the teachings, and we apply them to our daily lives, and in time, we feel their benefit and see ourselves becoming better people: more patient, more kind, more full of brotherly love.

But at the same time, we feel a strong affinity for those who walk the path with us; a strong bond with those who have gone before, and great hope for those who will come after. Increasingly, reason must confront a love – call it agape – that is founded on our intellectual understanding but whose walls soar high and strong with something more.

A Master Mason holds these seeming contradictions and difficulties lightly in his heart and mind. He treads a multi-dimensional path, and he occupies a liminal space where all possibilities and all apparent conflicts are subsumed into a reality that is all-encompassing and infinitely beneficent.

...in the hour of trial he fail not,

A Master Mason learns to cultivate a constant sense of being present in every moment. As a part of society, of course, he fulfils all the duties expected of him and this of necessity means considering the future and acknowledging the past.

But, as far as his inner life is concerned, a Master Mason strives always to be in the here-and-now, alive to every call upon his ability to reach out a hand to those in need.

He must be one to whom the troubled heart turns; the living example of upright behaviour, the beacon of light, the daily exponent of what it means to be a true brother to all. His life is lived by the principles taught to him: he regulates his time by the 24-inch gauge; he is upright, level and square, and he sets his bounds by the skirret and the compasses.

This is the daily practice of a Master Mason: to be ever mindful of Masonic principles and to cultivate them in every sphere of life in every moment of every day; for it is only when they are part of our very being that we can be sure that we will succeed, and find our way through every test and every trial of our fortitude and faith.

...a most serious trial of your fortitude and fidelity and a more solemn Obligation await you.

The ultimate test of a Master Mason's fortitude and fidelity waits for him at the closing hour of his earthly existence. All of his life is a preparation for this moment, and this is why a Master Mason works constantly on himself to cultivate the habits of serenity and faith.

A Master Mason spends his life preparing for death and he does so by living life to the full; by becoming a vehicle for the joy and goodness that are the results of surrendering one's ego driven desires to the unity of creation. Through knowledge, understanding and a disciplined daily practice of the cultivation of generosity and virtue, the Master Mason comes at last to a clear understanding that the Divine spark within his breast – his true, eternal self - needs have no fear of annihilation.

And with this knowledge comes peace profound; and certainty; and the ability to calm the worried and fearful hearts of others for whom the light of this knowledge has not yet dawned.

A Master Mason learns to be fearless in the face of death, but he also learns awe, reverence, and respect, acknowledging always that, like his Initiation into Freemasonry, he must take the next step in darkness and alone before he attains the light.

...to maintain and uphold the Five Points of Fellowship in act as well as in word:

Integrity is the watchword of a Master Mason and in all his relations he seeks to maintain and uphold the highest principles. The Five Points of Fellowship exhort us to be the very best we can be in our dealings with others and, more specifically, in our quest to perfect ourselves, it calls on us to recognise and honour the perfection – in all its stages – of others.

A fully realised Master is a powerful force in the world and when two come together it is a rare and beautiful thing. The Five Points of Fellowship give us a framework within which to operate in order to bestow that honour upon our self-realised brother, and to acknowledge his elevated place in our Masonic hierarchy. Here is a living example of our perfect principles; here is a teacher who can take us beyond ritual to a knowledge beyond words; here is a Master in whose footsteps we may tread to attain the heights to which we all aspire.

By living according to the Five Points of Fellowship, a Master Mason comes, in time, to embody their virtues. By according the highest of honours to his brethren, he becomes, at last, worthy of them himself.

...to seek the solace of your own distress by extending relief and consolation to your fellow-creature...

In a world where self-care has become the highest apparent good, the Master Mason is guardian of a great and noble truth. He understands the importance of self-care: he knows that to maximise the good that he can do in the world, he must maintain his mental, physical, and spiritual powers at their peak. But he also knows that self-care is not the end of the road, it is the beginning. Self-care is akin to preparing your vehicle for a long journey: making sure the oil and water are topped-up; checking the tyres, packing what you need; filling the tank. Having done all of that, the next stage is to drive away and if you do not do that, your preparations were pointless.

Self-care is the necessary preparation to a life of service, and this is a great secret that Masons preserve in a world of increasing selfishness and isolation.

A Master Mason aims to perfect himself, not for his own selfish gains, but to make of himself a clearer and more efficient vehicle for God's work of making the world a better place. He makes of himself a perfect ashlar, not to stand alone upon a shelf, but to take his place, however humble, in the great Temple fit for the indwelling of the Great Architect and Ruler of the Universe.

...to dedicate your heart...to His glory and the welfare of your fellow-mortals.

Having spent a lifetime on the road to perfecting himself, a Master Mason inevitably arrives at the top rung of Jacob's ladder. Here he finds himself, his hopes fulfilled, his faith tried, tested, and firm: perfect in all his parts and ready to become a building block in that great and glorious Temple.

Here, in this elevated position, what is left for him but to put into practice that crowning glory of Masonic achievement: charity.

And so, a Master Mason, having fully realised within himself the true unity of all life and having understood that the only worthy state of being is one of love, sets out to devote the rest of his life to manifesting and embodying that love.

A fully realised Master Mason has faced his demons. He has wrestled and overcome them, and he stands, at last, as a beacon of love and perfection, his heart a fitting vessel for the indwelling of that Divinity he has dedicated his life to serve.

The true Master, having overcome all the dangers and difficulties of material life, having proved himself strong, brave, and indomitable in spirit, is able, at last, to humble himself and become a servant to all.

...to contemplate the intellectual faculty and to trace it from its development, through the paths of heavenly science, even to the throne of God Himself.

Intuition and a heartfelt faith are key factors in a Master Mason's development and growth, but these private virtues should always be accompanied by intelligence and intellectual rigour.

A Master Mason is not afraid to put his life under keen examination and he knows that to start from a point of unshakeable faith and to end at the throne of God requires an infallible logical progression of enquiry and understanding.

It is true that some may consider faith to be unscientific, but lived experience is always valid and so, while the foundation of our Temple may be an intensely personal knowledge, the logical steps that take us from earth to Heaven are faultless: if we are God's children, then all are God's children. If all are God's children, then we are all brothers and sisters. If God dwells in me, then he dwells in all and if He dwells in all, then we are all the multifaceted expression of one great unity of life.

In moments of doubt a Master Mason can follow this train of thought and be guided directly from the bedrock of his faith to communion with all life and on to the throne of God Himself.

...contemplate, on your inevitable destiny,

A Master Mason has no fear of death. In fact, a fully realised Master learns to see death as nothing more than
the next step on the path; the next adventure of the
Spirit; the stepping-through of a doorway that leads to
more knowledge, more life and more light.

To die well takes a lifetime of preparation and it is
for this reason that a Master Mason cultivates a fully aware loving consciousness in all that he does. His
every breath is a meditation on the infinite; he inhales
joy and gratitude and exhales love. He understands
that death can come at any time and so he lives in the
world fully appreciative of its gifts and its beauty, but
also aware that he must be ready to let it go at any time.

Thus, a Master Mason strives to live his best life
at all times. He is happy and radiates happiness. He
loves lightly, knowing the difference between passion
and agape and he avoids thoughts, words and actions
which will compromise his readiness for death. He will
stay away, as far as is possible, from everything that de-
tracts from his soul's readiness to move on, and he will
always consider the legacy that he will leave behind for
those who love him and those who might aspire to follow in his footsteps.

...guide your reflections to...the knowledge of yourself.

Progressing through the Degrees of Freemasonry, we are led to consider the hidden mysteries of Nature and Science and then, more specifically their manifestation through the seven liberal Arts and Sciences. The serious student of Freemasonry takes these admonitions as more than symbolic lessons and focusses his meditation and his daily practice on understanding the lessons contained.

In the later stages, he is guided to a study of himself and encouraged to consider his own mortality. It is here that a Master Mason takes the first steps in self-realisation.

And it is here, in sight of the open grave, that the Master Mason begins to understand the connections between himself and all of Creation. It is here that he begins to understand himself to be a part of that great unity of life that encompasses all things and that is immortal, eternal, and Divine.

All knowledge of any value leads us, eventually, to self-knowledge; to a point where we stand, awestruck, looking up at the stars or out to sea or across to the mountains or just at the earth between our feet, and realise that we are a part of all that we can see, all that we love, all that brings us joy.

With gratitude to our Master we bend.

The path of a Master Mason can be lonely at times. All the Great Initiations are taken alone; each significant step is one that we ascend on our own merits and by our own efforts. But we also recognise that our path is one of Brotherhood and that, for long stretches, we walk in the company of like-minded men and women who nourish and support us, physically, mentally, and spiritually.

We also know that we are not the first to walk this path. Others have gone before us and they shine a light for us to see by, just as we must learn to shine a light for those who will come after us.

Within our religious traditions we all have teachers to whom we can look for inspiration and help, and, of course, within the annals of Freemasonry we are taught to revere King Solomon for his wisdom, King Hiram of Tyre for his strength and our Master, Hiram Abiff, who not only represents the beauty of our path, but who showed, by example, what it is to live fully by our Masonic precepts and obligations.

A Master Mason strives to be like all these great men and aims always to represent the wisdom, strength and beauty of the spiritual life. And to Hiram Abiff, who showed us how to be true Master Masons and how to manifest true godliness, we can offer nothing but deep and heartfelt thanks.

The 'Masonic Meditations' Series
by
Jonti Marks

Level Steps: 100 Meditations for Freemasons

Hidden Depths: 100 Meditations for Royal Arch Freemasons

Still Waters Volume I: Masonic Meditations on the Book of Psalms

Still Waters Volume II: Masonic Meditations on the Book of Psalms

365 Level Steps: Masonic Meditations for Every Day of the Year
(A lightly edited compilation of the previous four volumes.)

Level Steps Reflective Journals/Workbooks.

All available in print and electronic formats from your usual vendors.

Visit the author's website at:
www.masonicmeditations.com